ONE NATION
UNDER ARREST

ONE NATION UNDER ARREST

How Crazy Laws, Rogue Prosecutors, and Activist Judges Threaten Your Liberty

Edited by
Paul Rosenzweig and Brian W. Walsh

with an Introduction by
Edwin Meese III

© 2010 by The Heritage Foundation
214 Massachusetts Avenue, NE
Washington, DC 20002-4999
(202) 546-4400 • heritage.org

Printed in the United States of America

ISBN 978-0-89195-134-6

Cover design by Elizabeth Brewer
Interior layout by Ralph Buglass and Michelle Smith

TABLE OF CONTENTS

INTRODUCTION

Edwin Meese III

America is in the throes of overcriminalization: We are making and enforcing far too many criminal laws that create traps for the innocent but unwary and threaten to make criminals out of those who are doing their best to be respectable, law-abiding citizens.

A just criminal justice system, in the best sense of the word "just," has a twofold goal: to see that criminals are prosecuted, convicted, and appropriately punished and to ensure that those who are innocent are either not prosecuted in the first instance or, if mistakenly prosecuted, are not convicted.

The American criminal justice system is second to none and does an admirable job of achieving these twin objectives. Our law enforcement personnel, prosecutors, and judges in both the federal and state systems are some of the most dedicated and professional public servants one can imagine.

Yet key developments in criminal law and practice over the past few decades have raised troubling questions about the fairness of our criminal justice system as it affects the average American. It is time to confront these questions, analyze them, and subject them to serious, vigorous debate.

Before these questionable laws and policies cause irreversible harm to our system—and to the lives of untold numbers of Americans—it is also time to act.

Some stories about crime and punishment in America are told and retold. Allegations of socially and economically disadvantaged minorities suffering unjust conviction or police abuse are daily fare. Stories of criminals getting off—or getting off easy—are commonplace. And there is often some truth to the critiques that underlie these stories; no system is perfect, and the American criminal justice system is no exception to that universal rule.

But a deeper story about our criminal justice system is rarely told. It is a story that is subtler but raises greater threats to the fundamental freedoms of all Americans—black and white, rich and poor, young and old. Like the more well-known stories, this too is a story of injustice and of the relatively weak and powerless facing the authority embodied in the criminal law and criminal punishment: the greatest power that government regularly uses against its own citizens.

> The average American's deeply held beliefs about the freedoms he cherishes and the fundamental principles of his government are no longer as well founded as they once were.

The central character in this story is someone who used to be called "the average American." The average American is a man or woman who works hard and pays taxes. The average American cares for his family and is a good neighbor. Perhaps above all, he strives to stay on the right side of the law. Although not necessarily able to put them into words, the average American holds deep and often intuitive beliefs in basic principles about American government, including a belief that, if you do what's right, you have nothing to fear from your own government, and certainly not from the criminal justice system.

But the average American's deeply held beliefs about the freedoms he cherishes and the fundamental principles of his government are no longer as well founded as they once were. Today, he is far more vulnerable than ever before to being caught up in a criminal investigation and prosecution—and to actually being convicted and punished as a criminal—for having done something he did not even suspect was illegal.

This is the inevitable result of the strange path that American criminal law has taken in the past half-century. It has in fact developed along two divergent paths.

Two Roads Diverged in a Wood

The first path—the more familiar one—is the development of an elaborate, even Byzantine, set of procedures that protect people who are accused of traditional crimes of violence and property crimes: the type of crime that the average American ordinarily thinks of when he hears about, for example, rising crime rates or gang-related crime. Judges and legislators in the 1950s and 1960s dramatically increased the procedural hurdles that law enforcement had to overcome in order to convict a person of these inherently wrongful acts of murder, rape, robbery, burglary, theft, assault, and the like.

Americans are familiar with these "reforms," which exalted process over substance. They include the judge-made exclusionary rule that, as Judge Benjamin Cardozo said, allows "the criminal…to go free because the constable has blundered." That rule, along with convoluted *habeas corpus* proceedings, Miranda warnings for those who have already received them, and others, has become part of the warp and woof of our criminal justice system.

The first path of criminal law's development was also heavily influenced by Utopian theories of criminology which asserted that a large percentage of those who commit traditional crimes of violence and property crimes did so because they have suffered social and economic deprivation. Criminals, under this concept, should not be held fully accountable for their conduct. Many liberal judges began to doubt or even openly dispute the justice of traditional felony sentences: imprisonment and execution.

In the area of traditional crime, these trends have diminished. Today, the likelihood that the exclusionary rule and other judge-made procedural innovations will prevent a criminal from being punished is far greater than is necessary to protect the truly innocent from unjust conviction, but the likelihood that those who commit traditional crimes will be arrested and charged is also far greater than it was in the 1960s and 1970s. And those who are in fact convicted are far more likely to be sentenced to—and actually serve—significant time in prison. The deterrent effect of strict enforcement and strict sentencing is one of the reasons for the sharply reduced rate of traditional crime that has benefited the average American. The rate of serious violent crime has declined significantly from its peak in the late 1970s and 1980s.

The second path of criminal law's development over the past half-century is the newer, less traveled road. And that makes all the difference. It involves the creation of new crimes—thousands of them—that do not prohibit inherently wrongful conduct but, rather, punish what the average American would think of as unavoidable accidents, innocent mistakes, and other inadvertences.

The tales of injustice this second path has worked upon Americans are the stories rarely told. At the same time that judges were fashioning more and more procedural protections for defendants accused of traditional crimes of violence and property crimes, Congress and state legislators began to establish new patterns for criminal-law legislation. They created thousands of novel "crimes" that serve as snares and traps for the average American. These laws transform activities that until recently no one ever considered criminal—such as erecting a fence around your property, investing for your retirement, or disposing of used cooking oil—into potentially criminal conduct.

The jurists, policymakers, and practitioners, as well as a growing number of laypersons, who are now concerned about this modern trend describe it as "overcriminalization." *One Nation Under Arrest* reflects the scholarship and policy activity of a number of those legal experts. It explains the relevant history of criminal law and where we are, where we seem to be headed, and how we

The implications of such power in the hands of government officials are grim for all aspects of American life, from personal liberty to global economic competitiveness.

might be able to return to a more rational and restrained system of criminal justice. Most important, the authors of this book explain why overcriminalization represents a serious threat to both individual liberty and public safety.

This path takes American criminal law far from its moorings in the Anglo-American legal tradition. If followed to its logical conclusion, it leads to the point where criminal law and criminal punishment become nothing more than convenient and effective tools of government power. The implications of such power in the hands of government officials are grim for all aspects of American life, from personal liberty to global economic competitiveness.

The nature of the new "crimes" contrasts starkly with that of traditional crimes of violence and property crimes. The path of overcriminalization represents for some of our policymakers a misapprehension of the essential nature and purpose of the criminal law. For others, it reflects, sadly, a deliberate effort to remake society using criminal law as the agent of sociological change. For if one has a Utopian vision of society, then surely it follows that the most powerful force for compelling change—criminal punishment—ought to be used to bring about that Utopia.

But using the criminal process in a politicized manner to change society violates our nation's concepts of individual liberty, limited government, and consent of the governed. It is the method of a tyrannical state, not a democratic republic.

The Fundamental Elements of a Just Criminal Law

Some conduct should be criminalized, not merely because the best judgment of well-meaning government officials deems it to be worthy of punishment, but because it is inherently wrongful, regardless of any given official's personal views or professional judgment. Some of the most obvious examples include murder, rape, robbery, burglary, kidnapping, child sexual abuse, theft, extortion, and assault. Every government should and does criminalize these acts and others of a similar nature.

Because these acts are inherently wrongful, every failure to criminalize and punish them implicitly condones and even encourages them. Where effective criminalization or punishment breaks down, the resulting harms proliferate and threaten the fabric of civil society. As the examples of countless troubled nations illustrate, any city or nation in which no person's private property, physical safety, or life itself is effectively secure has little hope of fostering robust commerce and economic development. Its citizens' daily lives are consumed with protecting their personal security and preserving the most basic necessities of life.

But our legal traditions recognize that not every killing is a murder and not every taking of property without permission is a robbery or theft. For centuries, no person in the Anglo-American world could be convicted of an inherently wrongful act—or "guilty act"—unless he also had a "guilty mind." (The Latin term that judges and lawyers use for this is *mens rea*.)

- If you are carefully driving under the speed limit and unavoidably strike and kill a child who, without any warning to you, jumps out from between two parked cars, that is indeed a tragedy, but you should not be labeled and punished as a murderer.

- If you accidentally walk out of a store carrying an item in your hand for which you simply forgot to pay, that is a mistake, but you should not be labeled and punished as a shoplifter.

- If you are insane or suffer from a mental defect and cannot control your wrongful conduct or understand its wrongfulness, you have not formed the criminal intent and don't possess the guilty mind that makes you criminally liable for the crimes for which you otherwise would be punished.

Traditional crimes retain this historical guilty-mind requirement that protects the average American from criminal punishment for unavoidable accidents and other innocent mistakes. For crimes such as murder, rape, robbery, and theft, the government must prove beyond a reasonable doubt both (1) that the defendant was in fact the one who did the guilty act and (2) that he did so with the requisite criminal intent.

Until about 50 years ago, these two substantive protections against unjust criminal conviction and punishment were an essential element of virtually every criminal law on the books in America. These practical limitations on the scope of criminal law are assumed by and woven into the fabric of our constitutional protections against unjust criminal punishment. They are not as apparent to most Americans as the procedural protections that they see in almost every law-and-order movie or television show, like the reading of one's Miranda rights, but they are just as important—if not more so.

Thus constrained, American criminal law historically advanced the proper ends of government in safeguarding both liberty and security. Limiting criminal punishment to conduct that is inherently wrongful restricted governmental power in two important ways.

First, and most important, it served a normative purpose by keeping the range of governmental power small. Having few criminal laws and a short list of things not to be done limits the scope within which government can exercise its authority.

Second, it served a descriptive purpose by reflecting the beliefs and understandings that were common to the vast majority of our citizens—the very citizens who were subject to the criminal law.

These limitations in size and scope made our criminal law definite and knowable. Combined with the guilty-mind requirement, this greatly reduced the likelihood that anyone might stumble into punishment by an inadvertent or unconscious act. The average American was well equipped to know the law and to avoid transgressing it.

The "New" Criminal Law: The Road Less Traveled

Unfortunately for the law and its effects on the average American, an unprecedented politicization of American criminal-law policy and practice has taken place over the past 50 years. The criminal law has become a vehicle for social change instead of for the maintenance of social order. In lockstep with this period of increasing politicization, the size and scope of criminal law, at both the federal and state levels, has expanded dramatically. The average American, the average business person, and the average corporation have little or no hope of knowing all of the thousands of criminal-law statutes—and tens of thousands of criminal-law regulations—by which they must abide in order to remain on the right side of the law.

This is one of the primary reasons why it is no longer possible to avoid becoming a criminal by relying on one's conscience and general understanding of the law. Indeed, doing so would mislead the average American, since state and federal lawmakers have criminalized many forms of productive economic and social activity that, until very recently, were never considered wrongful.

A key reason for the deterioration of our criminal law is its sheer size and scope. In 1998, an American Bar Association task force estimated that there were well over 3,000 federal criminal offenses scattered throughout the 50 titles of the United States Code. Just six years later, a leading expert on the over-criminalization problem and one of the contributors to this book published a study estimating that the number was well over 4,000. As the ABA task force reported, the body of federal criminal law is "[s]o large…that there is no conveniently accessible, complete list of federal crimes."

> The ABA task force reported that the body of federal criminal law is "[s]o large…that there is no conveniently accessible, complete list of federal crimes."

Moreover, as if over 4,000 federal criminal offenses were not enough to criminalize any and every form of conduct Congress can imagine, Columbia law professor John Coffee has estimated that the federal government could use the criminal process to enforce as many as 300,000 federal regulations.

But the numbers only begin to define the problem. Quite literally, the scope of criminal law is now as wide as the regulatory scope of our governments—and in a world where governments increasingly run society, that scope has expanded to encompass virtually all human activity. It is only a slight exaggeration to say that potentially everything you do each day is subject to criminal law: driving, purchasing, gardening, and even, yes, eating.

Compounding the destructive effects of this explosion in the size and scope of the criminal law is the seemingly daily loss of the traditional substantive protections (rather than the more familiar procedural protections) that have shielded Americans from unjust prosecution and conviction. In multiple 20th century cases, for example, the Supreme Court held that the Constitution does not require a criminal conviction to be supported by proof of criminal intent or a guilty mind. This has had catastrophic consequences for American criminal law. Legislators at both the state and federal levels routinely enact criminal laws today that have no meaningful *mens rea* requirement. Because this fundamental protection is missing, Americans who had no intention of engaging in conduct that is inherently wrongful or of violating any law are routinely punished with criminal fines and imprisonment. The results are not much different from what they would be if legislators eliminated insanity as a defense or used language expressly criminalizing accidents and other unintentional acts.

> If everyone is potentially a criminal, then it is the government and its employees who decide which people to charge.

More fundamentally, legislators have made the criminal law into, essentially, a much rougher and more coercive version of civil law. But where civil law is designed to correct individual wrongs and make the injured whole, the criminal law is something more: an expression of social disapproval and opprobrium. One would think that the two should remain distinct—and so they did until recently.

Now, however, legislators routinely incorporate into many criminal statutes innovative doctrines that made sense only in the legal context in which they were first developed—that is, tort law where the remedy for wrongs committed is usually monetary damages. Tort-law doctrines are now used to make individuals criminally responsible for the acts of others who are not within their actual control and who did not act at their actual direction. These doctrines, going by names like "strict liability," "vicarious liability," and "*respondeat superior*" (Latin for a superior being held responsible), are now used to charge as criminals those who did not act with a guilty mind or who themselves did nothing at all wrong.

Thanks to these doctrines borrowed from tort law, the average American can now be punished as a criminal for crimes his employees committed—even if he implemented rules, training programs, and similar measures to prevent those employees from engaging in the prohibited conduct. The use of these tort-law doctrines in service of criminal prosecutions has transformed economically and socially beneficial conduct into act-at-your-peril activities. These innovative doctrines mean that even an inadvertent misstep by someone acting with all due care can result in a prison sentence.

The worst consequence, however, is possibly the most insidious: If everyone is potentially a criminal, then it is the government and its employees who decide which people to charge. With so wide a scope of possible criminal charges, we now face a situation where the discretion of the government determines who goes to jail and who goes free.

Where our government exercises that discretion with wisdom, justice will result; but, as reflected in the principles embodied in our Constitution and our concept of the rule of law, we insist on a government that is limited precisely because we doubt the unerring wisdom of officialdom. The comprehensiveness of criminal law now means that it may be deployed as a weapon against the disfavored or the politically unpopular without regard to the true nature of their conduct.

Wider Implications of Overcriminalization

Until the middle of the 20th century, American criminal law represented the distillation of wisdom from thousands of years of legal development. At least in its traditional form, it drew on lessons learned from many earlier systems of crime and punishment. American law's most immediate and obvious relative is the English legal system, itself a descendant of Norman French

deprivations of money, freedom, and—in the case of capital crimes—even life itself.

This system of prohibitions and punishments serves as society's ultimate bulwark against the evils of anarchy and against the exercise of real or perceived rights to avenge oneself when one has been wronged. Its application should be limited to actual threats to public order, not innocent mistakes. Misapplication and unwarranted expansion of the criminal law's force can result only in the dilution of that force and the deterioration of the criminal law's function as a protective bulwark for civil society.

> **Without limits protecting citizens from haphazard application of criminal punishment, law becomes a tool of oppression rather than protection.**

Without limits protecting citizens from haphazard application of criminal punishment, law becomes a tool of oppression rather than protection. As it diverges from commonly held ideas of justice, respect for the law declines, as does its moral force upon American society. Without that respect and force, law is far less able to further the ends of government in protecting the life, property, and liberty of the average American.

In conjunction with individuals and organizations spanning the political spectrum, my colleagues and I at The Heritage Foundation have been working for several years to raise public awareness of the problems of overcriminalization and to promote meaningful reforms before our criminal law traditions are irretrievably lost. Many legal scholars—and a large and increasing number of judges and lawyers—now recognize that American criminal law has deteriorated so badly and become so politicized that substantial reform is needed.

Much is at stake for our freedoms and the freedoms of future generations. The problems and proposed reforms in the following pages merit extensive study and debate by legal experts, policymakers, and the average Americans whose fundamental liberty is most at stake. Many constructive changes are possible that would make our justice system fairer and more just and that would do a better job of deterring wrongdoing and punishing real criminals. Taking the steps necessary to ensure that American criminal law once again routinely exemplifies the right principles and purposes will require much work, but the alternative is to squander the great treasure that is the American criminal justice system.

EDITORS' PREFACE

This is not a theoretical book. It is a practical book that is intended to serve as a clarion call for action. Much as we did in exposing "The Imperial Congress," The Heritage Foundation wants to shine a light on a little-noticed area of American political culture and then start the conversation about how to change that culture. To do that, we have to do two things: explain to the American people that there really is a problem and then show them that the problem is solvable.

To that end, this book is divided into three related parts.

Part I looks at the problem of overcriminalization through the eyes of its real-world victims: honest people caught in the labyrinth of a criminal law that no longer looks anything like the criminal law they were taught about in civics class. You will meet a Honduran lobsterman and an American orchid grower, a Medicare doctor and an honest businessman (yes, there really are some of those around), as well as several others. All of them have one thing in common: They were unjustly accused, caught up in the web of laws that today give prosecutors virtually unchecked power. Their stories are the stories of the innocent when the government comes and knocks on the door.

Part II gives you some of the more detailed historical and legal background of overcriminalization. Professors Rosenzweig, Lynch, and Baker explain the history of criminal law and how a pseudo-socialist movement of the mid-1900s hijacked venerable criminal law principles in the service of class-based aims. You will see firsthand the explosive growth in the sheer number of crimes being created by Congress and how prosecutors, in their unending effort to find new crimes, have distorted age-old doctrines, attempting to pervert them to their own ends. You will also see, through the examples of New York and Texas, how criminal law has been expanded in the states.

Part III tells you what you can do about it by outlining a robust, specific reform agenda. To get started, all you need to do is read this book. It will scare you, but fear is a great motivator for change, and we at Heritage are convinced that change is just ahead of us.

Finally, we wish to offer special thanks to Eric Lotke, who suggested the title, and to the members of the editing and publication staff at The Heritage Foundation, who were responsible for the production of this book.

CONTRIBUTORS

John S. Baker, Jr., is Dale E. Bennett Professor of Law and Director of the Hemispheric Trade Program at the Louisiana State University Law Center. Since 1999, he has also been an Invited Professor at the University of Lyon III (France) and has taught several summer courses on separation of powers with U.S. Supreme Court Justice Antonin Scalia. Professor Baker received his J.D. with honors from the University of Michigan Law School (1972) and his B.A. *magna cum laude* from the University of Dallas (1969). He also earned a Ph.D. from the University of London (2003). While a professor, he has been a consultant to the U.S. Department of Justice, the U.S. Senate Judiciary Subcommittee on Separation of Powers, and the White House Office of Planning. He served on an American Bar Association Task Force that issued *The Federalization of Crime* (1998). His writing includes the following books: *The Intelligence Edge: How to Profit in the Information Age* (with Friedman, Friedman, and Chapman; Crown Books/Random House, 1997); *Hall's Criminal Law: Cases and Materials* (with Benson, Force, and George; 5th ed., Michie, 1993); and *An Introduction to the Law of the United States* (ed. with Levasseur; University Press of America, 1992).

James R. Copland directs the Manhattan Institute's Center for Legal Policy, which seeks to communicate thoughtful ideas on civil justice reform to real decision-makers. He serves as managing editor of the Institute's PointOfLaw.com, a Web magazine that brings together information and opinion on the U.S. litigation system, and project manager for the Institute's *Trial Lawyers, Inc.* series of publications examining the size, scope, and inner workings of America's lawsuit industry. Before joining the Manhattan Institute, Mr. Copland was a management consultant with McKinsey and Company in New York. He earlier served as a law clerk for the Honorable Ralph K. Winter on the United States Court of Appeals for the Second Circuit. Mr. Copland earned J.D. and M.B.A. degrees from Yale, an M.Sc. in politics of the world economy from the London School of Economics, and a B.A. in economics with highest distinction and highest honors from the University of North Carolina at Chapel Hill.

Trent England directs the Citizenship and Governance Center at the Evergreen Freedom Foundation in Olympia, Washington. He was previously a legal policy analyst in the Center for Legal and Judicial Studies at The Heritage Foundation. Mr. England is admitted to the Washington State Bar. He earned a J.D. from the George Mason University School of Law and a B.A. in government from Claremont McKenna College. He lives with his wife and three children in Bremerton, Washington.

Andrew M. Grossman is a former analyst in the Center for Legal and Judicial Studies at The Heritage Foundation. He recently graduated from George Mason University School of Law and currently serves as a law clerk to the Honorable Edith Jones of the United States Court of Appeals for the Fifth Circuit.

Quin Hillyer, a senior editorial writer for *The Washington Times* and a senior editor for the *American Spectator*, has won awards for journalistic excellence at the local, state, regional, and national levels. He has been published professionally in well over 50 publications, including *The Wall Street Journal*, *The Washington Post*, the *Houston Chronicle*, the *San Francisco Chronicle*, *Investor's Business Daily*, *National Review*, *The Weekly Standard*, *Human Events*, and *The New Republic Online*. He was an original member of the executive board of the internationally acclaimed Louisiana Coalition Against Racism and Nazism, formed to halt the then-meteoric political rise of former Ku Klux Klan leader David Duke. Hillyer is a *cum laude* graduate of Georgetown University and a Fellow of both the Loyola University (New Orleans) Institute of Politics and Leadership Coastal Alabama.

Marc A. Levin is a director of the Center for Effective Justice at the Texas Public Policy Foundation, an Austin attorney, and an accomplished author on legal and public policy issues. His articles on law and public policy have been featured in publications such as *The Wall Street Journal*; *USA Today*; the *Texas Review of Law and Politics*, *National Law Journal*, *New*

York Daily News, Jerusalem Post, Toronto Star, Atlanta Journal-Constitution, Philadelphia Inquirer, San Francisco Chronicle, Washington Times, Los Angeles Daily Journal, Charlotte Observer, Dallas Morning News, Houston Chronicle, Austin American-Statesman, and *San Antonio Express-News*; and *Reason* magazine. Levin has served as a law clerk to Judge Will Garwood on the U.S. Court of Appeals for the Fifth Circuit and Staff Attorney at the Texas Supreme Court. In 1999, he graduated with honors from the University of Texas with a B.A. in Plan II Honors and Government. In 2002, he received his J.D. with honors from the University of Texas School of Law.

Erica A. Little graduated *cum laude* from the University of California at Los Angeles with a bachelor's degree in history and political science. She received her J.D. in 2007 from George Mason University School of Law, where she wrote on the *Federal Circuit Bar Journal* and worked in the Clinic for the Legal Assistance of Service Members. While completing her legal education, she worked as a Legal Policy Analyst at The Heritage Foundation's Center for Legal and Judicial Studies until returning to her native California, where she is currently practicing environmental law.

Tim Lynch directs the Cato Institute's Project on Criminal Justice, which under his leadership has become a leading voice in support of the Bill of Rights and civil liberties. His research interests include the war on terrorism, overcriminalization, the drug war, the militarization of police tactics, and gun control. In 2000, he served on the National Committee to Prevent Wrongful Executions. Lynch has also filed several *amicus* briefs in the U.S. Supreme Court in cases involving constitutional rights. He is the editor of *In the Name of Justice: Leading Experts Reexamine the Classic Article "The Aims of the Criminal Law"* and *After Prohibition: An Adult Approach to Drug Policies in the 21st Century.* Since joining Cato in 1991, Mr. Lynch has published articles in *The New York Times, The Washington Post, The Wall Street Journal,* the *Los Angeles Times,* the *ABA Journal,* and the *National Law Journal.* He has appeared on *The NewsHour with Jim Lehrer, NBC Nightly News, ABC World News Tonight,* Fox's *The O'Reilly Factor,* and C-SPAN's *Washington Journal.* He is a member of the Wisconsin, District of Columbia, and Supreme Court bars and earned both a B.S. and a J.D. from Marquette University.

Edwin Meese III holds the Ronald Reagan Chair in Public Policy at The Heritage Foundation, responsible for keeping the President's legacy of conservative principles alive in public debate and discourse. He also is the Chairman of Heritage's Center for Legal and Judicial Studies, founded in 2001 to educate government officials, the media, and the public about the Constitution, legal principles, and how they affect public policy. Before joining Governor Reagan's staff in 1967, Mr. Meese spent eight years as a Deputy District Attorney in Alameda County, California. In addition to being Governor Reagan's Executive Assistant and Chief of Staff from 1969 through 1974, Mr. Meese served as the governor's Legal Affairs Secretary from 1967 through 1968. From 1977 to 1981, he was Professor of Law at the University of San Diego and directed the law school's Center for Criminal Justice Policy and Management. During that same period, he served as Vice Chairman of California's Organized Crime Control Commission. As Counselor to President Reagan and his chief policy adviser from January 1981 to February 1985, he led the development of the Administration's policies for combating crime in America. Mr. Meese served as the 75th Attorney General of the United States from February 1985 to August 1988.

Paul Rosenzweig is the founder of Red Branch Consulting PLLC, which provides comprehensive strategic advice to companies, individuals, and governments in the areas of criminal law, homeland security, and privacy. He also practices national security and criminal law in a separate solo practice. Mr. Rosenzweig formerly served as Deputy Assistant Secretary for Policy in the U.S. Department of Homeland Security and twice as Acting Assistant Secretary for International Affairs. Before joining the Department, Mr. Rosenzweig served as Senior Legal Research Fellow in the Center for Legal and Judicial Studies at The Heritage Foundation, where his research interests focused on issues of civil liberties and national security and criminal law.

Dick Thornburgh is Of Counsel at K&L/Gates in Washington, D.C. He previously served as Governor of Pennsylvania, Attorney General of the United States under two Presidents, and the highest-ranking American at the United Nations during a public career that spanned over 25 years. All told, Mr. Thornburgh served in the U.S. Department of Justice under five Presidents, beginning as United States Attorney in Pittsburgh (1969–1975) and Assistant Attorney General in charge of the Criminal Division (1975–1977), emphasizing efforts against major drug traffickers, organized crime, and corrupt public officials. He is Chairman of the U.S. Committee for Hong Kong and a member of the board of advisers of the Russian–American Institute for Law and Economics.

Brian W. Walsh is the Senior Legal Research Fellow in The Heritage Foundation's Center for Legal and Judicial Studies. He directs Heritage projects on countering the abuse of the criminal law and criminal process, particularly at the federal level. His work also focuses on efforts to ensure that national and homeland security measures include protections for constitutional and other civil liberties. Before joining Heritage in 2006, Mr. Walsh worked on contract with the U.S. Department of Homeland Security; was an associate in the Washington office of Kirkland & Ellis, LLP; and served as a law clerk to Judge Pasco M. Bowman III on the Eighth Circuit U.S. Court of Appeals.

PART I

THE OVERCRIMINALIZATION PROBLEM

Trent England, Andrew M. Grossman,
and Erica A. Little

CHAPTER 1

A LOBSTER TALE
Invalid Foreign Laws
Lead to Years in U.S. Prison
(United States v. McNab)

David McNab is a Honduran citizen whose family has been in the fishing business for generations. McNab's business imported into the United States some of the spiny lobsters his company's vessels caught in Caribbean waters 100 to 350 miles off the coast of Honduras. Spiny lobster is not the same as the lobster caught off New England; it is far more plentiful and grows abundantly in the warmer waters of the Caribbean.

Two of McNab's business customers, Robert Blandford and Abner Schoenwetter, are United States seafood importers who sometimes purchased Caribbean spiny lobsters from him. Diane Huang worked for a California-based seafood distributor that purchased lobster tails from Blandford's company, processed them for distribution, and sold them to large American restaurants such as Red Lobster.

The story of how these four businessmen ran afoul of American criminal law began in February 1999 with an anonymous fax to the National Marine Fishery Service (NMFS), a division of the National Oceanic and Atmospheric Administration (NOAA) at the U.S. Department of Commerce. The fax stated that one of McNab's seafood shipments was scheduled to arrive in Bayou La Batre, Alabama, in two days. The fax alleged that the shipment contained "undersized (3 & 4 oz) lobster tails." It also claimed that, under Honduran law, the lobsters should have been packed in cardboard boxes but were instead packed in clear plastic bags.

Based on this strange, anonymous message, NMFS agents waited for McNab's ship and seized the $4 million worth of seafood—a huge sum for the company—upon the ship's arrival in Alabama. Without providing an explanation, the federal government held the ship and all of its contents for weeks and then confiscated McNab's 70,000 pounds of Caribbean spiny lobster and took it to a giant government freezer in Florida. There the

A spiny lobster—good to eat, but harvesting could cost you your liberty.

lobster tails sat for six months while NMFS agents scoured Honduran statutes and administrative regulations for some legal basis to hold the lobster meat and prosecute McNab and the importers.

After repeated phone calls, letters, and trips to Honduras, NMFS investigators eventually developed a basis for criminal charges (under a law known as the Lacey Act) against the four importers. They focused on three Honduran administrative regulations:

- The first regulation controlled the processing and packaging of fish harvested in Honduran waters. Written in 1993, this regulation required that exported seafood be packed in cardboard boxes. Nobody has ever been able to explain why cardboard boxes were required or has ever claimed that the requirement was a matter of health or food safety.

- The second regulation prohibited harvesting lobsters with tails shorter than five and a half inches. The nominal purpose of this regulation was to prevent the harvesting of juvenile spiny lobsters before they had a chance to reproduce—a sensible regulation in theory, since maintenance and management of fisheries are legitimate governmental concerns. Nonetheless, this must have come as a surprise to the investigating NMFS agents, since NMFS regularly published open market prices for two- and three-ounce Caribbean spiny lobsters from Honduras; that is, they were well aware, as the government's own expert admitted at trial, of an open public market for lobsters of two to three ounces that would necessarily have tails shorter than five and a half inches.

- The third Honduran provision prohibited destroying or harvesting "eggs, or the offspring of fish…or other aquatic species for profit." This regulation was obviously intended to protect the eggs of fish from being harvested, thereby disrupting the reproductive cycle at its inception.

Six months after sending the lobster to the cooler, NMFS agents finally had a legal standard to use to inspect the locked-up lobster tails. Fewer than one out of every 30 lobster tails turned out to be shorter than five and a half inches. Just 7 percent showed any evidence of having been egg-bearing lobsters. Despite these small percentages and the contradictory NMFS price lists, which seemed to approve of the public sale of small spiny lobsters, federal prosecutors used these violations of Honduran regulations as grounds for charging the importers and distributors under the Lacey Act.

The Lacey Act itself is a well-meaning law that prohibits the taking of any wildlife in violation of local, domestic laws and regulations. Its intent originally was to make it a crime for an American, for example, to hunt elephants in Kenya in violation of Kenyan wildlife protection regulations. Now this Act (with its modest penalties) was being deployed in this business context.

Charges based on these two technical violations (relating to young or child-bearing lobsters) alone would have allowed NMFS to seize only the relatively few lobster tails that were under five and a half inches or that showed evidence of bearing eggs, but federal prosecutors went on to charge that the entire shipment was illegal and formally seized all 70,000 pounds of lobster tails because they were packed in plastic bags rather than cardboard boxes.

Seizing millions of dollars worth of seafood and crippling McNab's business was still not enough to satisfy the government's view of justice. Federal prosecutors filed criminal charges against McNab and the three Americans who were destined to have received his lobsters. All charges

that because the Honduran president had not ratified the size restriction, it did not have the force of law.

Other witnesses, including a former Honduran Minister of Justice, testified that the egg-harvesting regulation was not intended to apply to sea creatures that just happened to be bearing some eggs when caught. The prohibition against harvesting or destroying eggs for profit was meant to do just that: prevent the intentional harvesting of eggs themselves. It was specifically targeted at the harvesting of turtle eggs, not lobster eggs that happened to be attached to the legs of some lobsters in a catch.

U.S. government prosecutors convinced the court to ignore McNab's extensive evidence and instead accept the testimony of a single Honduran bureaucrat, Liliana Paz. Her impressive-sounding title was Secretary-General of the Honduran Ministry of Agriculture and Livestock, but her primary official duties were to act as "an instrument of communication." She had neither the authority nor the expertise to render legal opinions. Yet, for reasons that remain unexplained, Ms. Paz testified that all of the regulations were valid and had the force of law.

Despite the apparent lack of intent by McNab and the importers to engage in any criminal or otherwise wrongful act (there was, for example, no evidence that McNab or the three importers knew that U.S. officials would deem clear plastic bags to be criminal smuggling devices), as well as significant questions about the validity of the Honduran regulations, all four defendants were convicted. Because of the add-on smuggling and money-laundering charges, the penalties were severe. In August 2001, McNab, Blandford, and Schoenwetter were each sentenced to eight years in federal prison. Huang, the seafood reseller, was sentenced to two years.

> In August 2001, McNab, Blandford, and Schoenwetter were each sentenced to eight years in federal prison. Huang, the seafood reseller, was sentenced to two years.

The U.S. Department of Justice touted the convictions in press releases, characterizing McNab as "the ringleader of a smuggling operation." These accounts were intended to portray McNab as deliberately and intentionally harvesting undersized and egg-bearing lobsters, never mentioning that the lobsters that fell into these two categories constituted just a small percentage of his catch. The Justice Department also neglected to mention that the only reason for declaring the entire shipment illegal and McNab a smuggler was that the seafood was packed in plastic bags instead of cardboard boxes. Only by the use of Orwellian Newspeak could a clear plastic bag—which is, of course, more transparent than the cardboard boxes called for under the Honduran regulation—conceivably be characterized as a device used by smugglers.

A press release issued by NOAA, the NMFS's parent agency, implied that the size and success of McNab's business was a key component of his "crime." NOAA's release

NOAA's release emphasized that McNab owned a "fleet of vessels, each of which can deploy thousands of lobster traps," as if this in itself was somehow wrongful.

emphasized that McNab owned a "fleet of vessels, each of which can deploy thousands of lobster traps," as if this in itself was somehow wrongful. Striking an even more bizarre note, NOAA declared that "[t]he wealth from McNab's vast harvest was denied to the common citizens of Honduras." McNab, a Honduran citizen, was apparently not "common" enough by the standards of certain NOAA bureaucrats.

After conviction, while his appeal was pending, McNab sought new evidence from Honduras that established his innocence and that of his three co-defendants even more strongly. Following the district court hearing on the force and meaning of Honduran law, McNab filed an action in the Honduran Court of First Instance of Administrative Law challenging the lobster size restriction. Several months after the end of the criminal trial in the United States, the Court of First Instance issued its decision. It formally held that the lobster size limit was void and declared that it had never had the force of law.

McNab's attorneys also discovered that the law authorizing the packaging regulations had actually been repealed in 1995. Under Honduran law, a regulation is automatically repealed when the authorizing statute is repealed. Even the prosecution's key witness on Honduran law, Ms. Paz, admitted this in a post-trial affidavit. Further, it became clear that the egg-harvesting provision had been repealed in a manner that, under Honduran law, operated retroactively. This repeal took place four years before the anonymous fax transmission that kicked off the NMFS investigation. Under Honduran law, the egg-harvesting regulation thus had no governing force over the four defendants' lobster shipment.

Finally, McNab filed a motion with the Honduran National Human Rights Commissioner challenging Ms. Paz's testimony about Honduran law. This Honduran office is charged with addressing complaints that the actions of government officials constitute "legal error." The Commissioner, Dr. Leo Valladares, is an internationally respected constitutional lawyer and human rights advocate. He issued a report, signed by the Minister of Agriculture (Liliana Paz's boss), stating that Ms. Paz's testimony constituted "an error of law." Valladares confirmed that the packaging regulation was repealed in 1995, that the size restriction had "never had the force of law," and that the egg-bearing provision had been retroactively repealed.

Through its embassy, the Honduran government directed this evidence demonstrating that the lobster defendants had violated no Honduran law to the U.S. State Department, asking that the Department forward it for review by the Department of Justice. The Attorney General of Honduras also filed an *amicus curiae* (friend of the court) brief during McNab's appeal to the United States Court of Appeals for the Eleventh Circuit (headquartered in Atlanta), providing this same evidence and explaining that McNab and the others had not violated any Honduran law.

The judges didn't care. On appeal, two out of the three judges on the panel effectively declared Honduras a banana republic, unfit to construe its own laws. This majority decided that it would be unwise to disagree with the American prosecutors' interpretation of foreign law, citing the "political question" doctrine. This doctrine limits the power of courts to meddle in the political affairs that the Constitution has assigned to the two elected branches of government. The

> On appeal, two out of the three judges on the panel effectively declared Honduras a banana republic, unfit to construe its own laws.

Eleventh Circuit's ruling ignored the holdings of other federal courts of appeal and essentially abdicated one of the most important roles of appellate courts: the job of determining the meaning of the written law.

Perhaps worst of all, the two federal appeals court judges who formed the majority appeared to believe that Honduran officials could not be trusted to interpret their own laws. This disdain for the democratically elected government of Honduras (all of these events happened many years before the current controversies in Honduras) somehow did not seem to apply to Liliana Paz, the Honduran bureaucrat who testified for the prosecution. In the interests of "finality," which appears to be more important to the judges than "justice," the Eleventh Circuit upheld the lower court on every issue. Because of the way the case was formulated for the jury, if the court of appeals had agreed with the Honduran government's assessment of its own regulations and found even one of the Honduran regulations to be invalid, all of the convictions would have been thrown out.

But let's step back and ask the more fundamental question: Even if one or more of these minor Honduran fishing regulations was still valid when McNab's ship set sail for Alabama in 1999, would criminal prosecution by the United States be justified? For supposed violations of lobster-related Honduran regulations, these four people had their lives and livelihoods destroyed. Despite strong evidence suggesting that David McNab and the other three defendants never intended to violate the law—traditionally a requirement for a criminal conviction—prosecutors and judges sent them all to federal prison.

> McNab has just been released from prison, where he spent eight years for violating Honduran regulations that the Honduran government itself certified did not apply to his actions.

In 2004, the Supreme Court of the United States declined to hear the defendants' appeal of the Eleventh Circuit's decision that affirmed their convictions. This essentially ended the possibility of their obtaining a victory from the American legal system.

Four people attempting to earn a living and support their families through legal commercial activities were sent to federal prison. Today, nearly 10 years after the U.S. National Marine Fishery Service received the anonymous fax and began investigating a shipment of lobster, one of them, McNab, has just been released from federal prison, where he spent eight years for violating Honduran regulations that the Honduran government itself certified did not apply to their actions. As of this writing, two of the others, Blandford and Schoenwetter, each have more than a year in prison remaining.

It is not possible to understand how this indefensible example of overcriminalization could be consistent with any just theory of American criminal law.

CHAPTER 2

CRIMINALIZING SUCCESS
The Prosecution of an
Honest American Businessman
(United States v. Cassese)

John Cassese is a hard-working businessman who faced the likelihood of years in federal prison for having made an honest mistake—a mistake his prosecutors agreed Cassese did not have the necessary information to avoid. Indeed, Cassese never tried to hide the fact that he bought stock in a computer company. He did not take any steps to deny making the stock purchases for which he was prosecuted, because he never suspected at the time he made them that they might be illegal.

Cassese made no false statements. He made no attempt to cover up his conduct. When, after the fact, he realized that the trades broke the laws, he readily admitted to the Securities and Exchange Commission (SEC) that he was responsible for a technical violation of the securities regulations. Without raising any objection, Cassese paid back the entire amount plus interest that he had earned from two securities purchases that technically violated SEC regulations. And without any challenge, he paid an additional civil penalty of $150,937.50.

Nonetheless, Cassese was charged with, tried (not once, but twice) on, and eventually convicted of federal criminal securities law violations. But for the bravery of a single federal judge who had the courage to throw out his conviction, Cassese might well have spent many years in jail. As it was, his reputation was tarnished, and years of his life were spent fighting the injustices of federal prosecution.

At the time Cassese made his fateful stock purchases, he was the Chairman and President of Computer Horizons Corporation, a computer and information technology services provider with annual revenues of $515 million. Cassese and two friends founded Computer Horizons in 1969.

Cassese was recognized not only for his material success, but also for his genuine care and concern for customers and employees.

Back then, the Internet did not exist, the development of the microprocessor was two years in the future, and the average computer was the size of several commercial refrigerators, costing hundreds of thousands of dollars. Over the next 30 years, Cassese labored to build Computer Horizons into one of the world's leading information technology services companies. Computer Horizons' engineers and other computer and information systems professionals helped design and develop a wide variety of telecommunications and computer information systems. Cassese saved Computer Horizons from a hostile takeover attempt in the 1980s and repositioned the company to become one of the key information technology service providers during the 1990s technology boom.

Cassese was recognized not only for his material success, but also for his genuine care and concern for customers and employees. In 1997, he was named New Jersey Entrepreneur of the Year. The following year, a leading Wall Street newspaper featured Cassese in a "Leaders & Success" column on its front page.

Cassese's stock troubles were only incidentally related to his Computer Horizons business. They stemmed instead from his personal purchases of the stock of one of his competitors, Data Processing Resources Corporation (DPRC). It all started in April 1999 when Computer Horizons began considering a merger with Compuware, another leading information technology services company. Ultimately, Computer Horizons rejected Compuware's offer.

At the same time that it was exploring merger possibilities with Cassese's company, Compuware was also conducting what it apparently concluded were more promising negotiations to acquire DPRC. The DPRC board approved a merger with Compuware in early June 1999.

On June 17, 1999, Compuware CEO Peter Karmanos called Cassese to inform him that Compuware had decided to acquire DPRC instead of

Computer Horizons. According to the judge who later presided over Cassese's criminal trial, the call with Compuware's CEO was brief, innocuous,
and unremarkable:

> On June 21, 1999, Karmanos spoke with Cassese, *whom
> he had never met, for the first and only time on a four-
> minute phone call.* During that call, Karmanos told Cass
> ese that (1) Compuware would not be doing a deal with
> Computer Horizons at that time, but might be interested
> in purchasing it in the future; and (2) that Compuware
> was going to announce a deal with DPRC instead. *Kar
> manos did not tell Cassese any details about the deal.*[1]

The next morning, Cassese purchased stock in DPRC. As a general
rule, it is perfectly legal to trade stock based on such non-public information about a merger. Cassese was an experienced corporate executive and
knew this. There are two exceptions to this rule, however.

First, such trades are not legal if the investor owes a financial duty to
either of the two merging companies. Cassese did not have any duty to
either company, and nobody has ever suggested that he did.

Second, stock purchases of this
sort are illegal if the merger is being transacted by means of a tender offer. A tender offer is simply a
public offer to purchase shareholders' stock for more than the current

**All three witnesses testified without
equivocation at trial that they never
said anything to Cassese about how
the merger would be transacted.**

market price. If a stock is trading at, say, $2 per share, a tender offer would
be an offer to purchase those shares at, say, $3 per share. One can, of
course, do a merger in any number of other ways.

In fact, the Compuware/DPRC merger was one of these forbidden
types—a tender-offer merger—so Cassese's purchases were illegal. But
Cassese didn't know that, because he didn't know that this was a tender-
offer merger, and nobody has ever said he did. The only three people the
government identified at trial as possible sources of any non-public information that Cassese knew regarding Compuware's merger with DPRC
were Compuware CEO Karmanos, another Compuware executive, and a
securities broker. All three of these men testified without equivocation at

trial that they never said anything to Cassese about how the merger would be transacted.

The first broker Cassese called the morning of his purchases was a friend at Morgan Stanley, but he was unavailable. Cassese then called his Merrill Lynch broker and placed an order for 10,000 shares of DPRC. When Cassese's Morgan Stanley friend called back later that day, Cassese placed a second order for another 5,000 shares. Both brokers later testified that these two trades were typical for Cassese. In fact, he had purchased stock in DPRC before, just as he had purchased stock in some of Computer Horizons' other competitors. Cassese never indicated to his brokers that he was trying to hide anything. He did nothing unusual, such as asking either broker to monitor closely DPRC's status or stock price.

Three days after Cassese received the information from Compuware's Karmanos, Compuware made its first public announcement of the DPRC merger. Unfortunately for Cassese, Compuware announced that the merger would be transacted by a tender offer. Cassese's Morgan Stanley broker reached him that same day with news of the merger—including mention of the tender offer. Surprised, Cassese immediately instructed the broker to sell those 5,000 shares. He then called his Merrill Lynch broker and had him sell his other 10,000 shares.

Cassese later asked whether it was possible to cancel the trades altogether, which would have wiped out any gain he might otherwise have made, but the transactions could not be cancelled. Because the announcement of the tender offer drove up the price of the stock, Cassese's sales of the two DPRC stock holdings resulted in a gain to him of about $150,000.

In February 2002, two and a half years later, the SEC filed a civil complaint against Cassese alleging insider trading in DPRC stock. Because the merger had been transacted by tender offer, Cassese had violated the civil law without even knowing it at the time. Generally speaking, there are two major differences between civil penalties and criminal charges.

First, unlike criminal prosecutions, the government does not have to prove every element of the typical civil violation beyond a reasonable doubt. Rather, the level of proof is only "by a preponderance of the evidence." The difference is proving something in a criminal case so that the jury is 95 percent sure (or more) that it happened versus proving it so that they are 51 percent sure that it happened in a civil case. Obviously, a civil case is much easier to prove.

Second, also unlike a typical criminal law charge, the government does not have to prove that the defendant acted with the intent to do anything wrong. In a civil securities case, an individual is "strictly liable" for his actions; in other words, he can be civilly liable even for accidentally or inadvertently violating the law. Again, that makes a civil case much easier to prove, and it is also why we use the civil law to correct minor wrongs and reserve the criminal law for more significant wrongs that threaten society.

Cassese knew he had made an inadvertent mistake. He immediately settled the civil case with the SEC. He paid back all profits from the DPRC stock sales, plus interest, and also paid a civil penalty equal to the gain on his DPRC investments. In all, Cassese paid the government $321,387.84. "I'm very well paid, and it looks stupid," Cassese told the Bergen, New Jersey, *Record* when asked about the SEC settlement. "I never tried to hide anything. If I made a mistake, I made a mistake." Cassese kept his job and position at the company he had founded 33 years earlier, and the matter appeared to have been settled.

While Cassese had been working to settle matters with the SEC, however, the Enron scandal had been unfolding. Flurries of state and federal investigations were launched into the affairs of public corporations of all sizes and into several Wall Street firms. Soon it became clear that telecommunications giant World-Com was self-destructing. In July

> "I never tried to hide anything. If I made a mistake, I made a mistake."

2002, President George W. Bush created the Corporate Fraud Task Force and signed the Sarbanes–Oxley Act, which dramatically increased public companies' federal reporting requirements.

Many pundits and business-school academics were claiming that the late-1990s boom had produced a culture of corruption within American business. Politicians accused regulators and prosecutors of having gone soft on corporate criminals. House Financial Services Committee Chairman Michael G. Oxley (R–OH), however, presciently warned that the increasingly hysterical

Senator Paul Sarbanes (D–MD) and Representative Michael Oxley (R–OH), authors of the Sarbanes–Oxley bill, which criminalizes business mistakes.

anti-business fervor threatened to "smother American businesses with red tape" and "punish those who have done nothing wrong."

In the midst of this hype and hysteria over an alleged epidemic of corporate wrongdoing, on March 13, 2003, the United States Attorney for the Southern District of New York—one of the members of the President's new Corporate Fraud Task Force—announced two criminal charges against Cassese.

Prosecutors normally have great discretion when they begin investigating possible wrongdoing. Most important, they can decide whether or not to pursue criminal charges against a particular person. This discretion can often serve as a critical safeguard in our justice system. Sensible prosecutors spend their time seeking criminal fines and imprisonment for people who intentionally commit illegal acts. They recognize that it makes no sense to punish someone criminally for an innocent mistake, especially a mistake for which they already have been sanctioned civilly.

Prosecutorial discretion can also be an important check against political expedience. Sometimes, however, this safeguard gives way to political pressure.

Both criminal charges against Cassese were based on the DPRC stock transactions made nearly four years earlier. One said that he had violated his financial duties to Compuware and DPRC; the other, that he had illegally traded stock in a tender merger. Cassese had, of course, settled the SEC's civil complaint a year earlier. Nevertheless, the government suddenly and inexplicably decided that he should pay even larger fines and go to prison too—for a maximum of 10 years for each of the two counts.

Two months before trial, District Judge Robert W. Sweet threw out the first of the two charges because the evidence was clear that Cassese was not an insider at Compuware or DPRC and owed no duty to either company. In his ruling on the dismissal, Judge Sweet pointed out a key reason to doubt the strength of the government's case: "It is interesting to note that the SEC determined it inappropriate to charge Cassese with [this violation] in the civil context." If the SEC had not even sought a civil penalty against Cassese for violating a duty to

Judge Robert W. Sweet, who heard John Cassese's case.

the companies, even though it would have been far easier to prove it in the civil context, he rightly doubted whether a crime had been committed.

In September 2003, Cassese was tried on the only remaining charge: alleged insider trading in violation of the Securities Exchange Act of 1934 based on the tender-offer mistake. At the end of the six-day trial, the first jury deadlocked during its deliberations. The jury in the second trial found Cassese guilty after a single day of deliberations. A Department of Justice press release extolled the verdict as an important victory against white-collar crime.

Cassese filed a post-trial motion asking the judge to disregard the jury verdict and enter a judgment acquitting him, arguing that in this context he could not possibly have had criminal intent since he did not know (and there was no evidence establishing that he did know) before he purchased DPRC stock that the merger would be conducted by tender offer. He further challenged the government's interpretation of the facts, asserting that "the evidence that the government claimed was proof that [he] acted willfully, actually showed his innocence."

In his opinion on the motion, Judge Sweet pointed out that while knowledge of a tender offer is not a necessary element of the crime, criminal intent is. In every similar prior case, different circumstances demonstrated the criminal intent of those convicted. But without any knowledge that the merger was by tender offer, Cassese had no reason to believe that his actions were illegal. He could not have had the requisite intent to commit a crime. Judge Sweet noted that Cassese was subject to strict liability in the civil context, but not in a criminal trial.

> **Without any knowledge that the merger was by tender offer, Cassese had no reason to believe that his actions were illegal.**

Criticizing the government's attempt to transform the securities laws into a "trade at your peril" regime, Judge Sweet reversed Cassese's conviction. Overruling a jury verdict in a federal criminal trial is a rare and courageous act for a trial judge. Given the federal prosecutors' tenuous theories of the law and the facts in Cassese's case, however, the evidence simply failed to indicate that the combination of Cassese's intent and actions constituted a crime. Cassese was not ignorant of the law: He knew, or thought he knew, that what he was doing was legal. He could not know until it was announced that the tender-offer format selected for the merger would cast legal doubt on his investments in DPRC's stock *after* he made the purchases.

The dangers of criminal law are well demonstrated by the Cassese case. None of the uncontradicted facts clearly demonstrating Cassese's lack of intent to commit a crime deterred the federal government from prosecuting him as a criminal. On top of the SEC's civil proceeding and penalties against him, the government subjected Cassese, his reputation, his business, and his family to the indignities and public reproach of two criminal trials.

Cassese nevertheless was one of the "lucky" targets of overcriminalization. Fortunately for him, the trial judge threw out the jury's verdict after concluding that, as a matter of law, the government's evidence was insufficient to support a conviction. The two criminal trials and the resultant enormous damage to Cassese's livelihood and reputation could have (and should have) been avoided. All that was necessary was for federal lawmakers to clarify the criminal intent component required by the federal securities law that the government used to prosecute Cassese.

But even in the face of an ambiguous law, we should expect more of our professional prosecutors. The judge was right to chastise the Justice Department for not interpreting the statute to require proof of criminal intent to prosecute someone as a criminal.

Cassese's case demonstrates the vast discretion and fearful power that prosecutors have to make decisions that can ruin virtually any American's business, livelihood, and reputation. At a more important and fundamental level, however, the case exposes the destruction of the deep moorings the criminal law used to have in Americans' common understanding of what is right and what is wrong, what is good and what is evil. Those common understandings originally justified a criminal conviction only when there was a combination of two crucial substantive components. No American could be convicted of a crime unless he (1) committed an inherently wrongful act (in Latin, *actus reus*) that constituted a serious threat to public order with (2) a wrongful motive or intent (*mens rea*).

These two substantive components of a crime were essential for a conviction in the Anglo-American world for centuries both before the American Founding and for well over the first 100 years of the new republic. Any time lawmakers pass a criminal law that dispenses with the traditional intent requirement, men and women like John Cassese who are both honest

> On top of the SEC's civil proceeding and penalties against him, the government subjected Cassese, his reputation, his business, and his family to the indignities and public reproach of two criminal trials.

and hard-working can find themselves facing prison time. This is true even if their alleged crime is a purely inadvertent violation that occurs while they are pursuing activities that produce social and economic benefits.

Historically, it was one thing to protect a person against unjust processes that could raise their probability of being wrongly accused and convicted. To guard against the possibility of such procedural injustices, the law developed the right against self-incrimination, the right to counsel, and the right to trial by jury, each of which is enshrined in the text of the Constitution.

The Framers, however, would never have considered it necessary to preserve in the text of the Constitution the historical *actus reus* and *mens rea* components of a crime. The Framers did not think to enshrine in the

Constitution a requirement that a crime must be composed of both a wrongful act and a wrongful intent because no one at the time would have imagined fashioning a criminal law that dispensed with the intent requirement. Defining "crime" in the Constitution would have been akin to inserting the definition of a "court," a "judge," or a "jury," none of which finds definition in the Constitution because the essential nature and character of each was assumed, based on longstanding practice and common experience.

In the world of global markets, multimillion-dollar businesses, and often cutthroat competition, Cassese stands out as an honest entrepreneur who created jobs for thousands of professionals and support-staff members, as well as honest, legitimate wealth for innumerable investors. Despite no indication that he ever acted with corrupt intentions, and despite abundant evidence that his trades were an honest mistake, federal prosecutors tried to send Cassese to prison for up to 20 years.

Criminal law is properly reserved for conduct committed with wrongful intent. Those who commit public wrongs with such intent deserve punishment. Those who accidentally or negligently injure others may be required to pay the injured party damages under the civil law. Yet a person who violates the law only because of a circumstance that is unknown to him cannot have wrongful intent and cannot deserve criminal punishment.

When political pressure or public opinion motivates prosecutors to disregard traditional limitations on criminal punishment, all Americans are endangered. If a defendant's lack of criminal intent is no longer a protection against prosecution, conviction, and prison time, how can anyone be safe from conviction? Getting tough on corporate criminals should mean getting tough on those who actually commit crimes—with criminal intent. Getting tough on corporate criminals should not mean criminalizing mistakes.

CHAPTER 3

BURNING BUSHES
Gardening Grandma Arrested for Failure to Prune
(Palo Alto v. Leibrand)

The David McNab story forces us to ask: What penalty should American law impose on those whom the American government (but not the Honduran government) deems to have transgressed Honduran regulations governing fishing? The story of the Palo Alto pruning police asks a similar question: How should the law treat a software engineer and grandmother whose most extensive brushes with the law have been traffic citations when she fails to keep the hedge surrounding the home she has lived in with her family for 36 years clipped shorter than two feet high?

The answer provided by the city of Palo Alto, California, was to have 61-year-old Kay Leibrand arrested and charged as a criminal. We kid you not.

Kay Leibrand and her husband bought their earth-toned Palo Alto bungalow on the corner of Waverly Street and El Dorado Avenue in 1966. The Leibrands were happy with their corner lot, and Mrs. Leibrand took a special delight in gardening with native California plants.

A few years after moving in, Leibrand planted xylosma seedlings between the sidewalk and the Waverly Street curb. Xylosmas are leafy, evergreen shrubs and are commonly used for hedges around gardens and sidewalks. Leibrand planted them to beautify the neighborhood and help muffle the noise coming from Waverly Street. A healthy line of neatly pruned bushes with shiny evergreen leaves soon sheltered her home and backyard from the sights and sounds of traffic.

Cuyamaca College photo

Xylosma. Kay Leibrand was arrested for criminal "failure to trim" these types of hedges.

Until its criminal enforcement action against the Leibrands began, the city had no record of any complaints about visibility at the Leibrands' intersection. Similarly, there was no record at all of any accidents at the intersection, much less any accidents related to the Leibrands' xylosma hedge.

Leibrand began a long fight with cancer in the 1990s. In September 2001, she returned from a trip out of town to find a Palo Alto "Notification of Violation" that had been left on her doorstep. It indicated that the city had received an anonymous complaint about the Leibrands' hedge. Leibrand was aware that her plants needed a trim, so she set about the task. Her work quickly restored the allegedly offending xylosma bushes to their usual well-kept appearance, which in 35 years had never before drawn a single complaint.

Nevertheless, a few weeks later, another Notification of Violation, this time sent by certified letter, informed the Leibrands that, in the city's view, the bushes remained in violation of the city's municipal code. The city cited an ordinance that required plants in the strip between the street and the sidewalk to be no more than two feet tall. According to this second notification, the Leibrands had to trim the shrubs or face "enforcement action," including "an administrative citation with a penalty in the amount of $500."

Leibrand did not want to be a scofflaw, but neither did she want to mow down her mature, well-kept xylosma hedge. After the letter from the city, she made sure once again to prune both the xylosma bushes and the rest of her plants carefully and neatly. The Leibrands checked the visibility at the intersection and verified that it was completely unimpaired by the hedge. Leibrand then contacted Palo Alto's Code Enforcement Officer and asked him to inspect the bushes himself to confirm that they were not a threat to visibility or safety.

Surprisingly, the Code Enforcement Officer refused. Leibrand's case had become "high-profile," he said, and he would not use the discretion he had been granted by state statute to grant her a waiver from this strict and unprecedented enforcement action by Palo Alto of the municipal code on hedge height. The officer told her to chop her bushes down to two feet or suffer the consequences.

Leibrand continued to try to appeal to city officials to act in a fair and reasonable manner. In a letter to Palo Alto's Chief Planning Official, she explained the situation. "If any plant over two feet tall in a planting strip is a safety hazard," she wrote, "then the city is indeed unsafe with…possibly hundreds of code violations." Leibrand noted that enforcement of the regulation based only on complaints guaranteed unequal and even biased enforcement of the law. This is especially true when, as did Palo Alto, a town or city refuses to use its discretion to see to it that enforcement actions follow the spirit of a law that is designed to ensure visibility and public safety.

The city's response to Leibrand's letter claimed that the Code Enforcement Officer had "considered both fairness and safety" and instructed her that the standards were "there to protect people from potentially unsafe situations." Surprisingly, the letter asserted that Palo Alto officials had no discretion with regard to enforcing the ordinance and reaffirmed the city's demand that Leibrand either cut the plants down to two feet or face prosecution.

According to this second notification, the Leibrands had to trim the shrubs or face "enforcement action," including "an administrative citation with a penalty in the amount of $500."

Leibrand was seriously ill and had already twice pruned the hedge to her typical exacting standard. She had also twice verified that the hedge did not hinder visibility in any direction. The city's enforcement officer had dismissed out of hand her request that he inspect her hedge himself. Leibrand decided to stand on principle: She would not do any further pruning.

Her letter in reply informed the city that she was seriously ill, pointed out that the weather was bad, and explained that the city had given her absolutely no reason to believe the hedge posed a safety hazard. She also pointed out that if the city was truly interested in safety, her intersection was plagued with stop-sign violations and high-speed traffic.

Reasonable and fair-minded city officials would have dropped the matter at this point. In fact, one of the most common defenses that is offered whenever a proposed criminal law is so broad that it can be read to criminalize conduct that no one would have considered wrongful under any rational standard is that the officials entrusted with enforcing the law can be trusted and expected not to charge crimes unless they are truly wrongful. This justification is offered even by well-meaning Americans who vociferously defend the principles of the American Founding: that the powers of government should be few and limited and that each governmental power should be subject to multiple checks and balances in order to prevent its abuse. Perhaps because such advocates of new overcriminalization are reasonable persons themselves and focus on all of the possible good the new criminal law could do and all the bad it would punish, they believe that any law-enforcement official would see things as they do.

> The pressure to achieve more—more arrests and convictions of more offenders under more (so-called) criminal offenses—affects all law enforcement officials at all levels of government.

Regretably, the real world rarely conforms to the visions of overcriminalization's advocates. Even reasonable law-enforcement officials are subject to pressures and temptations that can cloud their judgment and make it difficult to resist using the law in a manner that promotes their law-enforcement organization's interests, their personal self-interests, or their personal political or ideological views. In America today, no one's job is safe, even in government, and law enforcement officials are under pressure to perform. The pressure to achieve more—more arrests and convictions of more offenders under more (so-called) criminal offenses—affects all law enforcement officials at all levels of government. Power corrupts, Lord Acton noted. Unfortunately, it subtly corrupts even many who are well-intentioned.

The reality is that when in the mind of a government official (or his boss) the benefits of applying and enforcing an overbroad, unjust criminal law outweigh the harms, that official will probably apply and enforce it. Kay Leibrand's case illustrates this well. It is highly unlikely that the mayor or any member of the city council of Palo Alto had a case like Leibrand's in mind when they criminalized hedges over two feet high. (And if any of them did envision scenarios such as this and voted for the law anyway, they are unworthy of their offices.) Inevitably, however, one or more Palo Alto officials who reviewed the Leibrand dispute decided that the general purposes of the law, whether it was to maintain clear sight lines along the streets, to keep property values high, or to create a uniform look for the city, outweighed the harm of turning one of the city's long-time, law-abiding residents into a criminal.

Palo Alto officials thus referred the enforcement action to a Special Legal Counsel. According to Leibrand, the counsel failed to return any of her telephone calls and e-mails and disregarded the municipal code's provision for a hearing that would have allowed Leibrand to present her case. Instead, he dispatched two Palo Alto police officers to arrest Leibrand in her home.

On April 3, 2002, Kay Leibrand, a 61-year-old software engineer and grandmother, surrendered to the police. Her crime? She allowed her hedge to grow more than two feet high. Two Palo Alto police officers arrested her at her home, loaded her into the backseat of their patrol car in plain view of her friends and neighbors, and hauled her down to the Palo Alto police station. At the station, they fingerprinted Leibrand and compelled her to pose for mug shots. She was informed that she had committed a crime and must face the consequences. She might go to jail, or perhaps she would get off with just a fine. As a final indignity, before releasing her, the officers demanded a sworn statement that Leibrand—a Palo Alto resident for 36 years—would appear in court and not flee the jurisdiction.

As a last resort, Leibrand wrote to the city manager pointing out the strange way she was singled out and had never even been offered a hearing. The city's only response was to issue a press release celebrating this grandmother's arrest and providing salacious details of her arraignment.

The city's only response was to issue a press release celebrating this grandmother's arrest and providing salacious details of her arraignment.

On April 17, Leibrand was booked at the Palo Alto Police Station. She was arraigned the next month in Santa Clara County Superior Court, where she pled "not guilty." A criminal trial was set for February 10, 2003, but was delayed to allow the parties time to try to negotiate for a possible settlement of the criminal charges.

Eventually, the city of Palo Alto did settle with Leibrand. It is difficult to say whether it was Leibrand who gave in because of the risk she faced of criminal penalties or whether the city caved in rather than prosecute her in front of a jury of her fellow citizens for gardening-related crimes. Soon after the settlement, however, squat clumps of xylosma stumps appeared along Waverly Street where a healthy and attractive row of xylosma bushes had stood for years. To avoid a possible criminal fine or jail time, the Leibrands were also required to make a donation to a tree-planting organization.

In sum, officials of Palo Alto could enjoy the satisfaction of having "successfully" prosecuted one of its long-time residents and homeowners under a criminal statute governing the height of hedges. The citizens of Palo Alto were now safe in their homes from the grave dangers to society posed by 61-year-old Kay Leibrand.

Leibrand's case highlights some of the costs of runaway criminalization. Making trivial offenses like "aggravated failure to prune" into criminal offenses adds another burden to a criminal justice system that has far weightier problems to redress. It is certainly possible for poorly maintained properties to diminish the value of surrounding proper-

> The citizens of Palo Alto were now safe in their homes from the grave dangers to society posed by 61-year-old Kay Leibrand.

ties or to pose safety risks, but there is no need to address peeling paint, unmowed lawns, or overgrown hedges by using the criminal law when the civil law would suffice.

Let's see how: The civil law provides Americans multiple weapons they can use to combat, for example, vegetation that dangerously obstructs sight lines along their streets. Perhaps the biggest club the civil law provides is tort lawsuits for those whose person or property is allegedly injured as a result of poorly maintained private property. The possibility of large (indeed, sometimes unjustly large, but that is another story and another book) jury awards of damages is sufficient to deter all reasonably conscientious property owners from allowing their property to fall into neglect. For others, neighbors can bring lawsuits alleging that the neglected property interferes with their right to the full use and enjoyment of their own property and thus constitutes a nuisance under the law. If the problems with the offending property are extensive enough, a city or town may itself bring the suit, claiming that the property constitutes a public nuisance.

In addition to these tort lawsuits, cities and towns can pass zoning ordinances that specify mandatory maintenance standards, and officials may impose a civil fine that is commensurate with the severity of the zoning violation.

> There is nothing inherently evil about allowing a hedge to exceed a certain height, the paint on a garage door to peel, or a car in one's driveway to rust.

Finally, Americans may choose when they purchase residential or commercial property to enter into mutual covenants with their neighbors. Such covenants are common and constitute a legal ground to bring a civil lawsuit to compel recalcitrant neighbors to maintain their properties according to agreed-upon standards.

All of these legal tools or mechanisms for enforcing property maintenance standards afford an opportunity to impose a penalty on the offending property owner that is proportional to the offense. They also permit the alleged offender a meaningful opportunity to defend herself and her interests without exposing herself to the risk of criminal penalties that are far out of proportion to the nature and extent of her wrongful conduct—an opportunity Kay Leibrand never had.

The nature of the criminal law, by contrast, is such that it should be reserved for the most morally offensive conduct society faces. There is nothing inherently evil about allowing a hedge to exceed a certain height, the paint on a garage door to peel, or a car in one's driveway to rust. People who are ill, elderly, physically disabled, or just extremely busy trying to make ends meet can allow such things to happen with no wrongful intent whatsoever. Criminalizing such things trivializes the law, undermining the public's confidence in and respect for the criminal law.

The city of Palo Alto decided to use a criminal provision in its municipal code regulating the height of bushes

> Never before in the city's history had it prosecuted residents for horticultural excesses. (Ironically, "palo alto" actually means "tall tree" in Spanish.)

to make an example of Kay Leibrand and her hedges. In the midst of a "visibility project" designed to improve city appearances and safety, they broke out the blunderbuss of criminal law. Never before in the city's history had it prosecuted residents for horticultural excesses. (Ironically, "palo alto" actually means "tall tree" in Spanish.) During and after Leibrand's legal battle, she and her husband repeatedly produced photographs, taken at locations throughout Palo Alto, of similarly offending shrubs that Palo Alto and its police department chose to overlook.

Overcriminalization such as was present in Mrs. Leibrand's case leads to legal confusion, selective enforcement, and unfair prosecutions. Perhaps the most pernicious effect of overcriminalization is the threat such laws pose to honest and otherwise law-abiding people. The threat of broad regulations with criminal penalties hangs precariously overhead, threatening even the most law-abiding Americans.

The city of Palo Alto decided that general enforcement of its hedge height law would be too burdensome, so it created a complaint-based system. As one of Leibrand's letters to the city pointed out, this kind of enforcement—based on anonymous complaints from anyone who has a bad day or even a personal axe to grind—inevitably results in biased, vindictive prosecution. Overbroad laws that criminalize trivial "offenses" for which there are insufficient resources to carry out uniform, across-the-board enforcement thus end up being selectively enforced, effectively (at least in spirit) denying citizens the "equal protection of the law" guaranteed by the United States Constitution.

The battle is over at the corner of Waverley and El Dorado in Palo Alto. The xylosma bushes have been chopped down, casualties of Palo Alto's decision to overcriminalize. Leibrand, another casualty, noted that her backyard became a little less peaceful and a little noisier. Sadly, on July 20, 2003, five months after Kay Leibrand lost her battle with city bureaucrats intent on enforcing a trivial and unjust criminal law, she also lost her battle with breast cancer.

CHAPTER 4

NO GOOD DEED GOES UNCRIMINALIZED

Environmental Crimes Create a Legal Minefield

(Hansen v. United States)

In 1991, the financially troubled Hanlin Group, Inc., filed for Chapter 11 bankruptcy. Christian Hansen had founded the Hanlin Group nearly 30 years earlier, acquiring a chemical plant in Brunswick, Georgia, in 1979. Before the bankruptcy filing, that subsidiary, LCP Chemicals–Georgia, had been operated by Hanlin for over a decade.

LCP employed about 150 workers at the Brunswick plant. Some worked in two large buildings, called "cellrooms," where mercury cells were used to produce bleach, hydrochloric acid, and other chemicals commonly used by industry and in consumer products. Waste from this production process was separated, stored, and eventually removed from the facility.

With Hanlin in bankruptcy, LCP began struggling financially, cash flow became an issue, and the company had problems, particularly with maintenance and repair for its production facility. LCP nevertheless continued to hold safety briefings for employees, provide protective gear, and require regular urinalysis to monitor mercury exposure. The facility was equipped with a wastewater treatment system and had a permit to discharge water after it had been treated to remove chemical pollutants.

In order to ensure that the facility's water treatment system was never overloaded by production, LCP's discharge permit authorized the facility to hold water in the cellrooms until it could be treated and then released. Periodically, excess water began to accumulate in the Brunswick facility's cellrooms. After receiving an OSHA complaint, LCP constructed a board-walk to protect employees from standing wastewater.

Christian Hansen had some difficult decisions to make, and he needed someone he could trust to help his 30-year-old business weather serious financial straits. So he convinced his son, Randall Hansen, to serve as executive vice president of LCP. Randall was a smart, up-and-coming businessman with a young family and his own career direction. After doing some financial work for the Hanlin Group when younger, he had left in 1989 to pursue other opportunities. Randall nevertheless took the post with LCP to help his father get the Hanlin Group back on its feet. His father assigned him the daunting task of developing the business and financial plans necessary to turn around the financial condition of the chemical business.

The Brunswick plant was already suffering environmental problems when Randall Hansen was hired. Randall sought funds to repair the plant, but all requests had to go through Hanlin's board of directors, the bankruptcy creditor's committee, and the bankruptcy court. Nearly all the requests were denied. Randall sold unnecessary equipment and eliminated some jobs in an attempt to fund the needed repairs, but the moves proved largely ineffective.

> "Taylor stressed safety and strict adherence with LCP's training and safety programs, and assured employees the right to refuse to perform any activity if the employee felt it to be unsafe."

Cash-strapped, the Brunswick plant continued to struggle in an attempt to meet all its obligations. Alfred Taylor, an LCP employee since that company's founding, was the Brunswick plant's operations manager when Randall Hansen came in to help rescue the company. Two years later, Taylor was promoted to plant manager—something that Taylor will probably always regret.

According to the federal appeals court that reviewed Taylor's later conviction, as manager, "Taylor stressed safety and strict adherence with LCP's training and safety programs, and assured employees the right to refuse to perform any activity if the employee felt it to be unsafe." Unfortunately, the plant generated so much wastewater that it began occasionally to overflow through a doorway. Taylor promptly reported these unauthorized discharges of untreated water to LCP's board of directors and to the environmental protection division of Georgia's Department of Natural Resources.

Shortly after his promotion to plant manager, Taylor recommended temporarily suspending production to make major repairs and, if they proved unsuccessful or unfeasible, shutting the plant permanently. Randall later told Taylor that Randall would not be allowed to close the plant. Meanwhile, the unauthorized discharges continued, and Taylor continued to report them to state officials.

In April 1993, the Hanlin Group's directors removed Christian Hansen, Randall's father, from his positions as president, CEO, and chairman of the board but allowed him to remain employed with the company he had founded. Randall was given the CEO position. In July 1993, Taylor resigned as plant manager, and his responsibilities were assigned to Christian Hansen. Because of the continued discharges of untreated water, the State of Georgia notified LCP that it was preparing to revoke the plant's permit. Randall nearly sold the company on two different occasions, but both sales failed. After the second attempt, the Brunswick plant was closed. Randall unsuccessfully requested $1.5 million from the bankruptcy court for environmental cleanup.

> Shortly after his promotion to plant manager, Taylor recommended temporarily suspending production to make major repairs and, if they proved unsuccessful or unfeasible, shutting the plant permanently.

More than four years later, and as the statute of limitations was about to expire, federal prosecutors brought criminal charges against Christian Hansen, Randall Hansen, Alfred Taylor, and three other LCP employees at the Brunswick plant. The charges included (1) knowingly discharging pollutants in violation of LCP's permit under the Clean Water Act; (2) knowingly storing, treating, or disposing of hazardous waste without a Resource Conservation and Recovery Act (RCRA) permit; (3) knowingly endangering employees at the plant, such that they were placed in imminent danger of death or substantial harm; and (4) conspiring with other officers of Hanlin to violate these environmental laws.

Alfred Taylor and the two Hansens were convicted on nearly all counts. The other defendants entered into plea agreements before trial to secure more favorable sentences and testified against the Hansens and Taylor.

Christian Hansen was sentenced to nine years and one month in prison; Randall Hansen was sentenced to four years. Both were fined $20,000. Alfred Taylor was sentenced to six-and-a-half years.

Randall Hansen had come to LCP in order to turn it around and had continually—if unsuccessfully—fought with the board and the bankruptcy court for the resources necessary to prevent environmental violations. The evidence suggested that, rather than intending to break the law, Randall sought at every turn to bring the plant into full environmental compliance. He was nevertheless convicted because environmental crimes, like many of today's regulatory crimes, have very low requirements of criminal intent.

Likewise, Alfred Taylor was an advocate for employee safety and appropriately notified government authorities of improper wastewater discharges. After becoming plant manager, he had recommended that the plant be repaired or shut down. He resigned from his plant manger's position soon after his recommendations were rejected.

> The evidence suggested that, rather than intending to break the law, Randall sought at every turn to bring the plant into full environmental compliance.

There was no question that the plant had operated at times in violation of environmental laws, yet those violations could have been dealt with through administrative or civil enforcement. Those mechanisms are intended to prevent future violations and remedy whatever damage has been done. Administrative or civil courts emphasize the harm incurred because of regulatory violations but generally disregard the issue of intent. Unlike criminal courts, they don't mete out punishments, so there is no need to consider whether individuals actually deserve punishment. Criminal law, on the other hand, focuses on punishment and thus has historically applied only to those found deserving of such punishment because of their proven criminal intent.

Most of the charges against the Hansens also relied on the "responsible corporate officer" doctrine. Under this rule, executive officers of a company are responsible for the actions of their subordinates whether or not they knew of or authorized those actions. Christian Hansen was even convicted for events that occurred after October 1993, when he no longer held a position of authority within the company or at the Brunswick plant. Likewise, Taylor was convicted for occurrences at the plant after he had resigned from his management position. Randall Hansen was rarely in

Brunswick but was focused on restoring the finances of the entire corporation. Because the legal doctrine under which he was prosecuted does not require him to have had any wrongful intent, it did not make any difference whether he knew nothing about the discharges and fully performed every duty he had to perform to remain apprised of the plant's operations.

> Christian Hansen was even convicted for events that occurred after October 1993, when he no longer held a position of authority within the company or at the Brunswick plant.

Randall Hansen had joined the Hanlin Group in an attempt to help his father. He landed in a highly regulated industry where a complex web of laws and regulations virtually ensured some violations. Preexisting problems at the plant, a chronic lack of funds, and the bankruptcy process all limited Randall's courses of action. All three defendants were convicted against this backdrop. In many instances, the acts or events that led to the charges were far removed in time and space from the defendants. Nevertheless, their convictions and sentences were affirmed by the Atlanta-based U.S. Court of Appeals for the Eleventh Circuit. In 2002, the Supreme Court declined to review the case.

Randall Hansen tried to bring the Brunswick plant's operation into compliance with the law. His reward was spending almost four years in prison separated from his wife and young children.

CHAPTER 5

CRIMINALIZING KIDS
True Tales of Zero Tolerance and Overcriminalization

Lindsay Brown had good reason to be excited. It was May 2001, and she was just weeks from her graduation from Estero High School in Fort Meyers, Florida. The honor student and National Merit Scholar had an academic scholarship to Florida Gulf Coast University. She had spent the weekend moving into her own apartment.

Graduation would be an important milestone. As her mother recounted, Lindsay had been a lackluster student through middle school, unmotivated and undirected, but then she got serious. "All of a sudden, she decided that she wanted to graduate, she wanted to go to college," said her mother. "She did everything with graduation in mind." High school had transformed Lindsay into a model student who excelled in her science and English classes.

Everything seemed perfect until one Monday afternoon when a school security officer asked Lindsay to accompany him to the school parking lot. Lindsay had parked her 1991 Geo Storm in the wrong spot that morning, but that's not what the trip to the parking lot was about. Security officer John Scheall, also a county police officer, directed Lindsay's attention to her car's passenger seat. Sticking out from beneath it was a kitchen knife, just a piece of flatware, with a 5-inch blade and a rounded tip. Lindsay was puzzled, she recalls. Where did the knife come from?

She was whisked from the parking lot to the school's Resource Office for interrogation by the officer and top school officials: Why was the knife in her car? What did she plan to do with it? Lindsay didn't have any good answers, but the significance of the questioning was beginning to sink in. She was scared and hyperventilating, and the questions kept coming. Maybe her boyfriend had left the knife in her car, she told them. Under the pressure of their questioning, she wasn't sure. All she knew for sure was that she hadn't put the knife in her car.

And yet, there it was. Lindsay was arrested, handcuffed, and hauled off in police custody. She was charged with felony weapons possession and put in Lee County Jail, where she spent nine hours. The other prisoners in the lockup—real criminals—looked her over closely. "Honey, what are you doing here?" one asked. She was finally released after her parents paid $2,500 in bail.

After the initial questioning, the answer had come to her. It was so simple: During her move that past weekend, the knife had fallen unnoticed from one of the boxes. But that didn't matter. Regardless of how or why that knife wound up in Lindsay's car, the result would have been the same. It didn't matter whether she knew it was there or not, or what kind of student she was or what her teachers knew of her enthusiasm and good nature. It didn't even matter that her discipline record at the school was spotless.

> The other prisoners in the lockup—real criminals—looked her over closely. "Honey, what are you doing here?" one asked.

Lindsay was suspended from school for the last five days of classes. She was banned from the senior class breakfast, the yearbook staff party, and graduation ceremonies. School officials explained to her that she was getting off light. Had the knife been found a week earlier, Lindsay would have had to finish the year at an alternative school for delinquents. As it was, they would let her take her final exams.

Lindsay had run afoul of the school district's "zero-tolerance" policy. According to a district official, 26 separate offenses could lead to automatic disciplinary consequences. Bringing a knife onto school grounds—even a butter knife—was toward the top of the list, a Level 3 violation comparable to possession of a real weapon or an illegal drug. Estero's principal, Fred Bode, declined to make an exception for Lindsay's kitchen implement. "A weapon is a weapon is a weapon," he told the local paper. "We can't treat honor roll students differently than students with a 1.9 GPA."

A week after Lindsay's arrest, common sense finally made an appearance when State Attorney Joe D'Alessandro dropped the state's charge against her. He pointed out that the law required proof beyond a reasonable doubt that Lindsay knew the knife was in the car. "I just can't prove that she willingly and knowingly brought it on to the school grounds," explained D'Alessandro. Without knowledge of Lindsay's intent, he couldn't press criminal charges. A judge would eventually agree to expunge her criminal record.

Zero-tolerance policies are in force at most of the nation's public schools. As a spokesman for Lindsay's school district put it, "We are not the law. All we want are rules that will keep safety in the schools"—in other words, zero tolerance. But strict and indiscriminate rules inevitably create innocent victims like Lindsay Brown.

The zero-tolerance movement in schools began in earnest in 1994 with passage of the Gun-Free School Zones Act. The Supreme Court had found an earlier direct federal ban on guns in school zones to be unconstitutional. But in 1994, Congress and President Bill Clinton came up with a different approach, imitating other kinds of federal legislation, to allow the federal government to impose its policies on school districts across the nation.

> The 1994 Act required every state receiving federal educational dollars—in other words, all of them—to enact zero-tolerance legislation and expel students who have brought a weapon to school.

The 1994 Act required every state receiving federal educational dollars—in other words, all of them—to enact zero-tolerance legislation and expel students who have brought a weapon to school. The expulsions had to last for at least one year, though states could grant local school officials the ability to modify the expulsion requirement on a case-by-case basis.

What qualifies as a weapon under the Act is strictly defined. A weapon is an object which is "designed to or may be readily converted to, expel a projectile by the action of an explosive." Also included are "firearm silencer[s]" and "any explosive, incendiary, or poison gas," as well as bombs, grenades, missiles, and mines. Knives are not covered by the Act. The federal definition, however, is only a minimum requirement.

When state legislatures drafted legislation to comply with the Gun-Free School Zones Act, few limited their laws to the federal definition of a weapon. Provisions for possession of drugs, alcohol, tobacco, and knives were "obvious" and easy extensions of the law. Some states went further, including not just possession of contraband, but also certain behaviors. Intoxication, fighting, and even truancy suddenly became grounds for automatic expulsion in some states.

These policies easily won support from state lawmakers. After all, what legislator wouldn't want to oppose knives or alcohol in schools? After the federal enactment and corresponding state legislation, local school districts and individual schools followed up with their own zero-tolerance rules and regulations, again often expanding the scope of offenses and increasing the severity of punishments. Within little more than a year, zero tolerance swept the nation's schools.

Whatever initial resistance existed was washed away by growing public concern about school safety. After watching horrifying scenes from Columbine and elsewhere, many parents demanded action. Policymakers and school administrators often answered by creating, emphasizing, or expanding zero-tolerance policies. Many school officials also came to realize that such automated disciplinary policies allowed them to avoid complaints about unfair punishments or challenges to their discretionary decisions. No discretion meant no responsibility. Zero tolerance seemed to be here to stay.

> No discretion meant no responsibility. Zero tolerance seemed to be here to stay.

While cases like Lindsay Brown's have created a slowly growing backlash, most zero-tolerance policies remain in place. The Gun-Free School Zones Act was reenacted in slightly expanded form as part of the No Child Left Behind Act, leaving federal education dollars tied to state zero-tolerance policies for firearms in schools. Most zero-tolerance policies continue to reach far beyond guns, encompassing anything that resembles or might be used as a weapon, as well as both illegal and legal drugs and alcohol.

It is difficult to determine how many students are directly affected by zero-tolerance policies. In the 2003–2004 school year (the most recent year for which data were available at print time), 2,165 students were expelled nationwide for possessing a firearm at school. This number has actually been declining since 1996, according to U.S. Department of Education reports. The most recent data also showed a very high percentage of reported case-by-case "modifications" (46 percent of all cases).

Of course, the vast majority of these incidents involve weapons and would result in expulsion or another serious consequence under any other sensible school safety regime. Policies of zero tolerance, however, ensure that students without harmful intent will be punished along with the rest.

There are no national data for zero-tolerance punishments that are not gun-related. There is also no breakdown of which cases would likely be treated the same under any disciplinary regime and which cases are actually affected by zero tolerance. Certainly, many students punished for any zero-tolerance infraction committed their offense with nefarious intent and would be punished similarly under a non–zero tolerance disciplinary regime. Yet without considering student intent through case-by-case examinations, it is equally certain that numerous other Lindsay Browns will be caught in the zero-tolerance trap every school year.

> Four kindergartners were playing "cops and robbers" at their school. They pointed their fingers at each other. "Boom! I have a bazooka." None of the children were actually found to have a bazooka. But they were still punished.

Each one of the 55 million children in America's public schools confronts some kind of zero-tolerance policy. Many of those students are expected to memorize long and sometimes arbitrary lists of items and behaviors that could get them suspended, expelled, or even arrested. They must know exactly what is in their backpacks, pockets, lockers, and cars at all times lest they accidentally head off to school with a Girl Scout knife or a packet of aspirin and wind up in a lockup. Students, including elementary-school children, are expected to mind what they write and draw (in some districts, drawing a firearm can result in zero-tolerance consequences) and to be careful what they say. Indeed, in some schools, a playful childish threat can lead to harsh consequences.

On a March day in 2000, four kindergartners at Wilson Elementary were playing "cops and robbers" at their school in Sayreville, New Jersey. They pointed their fingers at each other and let their imaginations take over. "Boom! I have a bazooka, and I want to shoot you," was among the taunts that A.G. yelled. (His initials are all that is part of the public record.) Later, the *Atlanta Journal and Constitution* helpfully reported, "None of the children were actually found to have a bazooka." But they were still punished. The kindergarten students were suspended from school for "making threats," a violation of their district's zero-tolerance policy.

"Given the climate of our society, we cannot take any of these statements in a light manner," said school principal Georgia Baumann. "It may be just a game or something said in jest, but it can be taken differently by other children."

The district's superintendent, William Bauer, was even more direct: "This is a no-tolerance policy. We're very firm on weapons and threats."

Try explaining that to kindergarten-age boys, a parent might retort. For what it's worth, the school did try. Just a few days before the incident, Baumann himself had gone from classroom to classroom—even to the kindergarten classes—explaining to students that threats would not be tolerated.

Baumann was also responsible for informing the boys that they had violated the rules and would be punished with three-day suspensions. As one might expect of five-year-old children, they cried, no doubt puzzled that their playtime activity would lead to such serious consequences.

In 2003 at a Florida middle school, a sixth grader armed with a calculator was arrested for felony weapons possession.

Despite a wave of bad publicity, the district held firm and defended its zero-tolerance approach. In an interview with *The New York Times*, Assistant Superintendent Denis Fyffe asserted a connection between kindergartners' schoolyard games and Columbine-like school shootings. Fyffe explained that it was better to err on the side of caution than to "have a dead first-grade girl who was killed inside a classroom." "It was a well-thought-out decision, bearing in mind the age of the students and the type of infraction," said school board member Curtis Clark. "It was in no way a knee-jerk reaction."

Zero-tolerance policies deliberately ignore the distinction between wrongful intent and innocent intent, focusing mechanistically on acts alone. They generally apply to students regardless of age or other factors that are often exculpatory in the adult justice system. While perhaps an extreme example, the cops-and-robbers case is not unique.

In 2003 at a Florida middle school, a sixth grader armed with a calculator was arrested for felony weapons possession. Cortez Curtis's mother would later recall buying the inexpensive calculator out of pity for a roadside-stand salesman. The novelty item was not just for math, but included a variety of foldout tools. The evening before her son's arrest, she lent it to him for his homework. The next day, Cortez brought the calculator to school. He accidentally dropped it while working on his math, and a little pocketknife blade rotated partly out.

One of Cortez's classmates told the teacher, who initially could not even find the two-inch blade in the calculator. The teacher reported the incident to school administrators. They had Cortez arrested. The sixth-grader was booked into juvenile detention—all this pursuant to a zero-tolerance policy based on the Gun-Free School Zones Act.

> Eleven-year-old Jerry Preece, an honor student, was made a criminal for defending himself in the midst of an assault.

If school officials wanted to punish Cortez for inadvertently bringing his calculator-knife to class, they had ample school-based remedies (detention, suspension, even expulsion). The policy, however, required notifying law enforcement. Thus, the well-meaning 13-year-old was arrested as a felon for an unintentional, if careless, act that threatened no one.

English and American legal history, not to mention common sense, suggests that Cortez's actions are not the equivalent of a student who brings a switchblade to school and pulls it out to threaten another student. Zero-tolerance policies blindly deny any distinction between such acts, treating Cortez like just one more dangerous little thug.

Eleven-year-old Jerry Preece learned this difficult lesson at the beginning of sixth grade. Jerry, an honor student, had become the subject of a bully's unwanted attention. One day, after enduring taunts, punches, and shoves to the ground, Jerry finally socked the bully. River Road Middle School rewarded Jerry with a suspension, and the Potter County Sheriff's Office gave him criminal citations for disorderly conduct and fighting in a public place. Jerry was made a criminal for defending himself in the midst of an assault.

> Ironically, if Jerry had been an adult, it is nearly certain that his actions would not have been considered criminal.

Ironically, if Jerry had been an adult, it is nearly certain that his actions would not have been considered criminal. (Indeed, they might have been considered heroic.) It is well known, perhaps instinctive, that legitimate acts of self-defense are not criminal and do not deserve punishment. More than two thousand years ago, the Roman orator Cicero explained that logic, necessity, tradition, and "nature itself" all teach that there is a right to use force against an attacker. A person acting in self-defense, like Jerry punching the bully, does not have a wrongful or criminal intent. Like Lindsay and Cortez, Jerry fell victim to the zero-tolerance mindset targeted at school kids that punishes the innocent along with the guilty.

Other troubling cases abound. For example:

- A high school student arrested on four felony charges for conducting a common chemistry trick off-campus, making a plastic soda bottle burst;

- A sixth-grader with a manicure kit charged with possession of a weapon on school grounds; and

- A high school junior arrested on two felonies after a sketch of military planes attacking a school inspired a search of the student's car that turned up a utility knife used for the student's part-time job.

All of these cases exhibit willful blindness on the part of school administrators and local law enforcement officers to the lack of culpable intent on the part of the arrested kids.

Perhaps the height of absurdity, however, was reached in the case of 13-year-old Savana Redding, who was forced to strip to her underwear in the school nurse's office. She was made to expose her breasts and pubic area to prove she was not hiding pills. Was she thought to be concealing a dangerous weapon? No. Perhaps some illegal narcotic like heroin or methamphetamine? Again, no. The drugs being sought were prescription-strength ibuprofen, equivalent to two Advils.

"I guess it's the fact that they think they were not wrong, they're not remorseful, never said they were sorry," April Redding, her mother, told *The Washington Post* as she and Savana talked about the legal fight over that search, which in April 2009 reached the Supreme Court.

The principal at Safford Middle School still thinks the school was right. He told April: "There was an incident with some pills, and we had to find out if Savana had them, but you should be happy because we didn't find any on her,'" Redding recalled. "I got really upset and was telling him, "Why did you do this to her? How could you do this to her?"'

Thankfully, common sense eventually prevailed—but it took a decision of the United States Supreme Court to bring a bit of sanity to the situation. By a vote of 8–1, they held that the search of Savana's pubic area violated her Fourth Amendment right against unreasonable searches and seizures.

It should, of course, have been obvious to anyone that stripping a 13-year-old to search for Advil wasn't reasonable, but what is even more disturbing is that this case be- came a matter for the criminal law at all. If our underlying sense of proportion were not so out of whack, poor Savana's under- wear would never have become an issue of popular concern.

> It should, of course, have been obvious to anyone that stripping a 13-year-old to search for Advil wasn't reasonable, but what is even more disturbing is that this case became a matter for the criminal law at all.

Proponents of zero-tolerance policies typically claim that they serve the interests of safety or prevent biased enforcement. To innocent kids struck by this sword of supposed justice, however, the results are clearly arbitrary and unjust. Such policies foster cynicism and disrespect for the rule of law, undermining people's faith in the fairness of our system of laws—a faith that is essential for a free society.

To make school children the target of such morally arbitrary enforce- ment is particularly corrosive. The message of zero-tolerance overcrimi- nalization is that justice is amoral. It is not about the choices you make, but something like a roll of the dice that determines whether you will be hauled away in handcuffs. The mechanistic legalism of zero tolerance can send a child to jail for a forgetful slip, a well-meaning action, or even something entirely beyond his or her control.

Unfortunately, this is true across the board. Even firearms cases—sup- posedly the perfect application of zero-tolerance policy—aren't always clear-cut.

Consider the story of Davis, California's Adam Liston. In January 2004, Adam, an 18-year-old senior at Davis High School, dropped off a few friends at school on his way to the gun range with a new shotgun in his gun rack. Apparently, someone reported seeing the gun through Adam's truck window. The next day at school, the vice principal asked to search Adam's Ford F-250 truck, and Adam readily agreed.

Six police cars arrived, and officers swarmed Adam's truck. As they searched, he realized that he had made a major mistake. He forgot to take the shotgun, unloaded and still in its original box, out of his truck after target shooting the day before. Adam broke down in tears as officers pulled the gun from his truck and placed him under arrest. He was handcuffed and taken to the Yolo County Jail.

> Adam Liston forgot to take his shotgun, unloaded and still in its original box, out of his truck after target shooting the day before. He was handcuffed and taken to jail.

Adam was charged with two felony violations of California Penal Code § 626.9, possessing a firearm within 1,000 feet of a school. He was released on $25,000 bail, and on February 19, the school board voted 3–1 to expel him from Davis High School.

The *Sacramento Bee* pointed out that Adam "had been a model citizen since the first grade." He "had never been a discipline problem in school and…never had a run-in with the law." Adam maintained good grades and already had college plans. His mother was president of the PTA.

One of Adam's former teachers called him a "very thoughtful, very respectful, very charming and fine young man." When his mother resigned her PTA position in response to her son's "banishment," several other parents also resigned to protest Adam's treatment. The Davis High School Student Council delivered a letter from students to the Davis superintendent, stating the obvious: "Adam Liston is not a threat to this school district."

The expulsion hit Adam hard, given his closeness to the school's officials. "I can understand their initial concern about the gun," he said, "but every single administrator knows me and knows I would never hurt anyone…. They just threw me aside. They didn't look at my history. They didn't look at anything but the gun."

A collection of letters to the editor of the Sacramento newspaper expressed the community's outrage. The authorities acted without "common sense," several writers opined. Adam's act was "unintentional" and "an honest mistake." This kind of zero-tolerance enforcement perpetuates a "paranoid atmosphere" and is "morally bankrupt" and "a real travesty of justice." Another letter writer rhetorically asked, "Where is the criminal intent in this case?" The letters appealed to simple common sense: Forgetting to remove an unloaded shotgun from your truck before driving to school is not the same as intentionally carrying a concealed loaded pistol to class.

> "They just threw me aside. They didn't look at my history. They didn't look at anything but the gun."

The number of school administrators, police, prosecutors, and lawmakers who are willing to cast aside this critical distinction in favor of mechanistic "zero-tolerance" policies is alarming. An American Bar Association report on these policies was highly critical. School kids "care most about fairness," said one attorney quoted in the report. "When they see two students whose 'offenses' are vastly different being treated exactly the same, that sense of fairness is obliterated and replaced with fear and alienation."

Civil society flourishes where people young and old can rely on law to approximate justice as best it can. Law, at its best, provides protection and predictability, both of which are essential to progress and ordered liberty. When the objective of law strays from justice, both concepts are tarnished. Law, no longer the protector, becomes the oppressor. Justice is twisted into a rationalization or dismissed as a phantasm.

This was particularly evident in the case of Miles Rankin, a 12-year-old boy from Henry County, Georgia. After a student reported to his teacher that Miles had been showing his friends a two-inch pocket knife in the school bathroom, Miles, a dedicated student with good grades, was handcuffed and taken away in a police vehicle—in view of his classmates—to a juvenile detention center.

At a hearing in juvenile court, Miles was shackled and handcuffed as if he were a dangerous criminal. The judge presiding over the hearing, who also happened to be the attorney for the school board, decided that Miles should remain in the detention center. Miles's parents were unable to pick him up on conditional release until the following evening, after he had been imprisoned for over 48 hours.

> Law, no longer the protector, becomes the oppressor. Justice is twisted into a rationalization or dismissed as a phantasm.

Nor did his punishment end there. Following Miles's traumatic experience in the juvenile justice system, his middle school held a disciplinary hearing. The presiding officer began by asking the scared 12-year-old if he understood his right to a hearing and to confront the charges against him by calling witnesses and cross-examining witnesses called by the school. Though Miles's mother was in attendance, the transcript of the hearing demonstrates (understandably) that neither she nor her son was an expert in due process rights.

Miles was asked to sign an admission of guilt. He was clearly willing to admit that he brought the knife to school, but he and his mother did not know that the hearing officer would use Miles's admission to justify meting out severe punishment.

> The presiding officer began by asking the scared 12-year-old if he understood his right to a hearing and to confront the charges against him by calling witnesses and cross-examining witnesses called by the school.

None of the students who saw Miles with the knife reported feeling threatened or believing that Miles intended to do any harm with the knife. The school superintendent even acknowledged this, but under a zero-tolerance policy, such things are not considered. The hearing officer took the principal's recommendation and decided to apply the most severe punishment available: expulsion from school for the remainder of the school year with the option to attend an "alternative" school. Although the Rankin family appealed the punishment, the County School Board simply reviewed the transcript of the initial hearing and then affirmed the decision.

Unfortunately for Miles and his mom, expulsion was not the end of the punishment. The juvenile court found Miles to be "in a state of delinquency/unruliness and in need of treatment, rehabilitation or supervision." The court issued an abeyance and protective order which placed him under 30 days of house arrest, provided a curfew, and placed him on probation for 180 days. The court documents describe only that Miles carried a weapon on school property. There is no discussion of his intent or behavior with the knife.

In the effort to make schools safer, misguided school officials have established a disciplinary system that does students more harm than good.

According to the policy in Henry County, Georgia, mere possession of a weapon on school premises warrants expulsion as well as juvenile court action, regardless of the intent, purpose, or other relevant behavior of the student. The hearing officer is granted some discretion in determining the punishment, but Miles's case shows how unwilling many school officials are to deviate from prescribed harsh punishments.

> The end result of the zero-tolerance policy was the removal of a good student—a young child—who posed no threat to others and a serious traumatic disruption in his life and education.

Miles clearly disobeyed the rules by bringing the pocketknife to school, yet the punishment of expulsion and probation is severe and unnecessary. The end result of the zero-tolerance policy in this case was the removal of a good student—a young child—who posed no threat to others and a serious traumatic disruption in his life and education.

Story after story demonstrates how zero-tolerance policies stand justice on its head. It should be troubling to all, then, that zero tolerance is spreading far beyond the schoolyard. One last incident illustrates the point far better than any fictive story we could concoct.

It was a cool, clear October day in Washington, D.C., when the closing bell rang and 12-year-old Ansche Hedgepeth ran out the door of Alice Deal Junior High School. She stopped at a fast-food restaurant for an order of hot French fries and then headed for home. Ansche took the escalator down into the Tenleytown/American University Metrorail station to catch her train. In the station, she ate a single French fry. Moments later, the junior high student was in handcuffs and headed for jail.

Ansche had no idea that the Washington Metropolitan Area Transit Authority (WMATA) had picked that

> In the subway station, Ansche ate a single French fry. Moments later, the junior high student was in handcuffs and headed for jail.

Monday to kick off a week of "zero-tolerance" enforcement of "quality of life offenses" (eating or drinking, playing loud music, smoking, or littering). They had ordered that undercover officers automatically punish even minor infractions.

District of Columbia government photo

The Washington, D.C., subway, where Ansche Hedgepeth became a French fry criminal.

D.C. Code § 35-251(b) makes it a violation to "consume food or drink" in a Metrorail facility. For a first offense, an adult can be fined from $10 to $50. Only for a second offense can an adult legally be arrested. Minors, however, cannot be fined. Officers can either warn them or arrest them. The zero-tolerance enforcement policy made arrest the only option.

When an undercover officer saw Ansche eat the fry, he dutifully placed her under arrest. The 12-year-old girl was searched. Her jacket, backpack, and shoelaces were confiscated. Her hands were cuffed behind her back, and she was put into a paddy wagon and driven to the Juvenile Processing Center. Three hours after the arrest, Ansche was released into the custody of her mother.

Did the undercover officer overreact? According to the WMATA, the arrest was exemplary. "We really do believe in zero-tolerance," said Metro Police Chief Barry McDevitt. "Anyone taken into custody has to be hand-cuffed for officer safety," he explained. Even young offenders "can kill you, too." The pen may be mightier than the sword, but the French fry?

In a decision reluctantly upholding Ansche's arrest, then-Judge John Roberts of the U.S. Court of Appeals for the D.C. Circuit (now the Chief Justice of the Supreme Court of the United States) noted that she was totally compliant, never resisting, only crying throughout the process. She had never eaten in a Metrorail station before, nor had she ever been warned by an officer not to eat there. Roberts mocked the harsh,

And what was Asche's punishment for eating a French fry in a subway station? Counseling and community service. She now has an arrest record. There was also a chance that Ansche would be suspended.

zero-tolerance enforcement of the "serious offense of eating a French fry on a subway platform."

The future Chief Justice also lamented the "humiliating and demeaning impact of the arrest," suggesting that the WMATA "re-think any other 'foolish' operating procedures before subjecting—or continuing to subject—unwary users of mass transportation to the indignity and horror suffered by [Ansche]." The Supreme Court, in a decision likewise finding nothing unconstitutional about a similar incident, cited news reports of Ansche's treatment as an example of a "comparably foolish, warrantless misdemeanor arrest."

And what was Asche's punishment for eating a French fry in a subway station? Counseling and community service. She now has an arrest record. There was also a chance that Ansche would be suspended or kicked off her double-dutch jump-rope team at school.

As one of many letters to *The Washington Post* put it, "Kids are a messy bunch. But childhood is so special and there are more serious things to worry about than rules about where food can be consumed. A warning would have been sufficient."

In the face of public criticism, the WMATA rescinded its "zero-tolerance" policy that required arresting minor children for minor infractions—a small victory for common sense in the larger war against zero-tolerance policies and overcriminalization.

Judge John Roberts called the D.C. subway policy "foolish."

assist providers if they are struggling to comply with the complex billing and claim rules. The Medicaid claims that doctors submit are processed by contractors. Medicaid regulations and statutes state that contractors are required to "initiate focused provider education when a specific error is verified." As Mrs. Krizek knew, their psychiatry practice's Medicare and Medicaid contractors had an obligation "to notify a doctor if any problems with his billing were found and to educate him about proper billing methods."

Sadly, another Christmas proved that their confidence in the government and in their contracts was misplaced. They received a certified letter from a federal prosecutor on Christmas Eve, 1992. The letter announced that the federal government was prepared to file a lawsuit against both Dr. Krizek and Mrs. Krizek for an alleged 8,002 fraudulent Medicare and Medicaid reimbursements. Of course, this could be avoided, the letter offered, "in exchange for an appropriate cash settlement."

The Krizeks were shocked by the allegations. They made arrangements to speak with the Assistant U.S. Attorney assigned to the case. According to Mrs. Krizek, the prosecutor's response

> Mrs. Krizek stated in her congressional testimony, "[W]e had nothing to hide and I believed in the fairness of our adopted country's system."

was essentially, "We are the Government, we don't have to show you anything.... Pay us hundreds of thousands of dollars and we won't file suit."

Instead of caving in to what they viewed as "official extortion," the Krizeks decided to fight the allegations and demonstrate their innocence of any fraud or similar wrongdoing. The government reacted by calling a press conference to announce a "major health care fraud enforcement initiative," including a lawsuit against Dr. and Mrs. Krizek for thousands of fraudulent claims. The government suit sought $81 *million* from the Krizeks.

The fanfare and astronomical dollar figure helped to ensure that the story made the newspapers and local television and radio. The Krizeks had yet to set foot in court, much less to be found liable for anything, but their personal and professional reputations were already seriously injured.

In addition to 8,002 alleged violations of the False Claims Act, the government's complaint against Dr. and Mrs. Krizek alleged conspiracy to defraud the government and unjust enrichment. The alleged damages were $245,392 from the six years covered by the suit. The government also wanted the maximum $10,000 fine for each supposed violation, adding up to more than $80 million in punitive fines. Their theory of the case accused Dr. Krizek of providing medically unnecessary treatment and systematically overcharging the government by "up-coding" on Medicare and Medicaid claim forms.

Originally enacted in 1863, the False Claims Act was the Lincoln Administration's reaction to "a spate of frauds upon the government" by defense contractors during the Civil War. In a 1986 amendment, Congress increased the Act's ability to punish those who are found to have submitted false claims with fines greater than the amount of the false claims.

The alleged damages were $245,392 from the six years covered by the suit. The government also wanted the maximum $10,000 fine for each supposed violation, adding up to more than $80 million in punitive fines.

The 1986 revision also removed the requirement of specific intent to defraud the government. This revision turned the law into a regulatory sword of Damocles dangling over the heads of many well-meaning doctors (as well as anyone else doing business with the federal government). For any reimbursement form with a single mistake, a doctor can be forced to pay a $10,000 fine plus treble damages (three times the amount of the allegedly false claims). The False Claims Act's penalties are so severe that it is essentially a *de facto* criminal law; rather than simply recovering funds that the government allegedly lost, it severely punishes those who are found liable for making false claims.

Because of the massive scope of the allegations against the Krizeks, their case was tried on the basis of a mere seven-patient sample that was supposedly representative of 200 disputed Medicare and Medicaid reimbursements. After a three-week bench trial, the district court judge dismissed the charge of providing medically unnecessary treatment, finding the government's single witness completely unpersuasive in the face of Dr. Krizek's own testimony. The court held that the doctor was "a capable and competent physician" who cared for many people "afflicted with horribly severe psychiatric disorders." The court also noted that the government's witness had failed even to "examine or interview any of the patients, or speak with any other doctors or nurses who had actually served these patients."

On the issue of "up-coding," the court found the government's interpretation of the relevant policies to be irrational, unfair, and not supported by evidence. This part of the government's case turned on the Krizeks' frequent use of "Code 90844," corresponding to "45–50 minutes of individual psychotherapy," on reimbursement forms. Dr. and Mrs. Krizek believed that the rules were intended to include all of the time spent on patient care, including making records, analysis, and research, in or out of the presence of the patient. The government claimed that "[e]ven if as much as an hour of a physician's time is devoted to a patient's case, with half that time spent in a face-to-face psychotherapy session and the rest spent on related services, the doctor is only permitted reimbursement…for the 30 minutes spent face-to-face."

> The court noted that the government's witness had failed even to "examine or interview any of the patients, or speak with any other doctors or nurses who had actually served these patients."

The court once again found the Krizeks' witnesses "credible and persuasive" and largely dismissed the government's evidence. The court pointed to the testimony of a government witness who claimed that a doctor could make the same telephone call to a consulting physician either in the patient's presence or in a different room and that one scenario would be reimbursable and the other would not. The court wrote that the Medicare–Medicaid system "cannot be so arbitrary, so perverse, as to subject a doctor whose annual income during the relevant period averaged between $100,000 and $120,000, to potential liability in excess of 80 million dollars because telephone calls were made in one room rather than another."

With the two issues decided in their favor and the government discredited, it appeared that the Krizeks had prevailed. The court, however, decided to consider the Krizeks' billing methods in their totality.

With so many seriously ill patients, Dr. Krizek had largely left the billing to his wife. Faced with federal regulations more voluminous than the entire federal tax code, Mrs. Krizek did her best to fill out and submit the reimbursement forms appropriately. The Krizeks acknowledged that their billing methods were sometimes hurried and lacked the formal oversight or auditing that a larger medical practice might have enjoyed. While mistakes were possible and perhaps inevitable, the Krizeks have consistently maintained that they worked hard to obey the law.

After finding the government's witnesses unconvincing and its burden of proof unmet, the court went fishing into six years of Dr. Krizek's medical reimbursement forms. The judge held that the Krizeks had demonstrated a "reckless disregard of the truth or falsity of the information" in their bills to Medicare and Medicaid. Because the False Claims Act requires "no specific intent" (that is, no criminal intent or *mens rea*) to defraud, this perceived carelessness was enough to find the Krizeks in violation of the law. The judge announced that he would hold them liable for any claims submitted in excess of "nine patient-treatment hours" per day. As one article about the case noted, on "the billing side, Krizek won one battle, but he lost the war."

The nine-hour threshold resulted from the testimony of a single psychiatrist about his normal workload. The court ignored evidence that Dr. Krizek routinely worked long hours and occasionally had worked around the clock when filling in for an absent colleague. Instead of examining the evidence for proof of specific actual errors, the court arbitrarily shifted the burden of proof to the defendants. For any claim exceeding nine hours in one day, the Krizeks would have to prove their innocence. The case was referred to a special master to examine the records and produce a finding for the court.

> As one article about the case noted, on "the billing side, Dr. Krizek won one battle, but he lost the war."

The special master was faced with a daunting task. Only two of the seven billing codes created by Medicare and Medicaid for use by psychiatrists actually had specified time dimensions. Even for these two codes, the time windows were clearly estimates. The 90844 code was described by American Medical Association guidelines as 45 to 50 minutes of care but had been construed by the Inspector General of HHS to range from 37 minutes to one hour. The special master determined that he would charge Dr. Krizek 45 minutes for each code 90844. Adopting a formula invented by a single HHS junior investigator, the special master assigned time values to each of the seven codes.

After several months, the special master informed the court that he had found 264 days for which the bills indicated that Dr. Krizek spent more than nine hours providing patient care. This could be viewed as further support for the court's earlier finding "that Dr. Krizek worked long hours on behalf of his patients."

This should not have been a surprise, since many doctors routinely devote very long hours to their practices. Instead, the court ordered the Krizeks to reimburse the government $47,105.39 in damages. Because the court had never determined that any particular reimbursement was invalid, the only basis for the damages calculation was the special master's arbitrary selection of which claims might represent the patient care that was provided after the court's nine-hour limit.

> Almost begging the government to let the case end, the court chastised the government for continuing "to relentlessly pursue Dr. Krizek, who is at this point a broken and sick man."

The court inexplicably backpedaled and used another arbitrary standard when it came to assessing criminal-style punitive fines against the Krizeks. For these purposes, the court changed the standard and assumed liability only for claims in excess of 24 hours in one day. The calculations, however, continued to rely on the special master's questionable methodology. If the special master had used the HHS 37-minute minimum instead of the AMA 45-minute minimum, the court would have allowed Dr. Krizek to care for six more patients in a 24-hour period.

For the six years examined, there were three days for which the formula suggested more than 24 hours of patient care. While the Krizeks concede that errors were possible, they also presented credible evidence that on at least one of these occasions, Dr. Krizek had actually worked around the clock. Nevertheless, the court ordered the Krizeks to pay the maximum $10,000 fine for each of 11 reimbursements from the three days, plus $11,000 in court fees. In all, the court required Dr. and Mrs. Krizek to pay almost $170,000 in damages, fines, and fees.

Even after destroying Dr. Krizek's practice and crippling the couple financially, the government remained unsatisfied and appealed the trial court's decision. The Krizeks cross-appealed, and a federal court of appeals in the District of Columbia remanded the case to the trial court with instructions to apply a new definition of "claims" that reduced the fines from $110,000 to $30,000. The appeals court granted the government permission to present limited new evidence, although the trial court later accused the government of attempting a "fishing expedition." The trial court pointed out that Dr. Krizek had retired and was suffering from cancer. Almost begging the government to let the case end, the court chastised the government for continuing "to relentlessly pursue Dr. Krizek, who is at this point a broken and sick man."

Despite the district court's appeal to the government for mercy, the government again appealed and was successful in ratcheting the judgment back up to over $300,000. The Krizeks tried to challenge the decision, but their attempts were turned down on appeals to the D.C. Circuit and the U.S. Supreme Court.

The Krizeks' case illustrates the grave danger of obliterating the line between criminal and civil law. While the government suggested that the Krizeks were guilty of criminal acts, it declined criminal prosecution in favor of a civil lawsuit with the benefit of the False Claims Act's draconian financial penalties.

Dr. and Mrs. Krizek continued to live in their adopted homeland's capital, but Dr. Krizek's medical practice was gone.

This meant that government attorneys could get the advantage of the False Claims Act's punitive provisions without having to satisfy the criminal law's requirement of proving beyond a reasonable doubt that Dr. and Mrs. Krizek intended to commit a wrongful act. Instead, allegations built upon a relatively small number of careless bookkeeping errors became the basis for destroying Dr. Krizek's medical practice. By selecting the civil False Claims Act, the government also dramatically lowered its burden of proof from the high standard (beyond a reasonable doubt) necessary for criminal convictions to the lower standard (preponderance of the evidence) required in civil court.

Dr. and Mrs. Krizek continued to live in their adopted homeland's capital, but Dr. Krizek's medical practice was gone. He could no longer apply his international training and decades of experience in psychiatry to caring for the mental and emotional health of some of the District of Columbia's neediest residents.

Given that a society's use of the power to punish citizens through criminal law is one of the best gauges of that society's commitment to fairness and justice, it is understandable that the Krizeks now have some troubling questions about their adopted home. Testifying about their case before a committee of the U.S. House of Representatives, Mrs. Krizek reflected:

> We have both been intensely patriotic in our new country, [but] we must now step back and question whether what we have experienced at the hands of Government investigators and prosecutors meets any possible definition of democracy or due process.

CHAPTER 7

THE UNLIKELY ORCHID SMUGGLER
Criminalizing "Flowers 'R' Us"
(United States v. Norris)

George Norris, an elderly retiree, had turned his orchid hobby into a part-time business run from the greenhouse in back of his home. He would import orchids from abroad—South Africa, Brazil, Peru—and resell them at plant shows and to local enthusiasts. He never made more than a few thousand dollars a year from his orchid business, but it kept him engaged and provided a little extra money—an especially important thing as his wife, Kathy, neared retirement from her job managing a local mediation clinic.

Their life would take a turn for the worse on the bright fall morning of October 28, 2003, when federal agents, clad in protective Kevlar and bearing guns, raided his home, seizing his belongings and setting the gears in motion for a federal prosecution and jail time.

The Raid

Around 10:00 a.m., three pickup trucks turned off a shady cul-de-sac in Spring, Texas, far in Houston's northern suburbs, and into the driveway of Norris's single-story home. Six agents emerged, clad in dark body armor and bearing sidearms. Two circled around to the rear of the house, where there is a small yard and a ramshackle greenhouse. One, Special Agent Jeff Odom of the U.S. Fish and Wildlife Service, approached the door and knocked; his companions held back, watching Odom for the signal.

A typical orchid greenhouse.

Norris, who had seen the officers arrive and surround his house, answered the knock at the door with trepidation. Odom was matter-of-fact. Within 10 seconds, he had identified himself, stated that he was executing a search warrant, and waved in the rest of the entry team for a sweep of the premises. Norris was ordered to sit at his kitchen table and to remain there until told otherwise. One agent was stationed in the kitchen with him.

As Norris looked on, the agents ransacked his home. They pulled out drawers and dumped the contents on the floor, emptied file cabinets, rifled through dresser drawers and closets, and pulled books off of their shelves.

When Norris asked one agent why his home was the subject of a warrant, the agent read him his Miranda rights and told him simply that he was not charged with anything at this time or under arrest. Norris asked more questions—What were they searching for? What law did they think had been broken? What were their names and badge numbers?—but the agents refused to answer anything. Finally, they handed over the search warrant, but they would not let Norris get up to retrieve his reading glasses from his office; only an agent could do that.

It was as if he were under arrest, but in his own home.

Attached to the warrant was an excerpt of an e-mail message from two years earlier in which a man named Arturo offered to have his mother "smuggle" orchids from Ecuador in a suitcase and send them to Norris from Miami. Norris remembered the exchange; he had declined the offer and had stated that he could not accept any plants that were not accompanied by legal documentation.

The agents questioned Norris about the orchids in his greenhouse, asking which were nursery-grown and which were collected from the wild. Norris explained that nearly all of them had been artificially propagated; one agent, knowing little about orchids, asked whether this meant they had been grown from seeds.

The agents boxed and carried out to their trucks nearly all of Norris's business records, his computer, his floppy disks and CD-ROMs, and even installation discs and left him a receipt for the 37 boxes that they took. Then they left. Norris surveyed the rooms of his home. In his tiny office, papers, old photographs, and trash were strewn on the floor. Everything was out of place.

> The agents questioned Norris about the orchids. Norris explained that nearly all of them had been artificially propagated; one agent, knowing little about orchids, asked whether this meant they had been grown from seeds.

His wife arrived home shortly after the agents left. She had panicked when, calling home to talk to her husband, an agent picked up the phone and refused to put him on or answer any questions. It took the two of them hours to clean up the house and try to assess the damage.

A Passion Blossoms

George Norris, now 71 and arthritic, carries his large frame wearily. His gestures are careful, as if held back by pain or fear, and his stride slow and deliberate. And his voice, once booming, is now softer and tentative. Visibly, he is a man who has been permanently scarred by experience.

Yet his mood and movements become animated when he discusses the birth of his passion for orchids. His first was a gift, twice over: A neighbor had received the blooming plant, straight from the store, for Mother's Day, and she gave it to Norris after the flowers faded. At the time, he had a small lean-to greenhouse and dabbled in horticulture. He put it there and forgot about it. A year later, as he was doing the morning watering, his eyes were drawn to two stunning yellow flowers on stems shooting out of the plant. They were prettier than any other flowers he had ever seen.

He dove into the world of orchids with an unusual passion, reading everything he could find on the subject. One book extolled the diversity of species in Mexico. It was not so far from Houston, and his wife spoke fluent Spanish, so they planned an orchid-hunting trip. In every small town, the locals would point them to unusual plants, often deep in the woods. Norris managed to collect 40 or 50 plants, and their beauty and diversity were stunning. He was hooked.

That was 1977, years before an orchid craze would hit the United States. All of a sudden, Norris found himself part of a small, close-knit community of orchid enthusiasts and explorers committed to finding and collecting the unknown species of orchids from Asia, Africa, and South America. They communicated by newsletters and at regional orchid shows. While man had thoroughly covered and mapped the Earth's terrain, the world of orchids was still frontier, with exotic specimens being discovered regularly.

> Norris was part of a small, close-knit community of orchid enthusiasts and explorers committed to finding and collecting the unknown species of orchids from Asia, Africa, and South America.

Within a few years, orchids were taking up more and more of Norris's time and attention, and he had become dissatisfied with his work in the construction field. So he quit work and set off to see if he could make a living as a full-time explorer, finding orchids in the wild and introducing them to serious collectors in the U.S.

His new business was not initially a success. It took years to build up a mailing list of customers and credibility in the field. By the mid-1980s, he was beyond the break-even point, and from there, business kept growing. In 2003, revenues topped $200,000—a huge sum considering that most plants sold for less than $15.

Norris, meanwhile, was gaining prominence. Through word of mouth and after seeing his orchids in collections, more and more enthusiasts wanted to be on his mailing list, and he began to use his catalogue as a platform for his views on orchids, the orchid community, and even politics. Orchid clubs all around the South invited him to deliver talks and slideshows.

Norris made a name for himself as one of the few dealers importing non-hybrid plants, known as "species" orchids. He got commissions from botany departments at several universities that needed non-hybrid plants for their research, from botanical gardens, and from the Bronx Zoo when it needed native orchids to recreate a gorilla habitat. Years later, some of those orchids are still a part of the zoo's Congo Gorilla Forest.

Norris's work took him to Costa Rica, Peru, Ecuador, Mexico, and other countries where exotic species grew wild. On each trip, he tried to meet local collectors and growers, contacts who could lead him to the best plants. Some of these in later years would become his chief suppliers.

Rules at the time were lax. In Mexico, Norris explained, "You could collect as many as you wanted" and get permits for them all. And with that paperwork, importing them into the U.S. was a breeze.

As orchids became more popular, however, that would change.

"The Regulation Is Out of Hand"

Passion for the flower is not enough today to succeed in the orchid business. Moving beyond the standard hybrids sold at big-box stores requires either gaining a detailed knowledge of several complicated bodies of law or hiring attorneys. This is a necessity because the law is complicated and the penalties for getting anything wrong are severe: fines, forfeiture, and potentially years in prison.

Trade in orchids is regulated chiefly by the Convention on International Trade in Endangered Species (CITES), an international treaty that has been ratified by about 175 nations. Though initially conceived to protect endangered animals, the subject matter was expanded to include flora as well.[1]

Determining the law that applies to a particular plant is not always an easy task. Some species of orchids cannot be traded at all; others can. Exporters, however, often have a

> Exporters often have a tough time identifying plants, especially those collected from the wild. The result is rampant mislabeling of orchid species.

tough time identifying plants, especially those collected from the wild. The result is rampant mislabeling of orchid species. Usually, this has few consequences, because permitting agencies and customs agents, who tend to focus on animals and invasive species, rarely have the expertise to recognize the often subtle differences between varieties of orchids, especially when they are not in bloom.

In the United States, CITES is implemented through both the Lacey Act, a 1900 wildlife protection act that was amended in 1981 to protect CITES-listed species (this is the same law that got David McNab in trouble for lobster importation), and the Endangered Species Act (ESA). Both, in their original forms, covered only animals; plants were added later and made subject to the same restrictions as animals. Taken together, these laws prohibit trade in any plants in violation of CITES, as well as possession of plants that have been traded in violation of CITES.

Specific federal regulations lay out the requirements for importing plants. Every plant must be accompanied by a tag or document identifying its genus and species, its origin, the name and address of its owner, the name and address of its recipient, and a description of any accompanying documentation required for its trade, such as a CITES permit. The importer is required to notify the government upon the arrival of a shipment. After that, the plants are inspected by the Animal and Plant Inspection Service, a division of the U.S. Department of Homeland Security (it used to be part of the Department of Agriculture), which checks for possible infestations, banned invasive species, and proper documentation. Any red flags can cause a shipment to be turned back at the port of entry.

> The result is that minor offenses, such as incorrect documentation for a few plants, are treated the same as the smuggling of endangered animals and can lead to penalties far more severe than those regularly imposed for violent crimes and dealing drugs.

Violations also carry severe penalties. Under the ESA, "knowing" violations can be punished by civil fines of up to $25,000 for each violation, criminal fines of up to $50,000, and imprisonment. But proving a "knowing" violation is relatively easy. The government only has to prove that the dealer knew the basic facts of the offense, such as what kind of plant was being imported or that the CITES permit did not match the plant, though not the legal status of the plant, such as whether it was legal to import. Since few people import orchids by accident, the act of importation itself satisfies the criminal intent requirement of the law. The same conduct can also be punished under the Lacey Act, which allows civil penalties of up to

$10,000 for each violation, criminal fines of up to $20,000, and imprisonment for up to five years.

Importers also face possible legal penalties under more general federal statutes, such as those prohibiting false or misleading statements to government officials (imprisonment of up to five years); the mail fraud statute (20 years); the wire fraud statute (20 years); and the conspiracy statute (five years).

The result is that minor offenses, such as incorrect documentation for a few plants, are treated the same as the smuggling of endangered animals and can lead to penalties far more severe than those regularly imposed for violent crimes and dealing drugs. Because this legal risk is so great, many orchid dealers have stopped importing foreign plants—even those that can be traded legally—and others have sharply curtailed their imports.

Perversely, the result of this drop in legal imports has been a blossoming in black-market orchids, illegally imported into the country and commanding large premiums because of their rarity and allure. Meanwhile, those who continue to import plants through the proper channels, even if they do so with great care and top-notch legal advice, know that they could be ruined at any time by so much as a single slipup. As one academic ecologist put it, "The regulation is out of hand."

The fundamental problem may be that CITES is simply a poor fit for plants. As originally conceived, the treaty was intended to cover only endangered animals; plants were added toward the end of negotiations. The amendment was crude, doing little more than replacing "animals" in every instance with "animals or plants." An orchid picked from the wild, which could produce a thousand seedlings in short order, is subject to the same regulation as an elephant, a female of which species will produce fewer than 10 offspring in its decades-long lifespan; and by extension, that orchid and elephant are subject to the same means of criminal enforcement in the United States.

The difference, needless to say, is that elephant poaching may lead to that species' extinction, while picking the orchid will more likely lead to its species' preservation in the face of widespread habitat destruction. It is truly a perverse result that furthering the ends of CITES and U.S. environmental law carries the same massive penalties as frustrating them.

Business as Usual

George Norris was among that group of legal importers, counting on his common sense and understanding of orchids to see him through any legal risks. That would be his downfall.

Over the years, he had built relationships with orchid gatherers and growers around the world, and many became his suppliers. He worked the most with Manuel Arias Silva, who operated several nurseries in Peru and was known for cultivating the toughest species from the wild that few others could persuade to grow.

Norris had met Arias in the late 1980s, when Arias had just started his export business and was looking to build a customer base in the United States. The two hit it off immediately, and in 1988, Norris spent two weeks in Peru with Arias, collecting plants and surveying Arias's operations.

Their families also grew close. After meeting Arias's relations, Norris and his wife offered to take in two of Arias's sons, Juan Alberto and Manolo, who were badly scarred about their hands and faces from a fire years earlier, and to arrange plastic surgery for them. Kathy Norris persuaded a local hospital to donate its facilities, and Dr. David Netscher, a prominent surgeon and professor at the Baylor College of Medicine, agreed to do the work for $1,500 per child, barely enough to cover his expenses.

In 1993 and 1994, first Manolo and then Juan Alberto spent six months with the Norrises undergoing surgery, follow-up care, and recuperation. After that experience, the Norrises and the Arias family were in regular contact, exchanging family photographs and visiting from time to time.

Norris had other suppliers. One was Raul Xix, a native Maya in Belize who supported his 11 children and wife through odd jobs: building homes, tapping chicle trees, and collecting orchids from the jungle. Norris had befriended Xix on a trip and encouraged him to try his hand at exporting plants, a potentially more lucrative and dependable source of income.

Xix, Norris soon learned, had no business experience, could barely read and write, and knew little about exotic orchids. He would ship boxes loaded with all manner of flora, some not even orchids and many infested

Norris was among that group of legal importers, counting on his common sense and understanding of orchids to see him through any legal risks. That would be his downfall.

with ants, and though bearing CITES permits from Belize, few plants were correctly identified—not that it ever mattered.

Norris, charmed by Xix and admiring his work ethic, decided that he would be a regular customer and use their interactions to teach Xix the ins and outs of the business. Keeping that commitment was a challenge: Xix's first few shipments were a total loss, and others were turned back at the port of entry because of poor packing and infestations. But slowly, Xix became more reliable.

For Xix and Norris's other suppliers, paperwork was more of a hassle than growing or gathering orchids. In most developing nations, months pass between applying for and receiving a CITES permit. To compensate, orchid exporters request permits early, long before the plants are ready to sell. In that gap between applying for a permit and receiving it, some plants die and others thrive. Or a big shipment comes in from the countryside. Or a new family or species comes into fashion overseas.

Then the permits arrive, and the plants are ready to ship. Because of the delay, only rarely does the permit perfectly match the merchandise. There are always at least a few discrepancies. Going strictly by the book would mean giving up the lucrative foreign markets that account for nearly all profits. Importers face a similar dilemma. Fashionable plants come from foreign soil, and without imports, no boutique could attract collectors—that is, anyone willing to pay more than $15 or $20 for a flower.

> In most developing nations, months pass between applying for and receiving a CITES permit. To compensate, orchid exporters request permits early, long before the plants are ready to sell.

In the 1990s, what these collectors wanted were Phragmipediums, better known as tropical lady slippers. Phrags became popular in the early 1990s after all of the species in the family were uplisted to CITES Appendix I, a move that many in the orchid business attribute to commercial rather than preservationist motives. Demand for the flowers surged.

Arias had been breeding Phrags for years from plants that he had legally taken from the wild, but in Peru, Phrags were common and almost worthless. So in 1998, he turned to the export market. It would be months or even years, Arias guessed, before he was approved to have all of them listed on his permits.

Arias began including Phrags in the price sheets that went to his best for-eign customers. Norris ordered a few, along with hundreds of other plants. On the forms, they were described as Maxillarias, a type of orchid that Arias had cleared for export. Per usual industry practice, he received a separate let-ter matching the names on the permit with the plants' real identities.

Over time, Arias's nurseries received permits and CITES registration to grow many of the Phrags he had previously shipped under other names, and as that happened, he began labeling them properly in his shipments. But there were always at least a few in each shipment that were mislabeled because he had not yet received the proper permit.

However, it was a flower that Norris never actually imported that would lead to the investigation and his arrest.

If there is a rock star of the orchid world, it is the Phragmipedium kovachii. James Michael Kovach discovered the flower while on an orchid-hunting trip to the Peruvian Andes in 2002 and sneaked it back into the United States without any CITES documentation to have it catalogued by Selby Botanical Gardens' Orchid Identification Center, a leader in identifying and publishing new species. Two Selby staff mem-bers, recognizing the importance of the discovery, rushed out a descrip-tion of the new flower, christening it kovachii, after Kovach, and barely beating into print an article by Eric Christensen, a rival researcher who had been working from photos and measurements taken in Peru.

It was a flower that Norris never actually imported that would lead to the investigation and his arrest.

The most striking thing about the kovachii is its size. The plants grow thick leaves up to two feet in length. Flower stalks shoot up from the plant, rising two feet or more. But the real stunner is the flower: It is velvety, a rich pink-purple at the tips of its petals, brilliant white in the center. And the size! Some measure more than 10 inches across. The flower is a rare combination of grace and might, a giant unrivalled in its delicacy and el-egance. Lee Moore, a well-known collector, dubbed it "the Holy Grail of orchids."

Pictures circulated on orchid mailing lists, and discussion reached a fe-ver pitch. "People decided they would become excited beyond all reason," said one orchid dealer. "Everyone wanted it. It was a meteoric plant." Ac-cording to rumors, black-market specimens had sold for $25,000 or more.

The orchid fever was only heightened by the legal drama that had engulfed Selby Gardens and Kovach as a result of the find. The Peruvian government caught wind of the frenzy over the flower and, irked that its country had lost out on the honor of identifying the plant, pressed U.S. authorities to investigate for CITES violations. Eventually, criminal charges were brought against Kovach, Selby Gardens, and its chief horticulturalist, Wesley Higgins. All pleaded guilty, receiving probation and small fines.

Right after he heard about the kovachii, Norris contacted Arias to press for information about the flower, especially when it would be available for sale. With illegal trade in the flower already flourishing, Arias figured that he could get the right permits to collect a few from the wild for artificial propagation. Breeding the flower would not be easy—Phrags have a reputation for being difficult plants, and that is especially true of the rarer ones—but he had succeeded before with other tough plants and had a high-altitude greenhouse that would be perfect for the kovachii. Doing it legally could take a year or two, maybe even three.

Norris was more optimistic and ran with the information in his next catalog, boasting that he would have legal kovachiis for sale in a year, perhaps less—far sooner than anyone else thought possible. That caught the attention of an orchid researcher who had long believed that the U.S. orchid trade was overrun with illegal plants, threatening the survival of many species in the wild. Enforcement was a joke; there had been only one prosecution to date for dealing in illegal orchids. He decided to take a closer look at Norris's spring orchid specialties and brought Norris to the attention of the U.S. Fish and Wildlife Service.

Around that time, a new customer placed an order for four Phrags and specifically asked Norris to include the CITES permits for the flowers. It was an unusual request. Usually, the Department of Agriculture inspectors took the permits at the port of entry for their records. Except for the few times that shipping brokers made copies, Norris hardly ever received them with plant shipments. Assuming that the request was just a misunderstanding, he shipped the plants with a packing list but no permits.

Several days after the orchids were delivered, Norris received another e-mail from the buyer, asking again for the permits. The Department of Agriculture had them, Norris responded, but he would try to get a copy. That, thought Norris, was the end of the matter. The buyer made another order for more Phrags a year later and again asked for the permits. Once again, Norris shipped the flowers without them.

Unknown to Norris, the buyer in these transactions was working with Fish and Wildlife Service agents. Because of the controversy over the kovachii, the Service had a newfound interest in orchids. A few prominent prosecutions would serve as a warning to the rest of the tight-knit orchid community.

That informant's two transactions with Norris would serve as the basis for the raid on Norris's home.

The Prosecution

The raid occurred in October 2003, but George Norris was uncertain of his fate for the next five months, receiving no communications from the government. On the advice of friends, he wrote a letter to the Miami-based prosecutor who was probably overseeing the case, explaining that he had never imported kovachiis—this was at the time that others were being charged for importing the flower—and asking for a meeting to answer any questions. At the very least, he asked, could the government tell him what he was suspected to have done? After a few weeks, his computer was returned, broken, and Norris resumed business as best he could, taking orders and showing off his plants at shows.

> The Fish and Wildlife Service had a newfound interest in orchids. A few prominent prosecutions would serve as a warning to the rest of the tight-knit orchid community.

Meanwhile, Fish and Wildlife Service Agents were poring over the records retrieved from Norris's home, as well as others obtained from the Department of Agriculture. There was no evidence that Norris had ever obtained or sold a kovachii, but the agents did notice minor discrepancies in the documents. Some of the plants Norris had offered for sale were not listed on any CITES permits. Among those missing were three of the 10 Phrags in the informant's second order. The agents also found Norris's correspondence with Arias and Xix, which seemed to confirm their hunch: Norris had been engaged in a criminal conspiracy to skirt CITES and violate U.S. import laws.

Norris's business slowly recovered but suffered a devastating blow when Manuel Arias Silva was arrested in Miami one day before the Miami Orchid Show in March 2004. After that, everyone assumed that Norris would be next. Norris and his wife scrambled to sell Arias's flowers (mostly Phrags, by now properly permitted) at the show, earning just enough to pay his expenses and get him out of jail. With no one else to step in, they guaranteed Arias's $25,000 bail and $175,000 personal surety bond: He was now their responsibility. Rumors raged that Norris would be arrested on the floor of the show.

But it was another week before Norris was indicted. There were seven charges: one count of conspiracy to violate the Endangered Species Act, five counts of violating CITES requirements and the ESA, and one count of making a false statement to a government official, for mislabeling the orchids. Arias faced one additional false-statement charge.

> At the very least, Norris asked, could the government tell him what he was suspected to have done?

On March 17, 2004, Norris and his wife flew to Miami, where he voluntarily surrendered to the U.S. marshals. The marshals put him in handcuffs and leg shackles and threw him in a holding cell with three other arrestees, one suspected of murder and two suspected of dealing drugs. Norris expected the worst when his cell mates asked him what he was in for. When he told them about his orchids, they burst into laughter. "What do you do with these things, smoke 'em?" asked one of the suspected drug dealers.

The next day, Norris pleaded not guilty, and a day after that, he was released on bail. The Norrises returned to Spring, Texas, to figure out their next steps. Their business was destroyed; their retirement savings and home were on the line for the Peruvian orchid dealer who was now living in the spare bedroom; and Norris, 67 and in frail health, faced the prospect of living out his days in a federal prison. Still, Norris believed he had not done anything wrong and would win out in the end.

So they made a go of fighting the charges. Norris hired an attorney who, with most of his experience at the state or county level, quickly found himself in over his head with the complexities of international treaties, environmental law, and the intricacies of a federal prosecution.

In April, the attorney accompanied Norris to what turned out to be a proffer meeting, at which defendants are typically offered the opportunity to cooperate with the government in exchange for leniency. Norris had not been told what to expect and did not have anything to say when prosecutors asked what he was willing to admit. They peppered him with names of other orchid dealers, but Norris was not inclined to inform on them—not that he knew enough about their operations in any case to offer anything more than speculation.

After that, Norris got a more experienced—and much more expensive—attorney. With bills piling up and the complexity of the case and the resulting difficulty of mounting a defense finally becoming apparent, Norris took the step he had been dreading: changing his plea to guilty. "I hated that, I absolutely hated that," said Norris. Five years after the fact, the episode still provokes pain, his face blushing and speech becoming softer. "The hardest thing I ever did was stand there and say I was guilty to all these things. I didn't think I was guilty of any of them."

While Norris and his wife were focused on his case, Manuel Arias Silva was plotting his own next moves. By mid-May he had managed to obtain a new passport and exit visa from the Peruvian Consulate. On May 19, soon after they had returned to Texas from a hearing in Miami, Kathy Norris received a call from Juan Silva, in Peru, who was in tears. His father, he explained, had returned home to evade the charges against him in the United States. The Norrises would be on the hook for Arias's bail and bond—nearly $200,000.

"The hardest thing I ever did was stand there and say I was guilty to all these things. I didn't think I was guilty of any of them."

Based on Norris's transactions with Arias, as well as those with Xix, the government recommended a prison sentence of 33 to 41 months. Such a lengthy sentence was justified, according to the sentencing memorandum, because of the value of the plants in the improperly documented shipments. Two choices pushed the recommended sentence up. First, the government used Norris's catalog prices to calculate the value of the plants instead of using what he had paid for them. Second, it included all plants in each shipment in its calculations, reasoning that the properly documented plants—by far the bulk of every shipment—were a part of the offense be-cause they were supposedly used to shield the others.

On October 6, Norris was sentenced to 17 months in prison, followed by two years of probation. In the eyes of the law, he was now a felon and would be for the rest of his life. The sentencing judge suggested to Norris and his wife that good could come of his conviction and punishment:

> Life sometimes presents us with lemons. Sometimes we grow the lemons ourselves. But as long as we are walking on the face of the earth, our responsibility is to take those lemons and use the gifts that God has given us to turn lemons into lemonade.

Norris reported to the federal prison in Fort Worth on January 10, 2005; was released for a year in December 2006 while the Eleventh Circuit Court of Appeals considered a challenge to his sentence; and then returned to prison to serve the remainder of his sentence. Prison officials, angered by Norris's temporary reprieve, threw him in solitary confinement, where he spent a total of 71 days. He was released on April 27, 2007.

The sentencing judge suggested to Norris and his wife that good could come of his conviction and punishment.

The Aftermath

"Our home was ransacked by federal agents, my husband was prose-cuted and imprisoned, and our family is still suffering the consequences—all because my husband imported a few legal orchids into the United States with improper paperwork," says Kathy Norris. Readjusting to life outside of prison was tough for George, Kathy explains:

> He came home from prison and ate and slept and sat on the couch, staring at the TV—not really watching it. He would not water a plant, invite a friend over, initiate con-tact with the kids and grandkids. Nothing. And this went on for months.

George Norris has lost his passion for orchids. The yard behind their home is all dirt and grass, nothing more. The greenhouse is abandoned. Broken pots, bags of dirt, plastic bins, and other clutter spill off its shelves

Andrew M. Grossman photo

Kathy and George Norris in their greenhouse.

and onto the floor. The roof is sagging. A few potted cacti are the only living things inside it aside from weeds.

A dozen potted plants grace the Norrises' back porch; three or four are even orchids, though none are in bloom. Kathy waters them. "They're the ones I haven't managed to kill yet," she says.

The couple's finances are precarious. Following the flood of 1994, Norris rebuilt most of their home himself, but they had to refinance the house to pay for materials. Kathy had to make those payments and all the others while Norris was in prison, relying on her salary as director of Montgomery County's Dispute Resolution Center, which she ran on a shoestring budget. The same discipline now reigns at home.

Neither Norris nor his wife knows how they will face retirement with all of their savings used to pay legal expenses.

"I figured out how to live on as little as it's possible to live on and still keep the house," says Kathy.

Neither Norris nor his wife knows how they will face retirement with all of their savings used to pay legal expenses. "It might be possible to recover from such losses had we been younger," observes Kathy, "but at the ages of 71 and 66, there is not enough time and health to regain the loss." Arias's bond hangs over their heads as well, and the government has said that it will seek to enforce it. That threat keeps Kathy up at nights. She doesn't know what else they could give up, other than the house, or how they could possibly come up with the $175,000 still owed.

The hardest blow, explains Mrs. Norris, has been to their faith in America and its system of criminal justice.

Norris has already suffered the indignity of his grandchildren knowing that he spent over a year in federal prison and is a convicted criminal. What hurts him now is that he cannot introduce them to the hunting tradition—small game, squirrels, and rabbits—that has been a part of his family, passed from generation to generation. As a felon, he cannot possess a firearm. They sold off and gave away his grandfather's small gun collection, which he had inherited. In poor health and unarmed, Norris fears that he cannot even defend his own family.

But the hardest blow, explains Kathy, has been to their faith in America and its system of criminal justice. As she told the House of Representatives Subcommittee on Crime, Terrorism and Homeland Security in July 2009:

> I got raised in a country that wasn't like this. I grew up in a reasonably nice part of Dallas, I came from a family where nobody had been indicted for anything, and so had George. And the government didn't do this stuff to people. It wasn't part of anything I ever got taught in my civics books.

That lack of faith is almost visible in George Norris's frailty and fear. "I hardly drive at all anymore," he explained. "The whole time I'm driving, I'm thinking about not getting a ticket for anything…. I don't sleep like I used to; I still have prison dreams." He pauses for a moment to think and looks down at the floor. In a quiet voice, he says, "It's utterly wrecked our lives."

Probably any dealer in imported plants could have been prosecuted for the charges that were brought against George Norris. His crime, at its core, was a paperwork violation: He had the wrong documents for some of the plants he imported but almost certainly could have obtained the right ones with a bit more time and effort. Neither he nor other dealers ever suspected that the law would be enforced to the very letter so long as they followed its spirit.

Norris was singled out because he was in the wrong place at the wrong time. As controversy roared over the kovachii and prosecutors were gunning for a high-profile conviction to tamp down sales in truly rare and endangered plants, Norris bragged that he would soon have the extraordinary flower in stock. To this date, he has never seen one.

Armed with overly broad laws that criminalize a wide range of unobjectionable conduct, prosecutors could look past that fact. Burrowing through Norris's records, they found other grounds for a case. One way or another, they would have their poster child.

> Enormously complex and demanding regulations are regularly paired with draconian criminal penalties for even minor deviations from the rules.

This is the risk that all American entrepreneurs face today. Enormously complex and demanding regulations are regularly paired with draconian criminal penalties for even minor deviations from the rules. Minor violations from time to time are all but inevitable because full compliance would be either impossible or impossibly expensive. Nearly every time, nobody notices or cares, but all it takes is one exception for the hammer of the law to strike.

"If there is a lesson here, it is that overcriminalization has very real, very serious consequences for American families," says Kathy Norris. "If any good is to come of what happened to us, it will be that we help to make sure that more families don't suffer as we have."

CHAPTER 8

THE MYSPACE SUICIDE CASE
Are All Your Posts Crimes?
(United States v. Drew)

It is a legal cliché that "Hard cases make bad law"—that is, that courts are too often tempted by emotional facts and sympathetic parties to render decisions without thinking about the law they are making and its effect on future cases. The same could be said of the recent development of the criminal law: Legislators, prosecutors, and the public seem to believe that every bad act is a legal wrong, punishable just as traditional crimes like murder and theft and rape are punished.

But too often they overlook the far greater differences between traditional crimes and these new offenses. Pushing the criminal law beyond its historical bounds carries consequences that may not be apparent when the public mood is hot and vengeful, and only later is the result apparent: bad law. This pattern is repeated nearly every time Congress passes a narrow law to target some unlikely, newsworthy wrong or slight deviation from productive behavior.

The case of housewife Lori Drew fits the pattern perfectly. Drew was indicted under a federal anti-computer hacking statute for impersonating a young man on MySpace to gain the trust of an emotionally troubled teen, Megan Meier, who killed herself after the cruel joke spun out of control. The case contains all the hallmarks of overcriminalization and illustrates all of its common consequences:

- The decline of *mens rea* (guilty mind) requirements as a protection against unfair criminal liability;

- The arbitrary nature of modern criminal offenses that provide citizens with no notice that their conduct may be illegal;

- Extremely broad liability that threatens to make millions of honest citizens criminals;

- Politics and public opinion trumping ordinary prosecutorial discretion and traditional notions of justice; and

- The threat to liberty, the rule of law, and our civil society.

Drew's conduct was irresponsible, but it was not criminal. It may deserve social sanction, already dispensed in great quantity, and perhaps civil liability to Megan Meier's parents. But if Drew had been convicted under criminal law, virtually every Internet user would have faced the consequences.

The Death of Megan Meier

Prosecutors alleged that Lori Drew violated a federal anti-hacking statute when she created a fake MySpace account in violation of the Web site's terms of service.[1] According to the indictment, Drew created a MySpace account under the name "Josh Evans," whom she styled to be a 16-year-old boy recently moved to the area in eastern Missouri.

Drew's apparent aim was to find out why Megan Meier, a neighbor's 13-year-old child, had dumped her own daughter as a friend. Indeed, the St. Charles County prosecutor who investigated the case initially said it was Drew's "only" purpose. She may also have intended it as a joke: to "mess with Megan" as she believed Megan had done with her daughter. Drew's motives, the record indicates, were not clear-cut and seem to have shifted during the deception. This is not, after all, a bank robbery or a mugging for which motive, and thereby criminal intent, may be inferred simply from the facts.

> If Drew had been convicted under criminal law, virtually every Internet user would have faced the consequences.

At first engaging and flirtatious, "Josh Evans" suddenly turned mean one rainy October weekend. He shared some of Megan's private messages with her friends (for example, "aww sexi Josh ur so sweet if u moved back u could see me up close and personal lol") and posted public bulletins calling Megan "fat" and a "slut." Most and perhaps all of these messages, say investigators, were posted by persons with access to the account other than Drew.

The barrage continued that Monday when Megan logged in after school to see whether Josh had relented. Typing through tears, Megan fired back strongly worded replies, laced with strong language, at Josh and others who had taken his side in the dispute. Megan's mother was shocked by her "vulgar" responses and angrily demanded that she log off of MySpace. In a huff, Megan ran to her room and shut the door.

Megan's father checked his daughter's MySpace account the next day and recalls what he believes is the final message from Evans that his daughter read that evening: "The world would be a better place without you." (Federal investigators, however, were unable to confirm that text, or that Drew is the one who sent it, as the message was lost in the ether.) Twenty minutes after receiving that message, Megan hanged herself in her bedroom closet.

It took a year for the case to gel. Word of Drew's involvement emerged gradually, as did the scope of what federal prosecutors now call a conspiracy. Drew apparently did not act alone, but shared access to the account with her daughter, a family employee, and perhaps others. The facts are confused, and no one has been able to work out who exactly was responsible for which messages to Megan.

> The facts are confused, and no one has been able to work out who exactly was responsible for which messages to Megan.

That wrinkle, among others, was lost when word of the case became public in late 2007. The cable networks leapt on the story, dubbing it the "MySpace Suicide Case," following a report in the local paper. With the perils of the online world and "cyberbullying" on many parents' minds, the story found a ready audience. The strange fact of Drew's involvement—this wasn't just children taunting children—gave the story a villain. "Good Morning America" and "Today" sought out the families and the witnesses for exclusive interviews. Hundreds of articles, opinion pieces, and television spots followed.

An indictment, however, did not—at least not immediately. A spokesman for the local sheriff's department said that what Drew did "might've been rude, it might've been immature, but it wasn't illegal." Tina, Megan's mother, contested that conclusion in an interview with ABC News: "You cannot as an adult sit there and do that and hide behind a computer. It is a criminal act. We want to see her go to jail."

The county prosecutor, Jack Banas, also reviewed the case and declined to press charges. The evidence, he said, showed that Drew was probably not the one who had sent the messages that final day; more crucially, she lacked the requisite criminal intent to harass or stalk Megan. Drew's behavior simply did not violate any law. The local federal prosecutor announced that he had reached the same conclusion.

The result was outrage, both online and off. The hundreds of comments posted at that time to an online forum provided by ABC News seethe with anger at Lori Drew. This one is representative for its content, if not its relatively temperate tone:

> Put her [Drew] in jail!!!!!! What kind of example are we setting if an adult/parent can get away with such an atrocity! We as adults all know how hard being a teenager is especially for the girls. She should have known better and acted as a parent and not as some rebellious teen. She obviously has some growing up to do! I think jail would be a great place for her to reflect on the fact that her stupidity has taken the life of a young, sensitive teenager, and ruined the lives of her family members who have to go on without her.

Vigilantism also took root in online communities and spilled over into the physical world. Critics posted the Drews' home address and phone numbers on message boards, as well as a satellite photograph of their home. Some discussed planning attacks on the Drews. Their home was repeatedly vandalized, and they received hundreds of angry, sometimes threatening phone calls. Drew was forced to close her coupon book business after clients were inundated with e-mails and calls from across the country. Due to the publicity and bullying, Drew's daughter dropped out of school.

Vigilantism also took root in online communities and spilled over into the physical world.

As interest in the case and outrage that Drew would not face jail time reached a fever pitch in early 2008, federal prosecutors in Los Angeles, where MySpace is located, decided to conduct their own investigation. The grand jury's initial subpoenas, quite unusually, made the cable and network news reports as well as *The New York Times* and the *Los Angeles Times*. Following a run-up in the press, an indictment of Lori Drew was issued in February.

The Charges

That indictment laid out a total of four charges: three for violation of a federal criminal statute and one for conspiracy to violate that statute. The statute is 18 U.S.C. § 1030, commonly known as the Computer Fraud and Abuse Act, which criminalizes unauthorized access to computer systems. Similar statutes have been enacted in all of the states.

Though intended to criminalize hacking, the statute is loosely drafted—a problem that regrettably has received little attention until now. The provision that Drew was alleged to have violated (and allegedly conspired to violate) authorizes the prosecution of any person who "intentionally accesses a computer without authorization or exceeds authorized access, and thereby obtains…information from any protected computer if the conduct involved an interstate or foreign communication."

As Professor Orin Kerr of George Washington University School of Law explained in a thoughtful 2003 article, "unauthorized access" statutes, and in particular § 1030, cover a very uncertain scope of conduct due to the vagueness of the words "access" and "unauthorized."[2] The key question, writes Kerr, and one that had not been asked of the federal statute until now is whether these laws criminalize the terms of contracts governing the use of computer services or something more akin to criminal trespass or theft.

> Though intended to criminalize hacking, the statute is loosely drafted—a problem that regrettably has received little attention until now.

The charges against Lori Drew are of the former variety: She was alleged to have criminally violated the terms of her agreement with MySpace. MySpace, the indictment explains, is a social networking Web site where registered individuals can post profiles of themselves and meet and interact with other users of the service. To join and register an account, an individual must visit the Web site, fill out a form, and agree to abide by its "terms of service," an agreement governing use of the site. Many Web sites, and probably all social networking services, have terms of service and require users to agree to them by checking a box on a sign-up form. Few users, however, actually review these complex and often lengthy legal documents; indeed, the trend in contract law is that they are unenforceable.

Under the MySpace terms-of-service agreement, a user represents that "all registration information you submit is truthful and accurate" and promises to "maintain the accuracy of such information." In addition, the agreement states that certain content is prohibited, including conduct that "harasses or advocates harassment of another person"; "promotes information that you know is false or misleading or promotes illegal activities or conduct that is abusive, threatening, obscene, defamatory or libelous"; or "solicits personal information from anyone under 18."

Other prohibitions are even broader. For example, content that "provides any telephone numbers, street addresses, last names, URLs or email addresses" is also prohibited. So using MySpace to send a friend a message containing a link to a newspaper article would be a violation of the site's terms-of-service agreement.

The agreement itself appears to contemplate enforcement by MySpace. It states, for example, that "prohibited content," a label applied at "the sole discretion of MySpace.com," may be investigated by MySpace, which will "take appropriate legal action...including...removing the offending communication...and terminating the Membership of such violators." Similarly, the agreement explicitly reserves MySpace's right "to reject, refuse to post or remove any posting (including private messages) by you, or to restrict, suspend, or terminate your access to all or any part of the MySpace Services at any time." Though the agreement states that MySpace may report members to law enforcement authorities for "using the MySpace Services in a manner inconsistent with any and all applicable laws and regulations," it does not purport to make its own terms of the agreement into criminal law.

Yet it is for violation of those terms that Drew was charged. The indictment alleged that she accessed MySpace "without authorization and in excess of authorized access" on three occasions when she, "in violation of MySpace TOS [terms of service], accessed MySpace servers to obtain information regarding [Meier]." The conspiracy count elaborated on these charges, alleging specific instances when Drew and others collaborated to achieve the same end, such as when she and "the co-conspirators altered the 'Josh Evans' profile to flirt with [Meier]."

In early September, district court Judge George Wu denied two motions by Drew to dismiss the charges against her but held over a third for further consideration. Judge Wu rejected the arguments that the statute is unconstitutionally vague and that, as applied in this case, it unconstitutionally delegated the power to define what acts constitute a crime to a private party, MySpace. The case proceeded to trial in early October, and Drew was convicted of three misdemeanors for violating the MySpace terms of service, but not of the more serious felony charges for doing so with the intent to cause an injury.

She was lucky. Each of the crimes with which Drew was charged is a felony. If she had been convicted on all counts, Drew faced a possible 20 years behind bars and criminal fines of up to $1 million. As it is, she faced up to three years in prison potentially. The conviction could have also served as evidence in a civil suit, perhaps leading to additional liability, such as the payment of damages for wrongful death to Megan Meier's parents.

In the end, however, Judge Wu went further. At a hearing in July 2009, he decided to dismiss the charges against Drew completely. He reasoned that her conduct, though reprehensible, was of the sort that millions did each day: They used MySpace in violation of the terms of service. Read broadly, any "lie" on MySpace (saying you are 40 when you are really 45 was the example the judge gave) would have been a crime. This, he said in dismissing the charges, simply went too far.

> Read broadly, any "lie" on MySpace (saying you are 40 when you are really 45 was the example the judge gave) would have been a crime.

In his written decision, Judge Wu said that a criminal prosecution for violating a site's terms-of-service agreement "runs afoul of the void-for-vagueness doctrine." Among other reasons, Wu held that such a prosecution is invalid because defendants don't have fair notice that ignoring or violating a user agreement can result in criminal sanctions.

He also pointed out that MySpace's terms of service are so broad that many people apparently violate them. For instance, he wrote, "the lonely-heart who submits intentionally inaccurate data about his or her age, height and/or physical appearance" violates the site's prohibition against providing false or misleading information. In addition, "the exasperated parent who sends out a group message to neighborhood friends entreating them to purchase his or her daughter's girl scout cookies" breaks the site's rule against advertising to other members.

The Consequences

Though there is some question about Drew's involvement in the meanest messages sent to Meier, even in the kindest light, her actions were irresponsible and deserve social, and perhaps civil legal, sanction. That does not mean, however, that she did anything that is or should be a crime. In the harshest light, the accusations against her do not rise to that level. If all of the allegations against her are true, she treated a vulnerable teenage girl with cruelty and a malign heart; but kindness and compassion are not things that our society enforces by law, nor could it do so.

The tragedy of Megan Meier's suicide, and especially what has followed it, demonstrates well the means and risks of abuse of the criminal law. The public response to the episode prompted lawmakers in Meier's hometown, the state of Missouri, and the U.S. Congress to introduce legislation to curb "cyberbullying," although whether any of these proposals would actually reach Drew's conduct and, if they did, would

> If all of the allegations against her are true, she treated a vulnerable teenage girl with cruelty and a malign heart; but kindness and compassion are not things that our society enforces by law, nor could it do so.

withstand First Amendment scrutiny is uncertain. The public response also led no fewer than three teams of prosecutors to consider the case.

The resulting indictment is based on a crime of questionable legitimacy—a tortured reading of a poorly drafted statute—and the consequences of this charging cannot be overstated. Specifically, and proving that hard cases do indeed make bad law, the Lori Drew case offers five cautionary lessons.

Lesson #1: Lack of a guilty mind doesn't matter

Driving into a pedestrian by accident is very different from running down a person deliberately, though the result may be the same. One undoubtedly deserves criminal punishment, for it is murder, but the other may not if it truly was an accident not brought about by the driver's recklessness.

In this way, criminal intent (or *mens rea*) requirements sort criminals from those who brought about bad results but without the intent of doing so. Their use, however, is in decline at a time when the criminal law is growing at an exceedingly brisk pace. A significant percentage of recent federal criminal statutes, for example, lack *mens rea* protections altogether, and others contain weak or ambiguous mental elements.

This is a hallmark of overcriminalization. Lax or non-existent *mens rea* requirements make the task of prosecution far easier, but they do so at the expense of wrongful conviction and the blurring of the purpose of the criminal law.

Although the statute that Lori Drew was accused of violating contains a relatively strong *mens rea* requirement, the indictment all but ignored it. The law requires that a person "intentionally" accesses a computer without authorization. In the context of criminal intent, "intentionally" generally means either of two things: that a person (1) "consciously desires the result" and acts to achieve it or (2) "knows that that result is practically certain to follow from her conduct." Thus, accessing a system without authorization accidentally, or without knowledge of an authorization requirement, should not be the basis for criminal liability—at least as the statute would traditionally have been read.

> To meet this *mens rea* standard, the government should have been required to prove that Drew intended to access MySpace in knowing violation of the authorization that MySpace had granted to her in its terms-of-service agreement.

To meet this *mens rea* standard, then, the government should have been required to prove that Drew intended to access MySpace in knowing violation of the authorization that MySpace had granted to her in its terms-of-service agreement. This means that she must have (1) known of the agreement and its provisions, (2) known that her authorization to access MySpace was conditioned on her not violating those provisions, and (3) known that her conduct had caused her authorization to access the site to be revoked so that subsequent access would be without authorization.

If that standard had been applied, it is unlikely that Drew would ever have been charged.

First, there was no evidence that Drew had ever accessed or read the terms-of-service agreement. The indictment stated only that the agreement "was readily available" to all MySpace users, but that is not enough. The agreement is nine solid pages of legalistic text, at times all in capital letters, organized into paragraphs that regularly go on for half a page. One doubts that anyone save a lawyer could read and understand it or that any MySpace user, lawyer or not, would bother to try. The indictment did not even allege that Drew, who is not a lawyer, had ever seen it.

Second, the agreement itself was not really susceptible to the reading that violation of its terms would necessarily terminate authorization to access the site. MySpace states throughout the document that it "reserves the right" to remove any posting on the site and to terminate a user's access, but it does not state that access is conditioned on following the agreement's terms—in other words, that misconduct would automatically lead to a withdrawal of authorization. So even had Drew read and understood the agreement, she would still probably have lacked the requisite mental state because she would not have known that she lacked authorization to access the site.

> Even had Drew read and understood the agreement, she would still probably have lacked the requisite mental state because she would not have known that she lacked authorization to access the site.

This is as it should be. Whatever Drew intended to do, hacking MySpace was not it. Moreover, even if her actions did amount to hacking, she simply lacked the mental state required for conviction. This is how the criminal law, quite appropriately, protects those who lack "fault" from punishment. That protection is undermined, however, by the rigors and expense of defending one's self, as Lori Drew was forced to do.

Lesson #2: Citizens receive no notice of the law and what is forbidden

It is said that ignorance of the law is no excuse, but traditionally such ignorance was rare because criminal offenses had an intuitive moral basis. Until recent decades, the bulk of crimes concerned acts that were *malum in se*, or wrong in themselves. This includes murder, rape, and theft, all offenses that a member of society would know, without reading statutes or case law, are crimes. Thus, an individual could easily conform his conduct to the law's requirements, and those who ran afoul of the law, it could be said with some certainty, deserved society's condemnation and punishment.

But today, new criminal laws invariably concern conduct that is *malum prohibitum*, or wrong only because it is prohibited. *Malum prohibitum* crimes include things like shipping chemicals without the proper sticker on the box, violating a recordkeeping requirement, or driving (non-recklessly) above the speed limit. Because these acts are not morally wrong and are made so only by the passage of sometimes obscure laws, individuals often lack notice that their conduct may subject them to criminal liability. This modern trend makes strong *mens rea* requirements even more important today than they were in the past, not less.

The law that Lori Drew was accused of violating appears to address conduct that really is morally wrong, but its loose language has been twisted to give it a far broader coverage that extends beyond any reasonable person's expectations as to what, exactly, constitutes online criminal conduct. As Professor Kerr explains, legislatures enacting unauthorized access statutes saw them "as doing for computers what trespass and burglary laws did for real property," but translating that intent into statutory language proved difficult because the concepts of "access" and "authorization" online differ from their real-world cousins. The usual case—until now, all those brought under the federal statute have been "usual" in this way—does not confront this problem, because it concerns conduct that is analogous to physical intrusion, such as an employee installing malicious software on his employer's computers and a Russian hacker breaking into a Connecticut business's computers to steal proprietary information.[3]

> This modern trend makes strong *mens rea* requirements even more important today than they were in the past, not less.

The case against Drew was different. Under the prosecutors' reading of the statute, "unauthorized access" includes not only hacking, but also any access in violation of the terms of service, in effect turning the terms of certain contracts (those concerning access to online services) into criminal law. These contracts, however, are not written with the same clarity as most criminal law and often regulate conduct that has nothing at all to do with the concerns or purposes of criminal law.

A criminal statute containing similar commands would be void for vagueness under the Constitution. As the Supreme Court has said:

> [The requirement that the terms of a criminal law be clear is] a well-recognized [one], consonant alike with ordinary notions of fair play and the settled rules of law; and a statute which either forbids or requires the doing of an act in terms so vague that men of common intelligence must necessarily guess at its meaning and differ as to its application violates the first essential of due process of law.

Lesson #3: Everyone is a criminal

As the scope of criminal prohibition expands, so does the number of people who are, according to the law, criminals. The increasing criminalization of economic conduct in recent years, for example, means that many entrepreneurs engaging in socially beneficial conduct may, because they overlooked a regulatory requirement or made a simple mistake, face criminal charges and even conviction.

This concern is anything but hypothetical, as the stories in this book unfortunately demonstrate. As state legislators and the U.S. Congress criminalize more conduct, greater numbers of individuals are unwittingly being subjected to criminal liability. Even those who prevail find that they have had to spend substantial portions of their savings on legal defense and have lost years of their lives fighting charges that they had no reason to expect.

It is not at all farfetched to say that today, every American is a criminal—or would be if prosecutors chose to enforce all of the laws on the books. The federal mail fraud and wire fraud statutes, for example, are so broad that they ensnare an enormous amount of private conduct unrelated to traditional fraud offenses. Calling in sick to the office to take an extra vacation day, while not commendable behavior, should not be a criminal offense either; by statute, however, it is almost surely wire fraud. Similarly,

> As the scope of criminal prohibition expands, so does the number of people who are, according to the law, criminals.

conspiracy offenses, as used in the Drew case, are a way for prosecutors to go after those whose actual conduct violated no criminal law.

The amount of conduct that would have been criminalized if Lori Drew had been convicted on the prosecution's theory of the law is enormous, as is the number of Americans who would be in violation of the law. Any person who has exaggerated his or her height on a dating Web site profile, unwittingly linked to a file that happens to contain a virus on Facebook, or performed research for pay using Google has violated a terms-of-service agreement and could be prosecuted for it.

> It is not at all farfetched to say that today, every American is a criminal—or would be if prosecutors chose to enforce all of the laws on the books.

As pointed out in a friend of the court brief by the Electronic Frontier Foundation (EFF) in the Drew case, the majority of teenage MySpace users have submitted at least some false information to the site in violation of its terms of service, and some child-protection groups actually encourage children to enter false information online in certain circumstances to protect their privacy and guard against exploitation. The EFF brief, noting that Google's terms of service bar minors from using its services, reasonably supposes that the company "[s]urely...did not mean—or imagine—that tens of millions of minors in fact would never use its services to obtain information or do so at the risk of criminal liability."

Professor Kerr puts forward a particularly pointed example:

> Imagine that a website owner announces that only right-handed people can view his website, or perhaps only friendly people. Under the contract-based approach, a visit to the site by a left-handed or surly person is an unauthorized access that may trigger state and federal criminal laws. A computer owner could set up a public web page, announce that "no one is allowed to visit my web page," and then refer for prosecution anyone who clicks on the site out of curiosity. By granting the computer owner essentially unlimited authority to define authorization, the contract standard delegates the scope of criminality to every computer owner.

In short, broad criminal liability means that more good people—people who are honest and who do not infringe on others' rights or run roughshod over society's basic rules—will be treated as criminals to nobody's ultimate benefit. All that protects them from criminal sanction is prosecutorial discretion and restraint, but overcriminalization causes even that to break down.

> Broad criminal liability means that more good people—people who are honest and who do not infringe on others' rights or run roughshod over society's basic rules—will be treated as criminals to nobody's ultimate benefit.

Lesson #4: Politics controls

A prosecutor's power is awesome, for he has the discretion to bring the force of the state, which alone can legally abridge a person's freedom, to bear on an individual. As specified in the American Bar Association's Model Rules of Professional Conduct:

> A prosecutor has the responsibility of a minister of justice and not simply that of an advocate. This responsibility carries with it specific obligations to see that the defendant is accorded procedural justice, that guilt is decided upon the basis of sufficient evidence, and that special precautions are taken to prevent and to rectify the conviction of innocent persons.

In other words, a prosecutor's role, according to the ABA's Standards of Criminal Justice Relating to the Prosecution Function, is not to win convictions or to advance his or her own political advantage, but to do justice.

Although public interest and concern should play a role in a prosecutor's exercise of discretion—after all, it is the prosecutor's duty to direct his resources to combat serious threats to the community—it is no substitute for his independent analysis of the merits of the case. Only when a prosecutor is himself convinced that a charge is supported by probable cause and sufficient admissible evidence to warrant a conviction may he institute it. Any lesser standard risks subjecting the innocent to the great burden and expense of criminal prosecution.

The Lori Drew indictment arrived with the strong whiff of politics upon it. At least two teams of prosecutors in Missouri—one local, one federal—investigated and reviewed the evidence in the case, and both declined to bring charges for the reason that Drew's conduct had violated no law. Only at that point, when public outrage was at its height, did the U.S. Attorney's office in Los Angeles, a jurisdiction far removed from the case's natural Missouri locale, become involved in the case. The appearance, if not the reality, of improper motivation in the decision to charge is strong.

> A criminal charge that comes as a surprise simply demonstrates that the law is unclear, has provided insufficient notice, and has failed in its purpose.

That the L.A. prosecutors were more "creative" in charging than their Missouri counterparts is no answer, for the principal purpose of the criminal law is voluntary deterrence, which is built atop a foundation of certainty. That such creativity in charging is possible speaks to the great overbreadth of the criminal law in general and the vagueness of the statute in particular. A criminal charge that comes as a surprise simply demonstrates that the law is unclear, has provided insufficient notice, and has failed in its purpose.

Lesson #5: Fundamental values fall by the wayside

It is said that overcriminalization is a bipartisan pursuit: Republicans wish to appear tough on crime, and Democrats tend to be happy to see business leaders behind bars. Meanwhile, the Department of Justice and prosecutors lobby for broader offenses to ease charging and conviction, and the public pushes for new offenses to target the evil of the day. The result is that criminal offenses multiply with no natural constituency in opposition, and when a person whose hands are unclean is alleged to have committed a questionable offense, few public figures are eager to rise to the defense.

However, this dynamic is changing as more and more groups recognize the growing threat of overcriminalization to the rule of law, our civil liberties, and the economy. Overcriminalization may be good politics, but it is terrible policy, and that fact is slowly swaying opinion.

For conservatives, prosecutions like Drew's demean the rule of law.

First, such prosecutions decrease respect for the law across the board. As Professor John Coffee has explained, "The criminal law is obeyed not simply because there is a legal threat underlying it, but because the public perceives its norms to be legitimate and deserving of compliance. [T]he criminal law is a system for public communication of values." This function is sacrificed, however, as the criminal law expands to cover offenses that are unconnected to our values. As a result, the power of the law to influence conduct is reduced, leading to more crimes, including those of the *malum in se* (wrong in themselves) variety. Overcriminalization, in other words, is actually counterproductive.

Second, the growth in criminal law is a part of the overall growth of government at the expense of citizens' freedoms. At the federal level, the statutes at issue in cases such as *Lopez* (the Gun-Free School Zones Act), *Morrison* (the Violence Against Women Act), and *Raich* (the Controlled Substances Act) embody flawed notions of Congress's Commerce Clause powers that have allowed federal control to expand well beyond its constitutional limits, severely undermining the federal system and threatening individual liberty.[4]

Third, overcriminalization has become a brake on the economy. Today, corporate leaders face criminal liability for minor regulatory violations at every turn. American business is less vibrant and internationally competitive because of the liability and compliance costs imposed by ill-conceived criminal statutes and prosecutions.

> American business is less vibrant and internationally competitive because of the liability and compliance costs imposed by ill-conceived criminal statutes and prosecutions.

Those who are on the left share these concerns and have several of their own. Unbounded prosecutorial discretion, for example, raises the risk of abuses, such as racial discrimination and politically motivated cases. These liberals, like conservatives, see overcriminalization as a threat both to fundamental liberties, such as free speech and the right to speak anonymously, and to the rights of the accused.

Thus, it is no surprise that the EFF, joined by the Center for Democracy and Technology and Ralph Nader's Public Citizen, filed a brief on behalf of Lori Drew, making the case that a conviction on the government's "novel and unprecedented" reading of an anti-hacking statute would "convert the millions of internet-using Americans who disregard the terms of service associated with online services into federal criminals"—an end that would be "unwarranted" and unconstitutional. The government's theory, the brief concludes, would violate the First Amendment because of its restrictions on free speech and anonymous speech and the Due Process Clause because of its vagueness and lack of notice.

Indicting Lori Drew on the charges leveled against her was bad law, no matter what her transgressions had been, but the recent trend in criminal law—one of great expansion and few checks—suggested that a conviction on the government's excessively creative legal theory was not unlikely. Even though she prevailed, Drew still had to suffer the rigors of prosecution, a burden that any person would rightly fear.

If the facts are as alleged, Drew does deserve punishment, but it need not, and should not, be of a criminal nature. Social sanction, which has been dispensed in great quantities, and civil justice are the appropriate remedies to address conduct such as Drew's, which was both hardhearted and unkind. Criminal law is not the proper remedy for the simple reason that she committed no crime.

In the end, perhaps some sense may come out of the Lori Drew prosecution. In response to the dismissal, Representative Linda Sanchez (D–CA) lobbied fellow lawmakers on a House Judiciary subcommittee to back her proposed legislation dubbed the "Megan Meier Cyberbullying Prevention Act." The

> Criminal law is not the proper remedy for the simple reason that Drew committed no crime.

Act would make being a bully in cyberperspace a federal crime. At a recent hearing, however, it appeared that both Democrats and Republicans were skeptical of the need to federalize a bullying offense. In the end, if they decline the opportunity to expand federal criminal law in this way, Congress may finally have drawn a line in the sand to stop overcriminalization.

As for Lori Drew, in November 2009, the government quietly dropped its appeal of Judge Wu's decision dismissing the charges against her. After a long, tortuous journey, the criminal case against her ended with a quiet whimper.

CHAPTER 9

WHEN ART BECOMES A CRIME
A Crime of Mold
(United States v. Kurtz)

When Steven Kurtz awoke one morning in his Buffalo, New York, home to find his wife, Hope, unresponsive, he rushed to dial 911 and summon paramedics. It was May 11, 2004. He had no reason to expect that his wife's fatal heart attack and his call to the authorities would mark the beginning of a four-year odyssey to the belly of the criminal justice system.

The paramedics and police detectives who arrived at Kurtz's home that morning to tend to his wife found more than they expected. Off the upstairs bedroom was a small table on which was arranged a home laboratory containing Petri dishes and various items of lab equipment. The detectives spent hours—nearly the entire day—interrogating Kurtz about the equipment and his relationship with his wife and then called in local health department officials, who ran tests on the cultures in the Petri dishes. They were harmless.

Not satisfied with Kurtz's answers, however, and still suspicious of the lab, the police decided to call in federal authorities. The next day, three or four vehicles came screeching up to Kurtz as he walked across a funeral home's parking lot, intending to make arrangements for his wife's cremation. It was the FBI. Kurtz was detained on suspicion of bioterrorism and held for 22 hours.

While Kurtz was being questioned in a downtown Hyatt, his home was being ransacked. Agents from the FBI, the Joint Terrorism Task Force, the Department of Homeland Security, and the Department of Defense, as well as officers from the local police and fire departments and the state mar-

Biohazard technicians and armed FBI agents raided Kurtz's house.

shal's office, arrived on the scene and cordoned off the entire block with crime-scene tape. As the TV cameras looked on, federal agents wearing hazmat suits and bearing guns entered Kurtz's home and seized all of his equipment, as well as books, personal papers, and his computer. Authorities went door-to-door, questioning Kurtz's neighbors about his habits and their impressions of him.

Nine-Day Ordeal

Their search went on nine days, and the authorities even seized his dead wife's body, despite the fact that the local coroner had already determined that her death was due to natural causes. Then federal officials announced triumphantly that they had thwarted a major bioweapons manufacturing plot.

But Steven Kurtz, a professor of visual studies at the University of Buffalo, was no terrorist, "homegrown" or otherwise. He is an artist and activist who works in unusual media. As a review of one of his recent exhibits explains, "Kurtz has never been shy about challenging the establishment, using a blend of performance art and science with his Critical Art Ensemble [CAE] to stir debate about such things as genetically modified crops and germ warfare."

> Steven Kurtz, a professor of visual studies at the University of Buffalo, was no terrorist, "homegrown" or otherwise.

The CAE, which Kurtz co-founded in 1987, is an art ensemble that produces Web projects, books, and gallery shows intended to engage viewers on the impact of technology on modern life. Its exhibits regularly include computers and electronics, as well as cultured bacteria, which are sometimes thrown at audience members. According to one of the collective's members, "We're…tactical media. We're mainly interested in issues of cultural representation, how things are represented to the public, and what's the ideology and the subtext to how something is being represented."

At the time of his wife's death, Kurtz had been at work on three projects. The small laboratory was intended for an exhibit on genetically modified organisms contained in store-bought foods at the Massachusetts Museum of Contemporary Art (MoCA). Most of the Petri dishes and harmless bacteria growing in them were meant for an exhibit called "GenTerra," the subject of which was the genetic engineering of organisms. The rest of the Petri dishes, as well as many books and papers, were part of Kurtz's early research for "Marching Plague," a project critical of the development and use of biological weapons agents. Those bacteria, as well, were harmless.

Claims Unravel, but Investigation Continues

After more than a week of searches and analysis, the FBI determined that Kurtz's home presented no public health risk and never had. The agency further confirmed that his wife's death had nothing to do with anything Kurtz might have done in his lab. Kurtz returned home to find the place ransacked, the detritus of a rushed investigation—stacks of pizza boxes and piles of sports drink bottles, discarded hazmat suits, used chemical test-kits—strewn throughout. Many possessions were missing, apparently confiscated, including a draft manuscript for his book on biowarfare.

> After more than a week of searches and analysis, the FBI determined that Kurtz's home presented no public health risk and never had.

The authorities' initial terrorism claims unraveled almost immediately, but the federal investigation dragged on for weeks, with FBI agents questioning museum curators and university administrators with ties to Kurtz's art collective. Agents issued 10 subpoenas to shocked guests at the opening reception for the CAE's MoCA exhibit, which the artists had had to cobble together from materials that had not been seized from Kurtz's home.

One CAE member was subpoenaed on the street by an FBI agent and made to appear before a federal grand jury for an inquiry into a possible

charge of "possession of biological agents," a criminal offense
created by the Patriot Act. The
offense prohibits the possession of "any biological agent...
that, under the circumstances,
is not reasonably justified by a
prophylactic, protective, bona
fide research, or other peaceful
purpose."

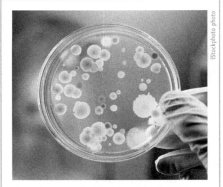

A petri dish of the kind found in Kurtz's home
and in high school labs across the country.

Kurtz and his allies believed
he had two sure-fire defenses to
that charge that would keep him
from being indicted.

First, the bacteria were completely harmless. Indeed, their safety had
been an essential component of the planned exhibit. "We were kind of de-
mystifying the whole procedure and trying to alleviate inappropriate fear
of transgenic science and redirect concern toward the political implications of the research," one CAE member told *The New York Times.* As one
leading biochemist explained in a letter to the lead prosecutor, the bacteria
found in Kurtz's home "are so
safe that they are cultured on
open lab benches and used in
public education." He continues: "You have more danger-
ous organisms likely growing on soft cheeses in your refrigerator."

> After all, Kurtz and his allies were
> artists, not belligerents, and their work
> was actually critical of bioweapons.

Second, the work done by Kurtz and his allies clearly fit into the "peaceful purpose" exception in the statute. After all, they were artists, not bel-
ligerents, and their work was actually critical of bioweapons.

The Indictment

It was a surprise, then, when nearly two months after the death of
Kurtz's wife, a federal indictment came down. Steven Kurtz and Rob-
ert Ferrell, a CAE associate who researches genetics at the University of
Pittsburgh, were charged not with possessing biological agents, but with
mail fraud and wire fraud. According to the indictment, Kurtz had used
Ferrell to purchase several strains of bacteria from an academic supplier,

American Type Culture Collection (ATCC), in violation of ATCC's terms of sale: that its customers be associated with

> The "crime," in essence, was breaking the terms of a private contract.

an approved lab or business, use the bacteria for research purposes only, and not distribute or transfer the bacteria.

The "crime," in other words, was breaking the terms of a private contract. Scheming to violate these contractual terms, under the prosecution's theory, was fraud, and both ATCC and the University of Pittsburgh were victims. And since Kurtz and Ferrell had discussed the matter over e-mail and the bacteria were shipped by mail, they could be prosecuted under the federal wire fraud and mail fraud statutes.

Just because the grand jury had declined to approve the charge that they had feared most—possession of biological agents—did not mean that Kurtz and Ferrell would get off easily. The fraud charges carried penalties of up to 20 years in jail and potentially $1 million in criminal fines apiece.

Kurtz and Ferrell vowed to fight the charges and were better positioned than most to do so. Their friends had established a defense fund to pay legal expenses, which would ultimately top $250,000, and the art world rallied on their behalf. Dozens of newspapers and magazines ran articles and columns on the case, most of them critical of the prosecution. Both of their universities stood by them. Few defendants in their position, Kurtz explains, would have the connections that they did and the resources and support needed to fight such a prosecution.

> Both of Kurtz's and Ferrell's universities stood by them. Few defendants in their position would have the connections that they did and the resources and support needed to fight such a prosecution.

A Reputation Ruined

Even so, the pressure and uncertainty eventually proved too much for Ferrell. The prosecution put a major blot on what had been a long and outstanding career during which he had contributed over 200 articles on the causes of diseases such as schizophrenia, muscular dystrophy, and diabetes. With criminal charges and the possibility of jail time hanging over his head, Ferrell, 64, was forced to curtail much of his research.

The prosecution also took a toll on his health. Previously diagnosed with non-Hodgkin's lymphoma, an incurable disease, Ferrell had undergone a bone-marrow transplant shortly after the indictment came down. The stress of the case contributed to a series of strokes, further weakening him.

In October 2007, Ferrell reached a deal with prosecutors and, in exchange for avoiding a prison sentence that would probably have killed him, pleaded guilty to a single misdemeanor count of mailing the bacteria to Kurtz. Ferrell was sentenced to a year of unsupervised release and a $500 fine. At Ferrell's sentencing hearing, the judge almost apologetically explained that this was "the most lenient sentence that I could give" under law.

> **The stress of the case contributed to a series of strokes, further weakening Ferrell.**

Kurtz, however, declined to plead guilty to a lesser charge and insisted that the government take the case to court. He argued that the indictment was defective because it failed to allege several elements of fraud: that the alleged victims—ATCC and the University of Pittsburgh—had been deprived of property and that he had intended to commit fraud. According to Kurtz, the prosecution had simply failed to demonstrate, even assuming the truth of the facts in the indictment, that he had done anything amounting to a crime under either of the fraud statutes.

Two Theories of Fraud

Chief Judge Richard Arcara of the Western District of New York heard oral arguments on Kurtz's motion to dismiss the charges in late 2007 and early 2008, at which time the prosecution put forward two theories of the fraud committed.

The first theory was plain fraud. ATCC and the university, prosecutors argued, were each deprived of two types of property—the bacteria and intellectual property rights in the bacteria—through Kurtz and Ferrell's scheme.

In a crisp page of analysis in its April 2008 opinion, the court rejected these arguments out of hand. The court observed that:

> [ATCC] was in the business of selling biological agents in exchange for money, and in this case it got what it bargained for. Ferrell, using the [University of Pittsburgh] account, paid ATCC for the biological agents. Therefore, ATCC was not deprived of the biological agents—it simply sold them.

As for the intellectual property, the court observed that "it is not clear what this allegation even means" and that it "appear[s] to be simply another way of saying that the defendant sought to obtain the biological agents from ATCC." Again, however, there was no evidence that Kurtz did anything to deprive ATCC of its intellectual property rights, such as reproducing the bacteria and selling them.

Finally, the University of Pittsburgh could not be a victim of fraud, since it never possessed the bacteria or had any property interest in them and, in any case, the indictment did not allege any type of fraudulent conduct directed toward the university.

Recognizing the weakness of its charges, the government belatedly put forward a "no-sale" theory of fraud as well. Under this theory, ATCC simply would not have sold the bacteria to Ferrell if he had not misrepresented the use to which they would be put: In other words, he and Kurtz used fraud to induce ATCC to make a sale it would not otherwise have made.

The court, relying on reasoning from a recent appeals court opinion, drew a distinction between "schemes that do no more than cause their victims to enter into transactions they would otherwise avoid," which are not crimes, and "schemes that depend for their completion on a misrepresentation of an essential element of the bargain," which are.

> There was no evidence that Kurtz did anything to deprive ATCC of its intellectual property rights, such as reproducing the bacteria and selling them.

The distinction can sometimes be difficult to draw. False claims made by a distributor to a manufacturer of military goggles that its products would not be sold to restricted nations "went to an essential element of the bargain between the parties" because illegal exports would have dire consequences for the manufacturer, and so could be criminally charged; but falsely claiming that one had been referred by a friend of a potential customer is not criminal fraud, because the misrepresentation "was not directed to the quality, adequacy or price of goods to be sold." In short, the false claims, to be chargeable as wire fraud or mail fraud, must have "relevance to the object of the contract."

In Kurtz's case, the inquiry was relatively straightforward. The prosecution, ruled the court, did not make a proper "no-sale" claim because it did not present *any* evidence that ATCC's terms of sale were an essential part of the sales agreement or that Kurtz and Ferrell had intended to violate the terms and thereby defraud ATCC. Indeed, the court observed, "the indictment does not allege that either [Kurtz] or Ferrell even knew about the transfer restriction" in the terms of sale.

The indictment, concluded Judge Arcara, did not spell out any scheme that actually amounted to a crime. He dismissed all charges against Kurtz.

A Bittersweet Victory

For Kurtz, the victory was bittersweet. Though he was ultimately exonerated, the government's misguided prosecution imposed enormous costs on him, Ferrell, and many other artists and scientists.

Kurtz, in particular, remains angry that he was denied the opportunity to mourn for Hope, his wife and artistic partner of 20 years, whose death launched the strange series of events that consumed him for four years. "I think all adults know the feelings of intense grief and depression that are brought about by the loss of a loved one," Kurtz told writer Ken Goffman. "But when you spice it up with the adrenalin and the hyperanxiety of being attacked by the full weight of federal forces, which in turn causes all your survival instincts to really kick in, you have a bad trip from which you are not going to come down for a long time."

> Kurtz remains angry that he was denied the opportunity to mourn for his wife and artistic partner of 20 years, whose death launched the strange series of events that consumed him for four years.

Dr. Patrick Moore, a professor of genetics at the University of Pittsburgh who has received many awards for his cancer research, laments the effect that the prosecution has had on his and his colleagues' research. Foreign collaborators, he writes, "have described to me their befuddlement over the Ferrell–Kurtz case," and this apprehension has stymied his labs' efforts to recruit foreign scientists to conduct genetic research in the United States. The case, he believes, "marks a low-tide for American scientists."

Moreover, the prosecution has impeded his research because shipments from biological agent suppliers are now reviewed multiple times and delayed out of the fear of criminal liability. In a letter to the prosecution, Moore is especially blunt: "You are interfering with my work on finding the cause of a cancer because of your prosecution."

Other cancer researchers likewise found the Kurtz prosecution unsettling. One prominent government scientist, who asked not to be identified, explained that "We share cells every day as a part of our research.... We couldn't replicate experimental results if we didn't." Further, "The suppliers are aware of it" but don't mind, because the purpose of transfer agreements is to prevent labs from competing against suppliers, not to keep them from sharing cells with other scientists engaged in the same work. If transfer agreements were enforced in that way, she said, basic research "would grind to a halt."

> The case, Kurtz believes, "marks a low-tide for American scientists."

Despite everything, Kurtz is proud that he was able to fight the charges against him and prevent the government from establishing a precedent that exchanging harmless biological agents and running afoul of other contractual terms are criminal offenses:

> [W]hat we were most worried about and why I wanted to fight this case to the end was this precedent, as we were talking about earlier. What should have been at best a civil suit, and it wasn't even that, the Department of Justice wanted to be able to say, "You know, whenever there's a contract dispute that involves the mail or internet"—and what contract dispute doesn't?—"we're going to have the right to come in and decide whether or not it's a civil case or, if we wanted [it] to be, however arbitrary, a criminal case. And then we are going to prosecute it as a criminal case...." So, you know, if you filled out a warranty card wrong and mailed it in, that could now be a twenty-year jail sentence. That's what they were after, and happily the judge ruled against them and said this is an abuse of the law and that mail fraud cannot be used this way. So the precedent went our way and narrowed the law instead of expanding it.

The law, however, remains almost unimaginably broad. Despite Kurtz's successful defense, prosecutors continue to use the federal mail and wire fraud statutes to go after contractual violations, local-government patronage politics, minor regulatory violations, and other conduct that may not warrant civil lawsuits, let alone criminal prosecution. Thus, as in the Drew case discussed in Chapter 8, a prosecutor can still bring charges based on a violation of a Web site's terms of service—terms that many courts refuse to enforce in contract lawsuits.

Prosecutors still wield the unbridled discretion to bring criminal charges against almost any individual, whether or not he or she has done anything typically regarded as a crime.

In short, prosecutors still wield the unbridled discretion to bring criminal charges against almost any individual, whether or not he or she has done anything typically regarded as a crime. Most of these defendants, like Dr. Ferrell, accept plea bargains to avoid the risk of lengthy sentences. A few, like Kurtz, have the resources and stamina to fight the charges, at great personal expense, and actually win—but they are the rare exception that proves the rule.

CHAPTER 10

KRISTER'S STORY

Quin Hillyer [1]

Krister Evertson is the kind of man all good conservationists should honor. His life's work was to try to invent an economical, clean-energy fuel cell that could generate power without polluting the air. By this decade, he was using what amounts to borax detergent to try to invent a mass-producible fuel cell, but back in middle school in Hawaii, he started making fuel cells by using coconut milk. He came in third in the state science fair in high school in 1971 for his efforts. "If you were shipwrecked on a desert island," he told a congressional hearing on July 22, 2009, "you could use wild coconuts to power a radio and listen to the news back home."

Krister Evertson

So much for idealism. On May 27, 2004, while Evertson was preparing in Wasilla, Alaska, for a private gold-mining expedition to raise more funds for his research, federal agents in two black SUVs, waving assault rifles, forced his car off the road. Manhandling him as if he were a terrorist, they arrested, interrogated, and jailed him. For what? Putting the wrong shipping—with the correct instructions, mind you, but still the wrong label—on a box of raw sodium that he sold on eBay.

That was the beginning of a bizarrely convoluted legal saga that continues to this day. In the meantime, his life's work has been ruined, more than $100,000 of materiel for that work was summarily destroyed for no good reason, and he was forced to spend 13 months in a federal penitentiary in Sheridan, Oregon, as federal prisoner number 15003-006. All because prosecutors ran amok in enforcing bureaucratic gobbledygook against one of the most well-intentioned souls you'll ever find.

Before that May day in Alaska, Evertson had no history of legal problems—none at all. And he had a long history of doing charitable good works, especially in teaching sign language to deaf young people, a talent he learned while coping with a severe stutter that partially lingers to this day. Hometown newspapers even celebrated his volunteer work long before anybody knew that overzealous prosecutors would put him in the position of needing testaments to his character.

Federal officials repeatedly have treated him as if he is a menace to society. Why?

Evertson is described in federal court documents as a "good-natured, kind, gentle person." Yet federal officials repeatedly have treated him as if he is a menace to society. Why?

In the early years of the current decade, Evertson was splitting his time between Wasilla, where his aging mother lived and where he mined for gold, and Salmon, Idaho, where his sister lived. It was in Salmon that he spent $100,000 of his family's money seeking to create the mass-producible fuel cell by mixing pure sodium with borax. Given a chance, Evertson will expound at great (and convincing) length about why his invention will work under the right conditions. He'll tell you with pride about the breadth and depth of his research and, with disarming frankness, about his setbacks. It seems that nobody doubts his basic science, but that the only question is about how practical it is for widespread use by the general public.

Evertson also will explain, with great scientific precision, about how safe his ingredients are unless handled quite stupidly. He'll readily admit that pure sodium is a metal that, when in direct contact with a certain amount of water, can explode. Yet it is safe enough that it can be easily bought online when it is packaged correctly; that is, surrounded by an oil solution that protects against water. Evertson had legally purchased 10 metric tons of sodium from a dealer in China. Yes, 10 tons. From China. Safely and legally and openly.

But Evertson ran out of money in Idaho before his experiments bore fruit. He therefore carefully stored all his materials, machines, and byproducts in stainless steel tanks, with most of the sodium either surrounded by oil and plastic or in its original, legal packaging from China. He then moved all these materials half a mile down the road to the Steel and Ranch Supply Facility, an industrial supply company owned by a friend. There were no leaks; there were no spills; there was no danger of leaks or spills. Undisturbed, the stuff could have sat there in safety for year after year after year.

Evertson paid rent in the form of two 1,000-pound sacks of borax, which his friend could resell for a profit. He said he planned to return once he raised enough money to restart his experiments. He moved to his mother's house in Wasilla, taking a few dozen pounds of sodium with him, and began selling the sodium on eBay to raise funds to finance a new gold-mining expedition.

Evertson in high school

Again, he did this on eBay. It wasn't a black market. There was no attempt to hide anything. There was no reason to expect there was anything wrong with it. Packaged correctly, pure sodium can be, and is, shipped anywhere on the globe without difficulty.

Nevertheless, that's where the troubles began. Because of its potential explosiveness, pure sodium is not allowed to be shipped by air, even if packaged entirely correctly. Evertson knew that. That's why, when he received eBay orders for the stuff, he packed the sodium so carefully that nobody ever claimed that it was anything but safe (even for a plane ride). He then checked the form on the UPS packaging that said "ground transportation only." In short, every action he took showed entirely innocent intent.

But there was one problem: Evertson didn't know that in Alaska, because of the distances involved, UPS actually ships "ground" packages by air. So, through no intent whatsoever, and even though he checked the box for "ground" shipping, Evertson had shipped a hazardous material on an airplane. For that "crime," the feds forced his truck off the road as if they were from "Miami Vice" and Evertson an armed drug dealer and arrested him without explanation.

No amount of subsequent protestation could convince the feds to drop the case. This was, after all, post-9/11. The feds had become hyperalert to airplane dangers. Any 90-year-old grandma bodily frisked at a major airport could tell you that. As with the grandmas, so with Evertson's case: No common sense was allowed. The federal

> **The feds forced his truck off the road as if they were from "Miami Vice" and Evertson an armed drug dealer and arrested him without explanation.**

agents wanted Evertson to plead guilty. They wanted a scalp. He wouldn't give it to them. They took the case all the way to trial. Oops. Mistake. A jury, seeing all the obvious signs of an entirely innocent error on Evertson's part, found the defendant not guilty of any charges.

Even then, all wasn't well because it didn't end well. The feds don't like to lose. If you're innocent of one charge, they'll find another. And they did.

What happened was that, during the agents' initial interrogation of him, Evertson had been extremely forthcoming about his entire situation. FBI notes at the time confirm as much. As he said at the congressional hearing, "I made a mistake on that day when the agents arrested me in 2004: I told the truth. When they asked me about the sodium, I told them that I had more in storage, for making fuel cells."

Federal authorities in Alaska sent word to the Environmental Protection Agency office in Idaho, which promptly dispatched its agents to the industrial supply facility in Salmon where the materials were stored. The owner of the site, Evertson's friend, truthfully said he hadn't heard from Evertson in a while and didn't know when Evertson intended to claim the materials. By the EPA's reckoning, apparently, that meant that the materials were "abandoned." The EPA agents treated the materials like a Superfund site. They cut open his steel drums, cleared away a perimeter—and, by their own account, ended up spending some $430,000 disposing of every bit of Evertson's painstakingly assembled experiments.

"They never told me; they just did it," Evertson said in a 2008 interview from his Oregon prison. "It's like Chicken Little: They run around like the sky is falling.... It's like the perfect storm of misunderstanding and

Evertson's office after it was "searched."

unfounded fear and they never asked me about it. I could have told them in one minute exactly what to do with it."

Despite his acquittal in Alaska, federal authorities, based on strained readings of EPA regulations, charged Evertson in Idaho for allegedly illegally transporting his materials—the whole, measly half-mile—from his home to the storage facility and for improperly storing "hazardous waste." Never mind that, until the EPA cut open the steel drums, no hazard actually existed.

"My expert witness said the stainless steel container could safely contain the intermediate process stream indefinitely, that means forever," Evertson explained. "The stainless steel was 3/8 of an inch thick. I bought it from the Long Beach, California Naval Yard. It was completely enclosed. I could have neutralized all of it for $200."

Also never mind that Evertson clearly had saved the material for future use rather than actually abandoning it and that, by statutory definition, the material is not "waste" if it is not "abandoned." Evertson had told them as

> Never mind that, until the EPA cut open the steel drums, no hazard actually existed.

much. He volunteered it while being interrogated for the original charge of improper labeling. That's how they knew about the materials in the first place and why they knew, from the pride he expressed in his work, that he intended to return to Idaho to complete his experiments.

Additionally, never mind that, in the words of Evertson's appellate brief, none of the materials were "discharged into the air, land or sea," and the government failed to produce any evidence "that the defendant intended this to happen." Finally, never mind that the judge's instructions to the jury about what constitutes "hazardous waste" intended for "disposal" were inexact at best. Indeed, the brief notes, "the EPA witness, Marc Callaghan, testified that the materials became hazardous waste [only] when the EPA disposed of them."

Evertson's appellate brief summed up the absurdity of the whole case by quoting from a decision of the U.S. Court of Appeals for the D.C. Circuit in 2000: "To say that when something is saved it is thrown away is an extraordinary distortion of the English language." And, one might add, a distortion of reason, of justice, and of the law.

> According to the court decision, "To say that when something is saved it is thrown away is an extraordinary distortion of the English language." And, one might add, a distortion of reason, of justice, and of the law.

At trial, Evertson was represented by a public defender who advised him not to testify. Evertson wanted to testify on his own behalf, even if he stuttered, but his counsel told him no. Evertson then expected the judge to ask him personally, not just his lawyer, whether he wanted to waive his right to testify in his own defense. That is, after all, the usual, but not absolutely necessary, practice.

Evertson planned to ask to testify anyway, but the judge never asked him, and the prosecutors scared the jury so badly about the explosive properties of improperly stored, pure sodium that the jury, according to subsequent claims by Evertson's later lawyers, never was properly directed to consider the key issue of whether the "waste" was both "hazardous" in its stored condition and "abandoned" (as if to leach into the environment) rather than saved for future use. There is, after all, no crime against storing pure sodium. It's a legal substance.

On October 22, 2007, the jury found Evertson guilty, and he was sentenced to 21 months in the federal penitentiary. He served 13 months behind bars and the rest in a halfway house.

The Washington Legal Foundation tried to appeal Evertson's case to the U.S. Supreme Court on the grounds that the judge's instructions to the jury were misleading. The jury never was asked to determine whether the materials were "abandoned"—necessary, by law, to consider them "waste"—and never was asked to determine for itself, rather than taking the EPA's word for it, that they were indeed "hazardous waste." The jury also was never asked to assess Evertson's intent or, in this case, his clear lack thereof.

> The jury also was never asked to assess Evertson's intent or, in this case, his clear lack thereof.

The appeal always had a high hurdle to climb. The public defender at Evertson's Idaho trial never objected to the improper jury instructions. The Supreme Court thus could easily believe that the grounds for appeal had not been properly preserved. In any event, the high court did not agree to hear the appeal.

The Washington Legal Foundation now is moving for a new trial on the grounds of "ineffective assistance of [Evertson's] trial counsel." Such new trials are granted infrequently. Meanwhile, Evertson lives in a trailer back in Idaho, all but broke and without the chance to renew his scientific passion. The terms of his supervised release preclude him from continuing work on his invention for three years.

> "I was an American inventor. And I was a law-abiding citizen. For following my dream, I wound up in prison."

In his testimony to Congress, Evertson summed up the situation he faces if he is not awarded a new trial:

> I will not regain my rights to vote, serve on a jury, or own firearms. I was working on fuel cells, trying to improve the environment and the world. I was an American inventor. And I was a law-abiding citizen. For following my dream, I wound up in prison. My story proves that these things can happen to any person. There are too many laws that put ordinary, well-meaning Americans at

risk of criminal prosecution and conviction. An old saying comes to mind: "One man's trash is another man's treasure." I had treasure; the EPA said it was trash. And so I lost my treasure. And that is why I am testifying today. Please protect our treasure, our freedom.

CHAPTER 11

LEGISLATION THAT SHOULD BE CRIMINAL
Equal-Opportunity Legislative Foolishness

So far, we have reviewed a number of cases involving prosecutions that can only be characterized as overzealous and unwarranted. For the most part this reflects the reality that overcriminalization is often the result of an unjust exercise of prosecutorial authority: Though the law permits the prosecution to be initiated, a wise and just prosecutor with a true sense of what constitutes a crime would refrain.

That, regrettably, is only half of the story. The laws prosecutors enforce all come from somewhere, and that somewhere is complacent legislatures whose members are happy to pass overly broad laws that devolve authority to unelected prosecutors. In doing so, they can claim to have "done something" about the crime problem while artfully passing the buck for hard enforcement decisions to the executive authorities. The making of criminal law is not, sad to say, a profile in courage.

When it comes to passing unreasonable or even downright crazy criminal laws—often the poison fruit of good intentions—neither Congress nor the state legislatures have a monopoly. Examples abound of both state and federal criminal laws that might be laughable if the potential consequences of violating them were less serious.

These are not laws that have been on the books since the 1700s or 1800s and are often featured in stories on American public radio illustrating all of the antiquated, rarely enforced statutes that legislatures have never bothered to expunge from the books. They are late 20th and early 21st century legislative acts. The following are some chilling examples.

Laws Imposing Radical Policy Agendas for the Treatment of Animals

In several states, noble intentions to protect animals from cruelty and abuse have motivated legislation creating new criminal laws. Despite the well-intentioned goal, such laws often demonstrate little respect for historical conceptions of the proper use of the criminal sanction or for long-standing and well-accepted principles governing the conduct of mankind toward animals.

Sometimes such legislation is drafted so loosely that it could easily be interpreted as criminalizing all hunting. Although Americans hold a variety of opinions about hunting and how people should generally treat animals, relatively few Americans find fault with the idea of legal hunting. In America, public land and the animals living there are just that: public.

In 2005, New York State Assemblyman Alexander Grannis nevertheless introduced New York State Assembly Bill 1850A. The text of the bill states that "a person is guilty of aggravated cruelty to animals when...he or she intentionally kills...an animal or wild game [or] wild birds." One need not be a card-carrying member of the National Rifle Association to know that hunting, by definition, is the pursuit of game "so as to capture or kill." Grannis said, and the bill states, that there is an exemption for lawful hunting, but making his proposed language the law could lay the groundwork to make hunting in New York State a felony. Indeed, a conviction under Grannis's proposed law could result in one year in jail and a $5,000 fine. At the end of the legislative session in 2006, the bill was allowed to die in the agriculture committee.

> Sometimes legislation to protect animals from cruelty is drafted so loosely that it could easily be interpreted as criminalizing all hunting.

Similar legislation was proposed in—of all places—Texas. In 2005, Republican state Representative Toby Goodman introduced House Bill 326, which would make it a crime to "cause serious bodily injury to an animal." This language would cause a dramatic change in traditional, widely accepted practices. Under current law, wild creatures are not defined as protected "animals." Bill 326, however, would eliminate this explicit hunting exemption and define an "animal" as any "nonhuman mammal [or] bird." There can be no doubt that if Goodman's bill becomes law, hunting might one day be considered a criminal offense—punishable by a prison sentence of up to one year and a $4,000 fine. This bill, too, failed without ever coming up for a floor vote.

Examples abound of absurd legislation criminalizing unquestionably ethical treatment of animals. In West Hollywood, it is illegal to declaw your cat. In Montana, it is illegal to *pretend* to abuse an animal in the

> There can be no doubt that if the Texas bill becomes law, hunting might one day be considered a criminal offense— punishable by a prison sentence of up to one year and a $4,000 fine.

presence of a minor. It may be thoughtless and unkind to frighten a child in this manner, but the law is trivialized and reduced to a joke if it criminalizes acts that are merely thoughtless or unkind. Perhaps Montana legislators' next act will be to make it a crime to forget to send one's niece or nephew a birthday card or present.

It is unreasonable to support or encourage cruelty against animals. Most reasonable people also understand that traditional hunting is not a crime. Nevertheless, some legislators and small special-interest groups push an agenda that would criminalize whatever they personally dislike. This breaks with centuries of legal doctrine, not to mention common sense.

For hundreds of years, the Anglo-American common law has required both a guilty mind (criminal intent) and a bad act (criminal conduct) in order to convict a defendant. Premeditated, unjustified killing of another person—*not* premeditated pheasant hunting or salmon fishing—should be a crime. Unless one accepts the radical animal rights activists' argument that eating meat requires "murdering" an animal, there can be no principled basis upon which to outlaw all hunting.

Americans have fought back. Alabama, California, Minnesota, Virginia, and Wisconsin have passed amendments to their state constitutions to preserve their citizens' hunting and fishing rights and to protect those who hunt or fish from being prosecuted as criminals. Pennsylvania and Arkansas are considering similar amendments. Nevertheless, special-interest groups continue their attempts to insert a radical agenda into the law books.

In the midst of the war on terrorism and crucial debates about homeland security and immigration reform, activists at the federal level have convinced Members of Congress to attempt to criminalize horsemeat.

They want federal law enforcement—the same professionals we rely on to investigate kidnappings and prevent terrorist attacks—to stop people from buying and selling meat that comes from horses.

Although most Americans may find the idea of eating horsemeat objectionable, low-carbohydrate dieters in particular might want to reconsider. Horsemeat has far fewer calories than beef, and it is low in fat and high in protein. It seems made to order for the recently fashionable South Beach and Atkins diets. According to the one U.S. Department of Agriculture press release promoting the dietary benefits of horsemeat, it has "a flavor somewhat between that of beef and venison." Despite horsemeat's positive dietary characteristics, however, as well as its acceptance in much of Europe, a small but vocal herd of horse lovers and animal rights activists has been riding Congress for years to stop "the horse holocaust."

> The fact that most Americans might be offended by horsemeat entrées on a restaurant menu is a poor reason to make such a choice a crime.

More than 20 U.S. Senators and 200 Members of the House of Representatives have co-sponsored the American Horse Slaughter Prevention Act—which, ironically, is not aimed at preventing horse slaughter. It does nothing to stop horses from being killed for dog food, glue, or as a Godfather-style warning by members of organized crime. The Act would only outlaw the killing of, or commerce in, horses for "human consumption."

The legislation also smacks of cultural imperialism. While the number of Americans eating horsemeat steaks may be almost zero, equine entrées are popular in other countries, especially Italy, France, and the Netherlands. These nations' acceptance of culinary diversity was particularly important during the mad cow scare, when horsemeat replaced beef for many Europeans. Outside of Jewish and Muslim areas, horsemeat has historically been common fare.

> Once Congress starts criminalizing foods, the only meat left may be pork.

Despite its current unpopularity, consumption of horsemeat in America has a long and, until recently, uncontroversial history. Some Native Americans ate horsemeat. Among other sources, this is documented by Lewis and Clark's record of a gift from northwestern tribes of "20 pounds of very fat dried horsemeat." The fact that today most Americans might be offended by horsemeat entrées on a restaurant menu is a poor reason to make such a choice a crime.

Passing special-interest legislation to sanctify Flicka and Black Beauty would set a terrible precedent. After all, why should horsemeat be singled out for congressional action? As one Illinois state legislator challenged when considering similar legislation, "If you can eat…Bugs Bunny and Bambi, why can't you eat Mr. Ed?" Once Congress starts criminalizing foods, the only meat left may be pork.

Lewis and Clark ate horsemeat they received from Native Americans.

Some of the supporters of the horse bill argue that horsemeat is unsafe or that the process of converting stallion to steak is particularly inhumane. Even if true, these are not arguments for criminalization. Health concerns, if valid, can be satisfied through regulations as they are with any other kind of food product. After several E. coli outbreaks, Americans know that beef and even spinach can be processed in unsafe ways that make people sick, and if threats to human health are the measure, we ought to be criminalizing beef (to prevent mad cow disease) or pork (to put a halt to swine flu). Thus far, there has been little outcry to pass federal criminal laws against beef, pork, or spinach production.

The Horse Act could even brand as criminal those who sell or transport horses without knowing that the buyer intends to kill them and market horsemeat for human consumption. Someone who buys meat without realizing that it is from a horse could also face charges under the bill. Such sloppy legislation allows lawmakers in Washington to transform well-meaning people into outlaws.

> Someone who buys meat without realizing that it is from a horse could also face charges under the bill.

Fortunately, in the current session of Congress with rather more important things to take care of (like a financial crisis and a war), the Horse Act has not yet reared its head again. Perhaps Congress has grown wiser as time has passed, and learned to simply say "neigh" to silly legislation like this.

Criminalizing News Stories That Rely on Forged Documents

Some legislators seem to believe they must keep making new laws, perhaps to show their constituents just how busy and useful they are. In

Some legislators want to make mistaken news reports, like the ones Dan Rather made, into crimes.

one example, after CBS News broadcast a later discredited story alleging that George W. Bush, when he was in his twenties, had improperly used wealth or political influence to secure his Texas Air National Guard position, one U.S. Senator wanted to criminalize bad reporting. The legislation would have closed a "loophole" by allowing "prosecution of both the creators and propagators of forged federal documents." The proposed law stated that a person who "utters or publishes as true…inconclusively verified" federal documents could be imprisoned for up to 10 years.

If this bill had become law, intentional deceit would not have been a prerequisite for obtaining a federal criminal conviction of a journalist, but intentionally passing off forged government documents for financial gain is already a federal crime under various statutes, and state laws uniformly prohibit slander and libel even though our traditional reverence for political speech means that political officials end up with little protection. Is it really a good idea to commit federal law enforcement resources to policing stories by CBS News? Should lazy or biased journalists go to federal prison?

Forging United States military records to smear the President of the United States in his reelection campaign is a grave injustice to the American people. The irresponsibility of CBS News and the co-conspirators was outrageous. But the system ultimately worked. CBS paid a high price in lost credibility and lower ratings. This translates to lost advertising revenues, a market-based penalty imposed, without need for government intervention, upon all those who try to pass off a forgery as the real article.

Is it really a good idea to commit federal law enforcement resources to policing stories by CBS News?

Not every offense or injustice justifies Congress's fashioning a new criminal law. The national government has developed a bad habit of aggrandizing itself by federalizing criminal law, traditionally considered the nearly exclusive purview of the states.

Trivial State Criminal Laws

The states have their own problems. In New Mexico, Governor Bill Richardson labeled 2004 "the year of the legislature." Santa Fe lawmakers had no problem living up to that title the following year when they passed the Recycling and Illegal Dumping Act. This bill created a new batch of misdemeanors and felonies related to scrap tires or tire-derived products in New Mexico. Possession of old tires in New Mexico can now result in a person's being given jail time and being slapped with the moral and societal censure that comes with being convicted as a criminal.

> Possession of old tires in New Mexico can now result in a person's being given jail time.

Overcriminalization is a slippery slope toward oppressive, centralized government power. Examples abound of outrageous applications of criminal law to trivial conduct:

- In Idaho, a man was arrested for dumping dirt in a forest.

- In Washington, D.C., a pregnant woman was arrested in a Metro (subway) station for speaking too loudly on her cellular phone.

- In Florida, a woman was arrested for inadvertently leaving a bag of marshmallows at a campsite while vacationing in Wyoming's Yellowstone National Park a year earlier.

Using the vague justification of protecting public health, safety, or welfare, government now criminalizes an almost unlimited array of offenses. It is politically popular for a legislator to be able to say that he has voted to make some supposed outrage a new crime.

In the meantime, regulatory agencies and powerful special-interest groups rally behind the simple phrase "There ought to be a law," and once a "criminal" act is identified (e.g., storing tires on private property), over-

> Overcriminalization is a slippery slope toward oppressive, centralized government power. Using the vague justification of protecting public health, safety, or welfare, government now criminalizes an almost unlimited array of offenses.

criminalization advocates need only contact a sympathetic lawmaker to translate their agenda into law. Experience demonstrates that relatively few of his colleagues will be willing to go on record as having opposed criminal punishment for those who pollute, lie over the airwaves, or engage in other improper behavior that is nevertheless unworthy of criminal sanction.

This desire to deem as criminal all offensive or unwanted behavior infects average citizens. In Port Orange, Florida, 15-year-old Luke Porto tossed a half-eaten Milk Dud out of a car window. The penny-sized piece of chocolate struck another vehicle's windshield but did not cause any damage. Nevertheless, the motorist pressed criminal charges against Porto. Fortunately, state officials eventually decided not to prosecute and instead sent the case to arbitration.

It is difficult not to see this story as an indication of how legislators and other government officials have abdicated their responsibility to understand and to demonstrate to Americans the proper scope and application of the criminal law.

Using Criminal Law to Protect Entrenched Businesses

Many states require approximately 1,700 hours of training to become a licensed paramedic, 300 hours of training to be a firefighter, and 500 hours of training to become a police officer. So any job for which a state mandates 3,200 hours of training must be even more complicated or dangerous. Right? Not necessarily.

Some states now require approximately 3,200 hours of training to become a licensed hair braider. Conducting a hair-braiding business without a license is a criminal offense. Even accidentally violating such regulations can turn well-meaning small-business owners into criminals.

For many urban women, particularly immigrants from Africa and the Caribbean, hair braiding is an excellent way to earn a living. It requires almost no initial investment, can pay a relatively high hourly wage, and allows a flexible schedule. But some established full-service salons have pressured their state regulators to go after hair braiders for failing to secure a cosmetology license—despite the fact that hair braiders do not use chemicals, razors, or any of the other potentially hazardous tools often found in a regular hair salon.

A Mississippi law required 3,200 hours of coursework just to *apply* for a hair-braiding license. Any violation was considered a crime. Hair braiders challenged the law in court in 2004 and won. The court required the law to be rewritten with more freedom and less economic protectionism. California law required at least nine months of full-time study at a

In Mississippi, it takes more than 18 months of full-time school to be allowed to braid hair.

cosmetology school. This training often costs over $5,000. A court in California found that the licensing requirement was irrational and struck it down.

Legislators may actually believe they are protecting consumers when they write such laws, but often they are merely a result of prodding by special-interest groups representing established businesses. Sadly, some entrepreneurs, once they have achieved their own success, become intent on stifling competition from start-up businesses. In practice, many business licensing laws do nothing to protect consumers. They merely raise prices and reduce the quality of products and services by restricting competition.

In most states, failing to navigate successfully through the licensing bureaucracy in order to fulfill all requirements is a criminal offense. Business owners who do not comply can be bankrupted with fines or even jailed.

In Utah, the Pleasant Grove City Police arrested eight people for "soliciting without a license." Soliciting what? Drugs? Prostitution? Far from

> In most states, failing to navigate successfully through the licensing bureaucracy in order to fulfill all requirements is a criminal offense.

it. They were going door-to-door selling vacuum cleaners. Police rounded up the otherwise law-abiding salesmen for violating a provision of the city code requiring them to provide fingerprints and post a $1,000 bond—just to sell vacuums. They sued the city of Pleasant Grove, arguing that the licensing regime violated their rights to freedom of speech and to earn a living.

In July 2005, the Denver-based U.S. Court of Appeals for the Tenth Circuit agreed with Pleasant Grove's vacuum salesmen. The city claimed that the purpose of the law was not to harass and discourage businesspersons but to prevent fraud and burglaries. However, during a hearing, a Pleasant

Don't sell flowers without a license in Louisiana.

Grove City police captain admitted that the fingerprints required for a sales license never had been used—not to prosecute a crime or for any other purpose. The fingerprinting and expensive bond were just methods for protecting established businesses against low-overhead competitors by creating time-consuming and complicated procedures with criminal penalties for non-compliance, whether intentional or inadvertent.

The Louisiana legislature has taken silly and abusive regulations even further. Would you like to open a flower shop in the Bayou State? First, you will need a state-issued florist license. To get the license, you must pass the state florist exam—which just happens to be graded by established florists. It is no surprise that the testing criteria are entirely subjective or that the passage rate for the florist exam is lower than the passage rate for the Louisiana state bar exam to become a lawyer.

The justification for providing economic regulation generally is to protect the "public good," but in many cases it is clear that lawmakers are simply protecting established businesses from competition. No one should be branded a criminal for practicing floristry without a license. Salesmen should not be treated like felons in the course of trying to sell a useful product to earn an honest living for their families. Women who want to braid hair for a living deserve the freedom to do so without being crushed by senseless regulation. Instead, the government's role should be to celebrate the distinctly American entrepreneurial spirit and encourage the creation of new businesses.

There certainly are occupations that call for high training standards and government oversight, but hair braiders and vacuum cleaner salesmen are not paramedics or pilots, and the criminal law should never be used to punish inadvertent or accidental violations. When it comes to the normal, industrious activities of everyday Americans trying to do everyday jobs, the criminal law should be held at bay.

PART II

HOW WE GOT WHERE WE ARE

CHAPTER 12

THE HISTORY OF CRIMINAL LAW

Paul Rosenzweig[1]

Part I of this book has given us anecdotal evidence of the problem of overcriminalization. The true stories recounted therein ought to be enough to scare even the most law-abiding American and convince him that his continued freedom is as much at the sufferance of prosecutorial discretion as it is as a consequence of his own law-abiding behavior.

But recognizing that a problem exists is only the first step to resolution. The next is to develop an understanding of how the problem was created and what its causes were. By now, the reader will have a general idea of what has happened: The traditional criminal law requirements of a guilty mind and personal responsibility have been eroded.

In this chapter, we explain in more detail how that came about, beginning with a short history of the development of criminal law from its original, "conservative" application under the common law in England and early America to its broad, "liberal" application in America today. The changes that have occurred can best be understood through the prism of yet one more case of overcriminalization: the case of Edward Hanousek.[2]

Hanousek was employed as roadmaster by the White Pass & Yukon Railroad, whose railway runs between Skagway, Alaska, and Whitehorse, Yukon Territory, Canada. As roadmaster, Hanousek was responsible under his contract for "the safe and efficient maintenance and construction of track, structures and marine facilities of the entire railroad."

One of the projects under Hanousek's supervision was a rock-quarrying project at a site alongside the railroad. The project involved blasting rock outcroppings, working the fractured rock toward railroad cars, and loading the rock onto railroad cars with a backhoe. Hanousek's company hired Hunz & Hunz, a contracting company, to provide the equipment and labor for the project.

At the site, a high-pressure petroleum pipeline ran parallel to the railroad within a few feet of the tracks. To protect the pipeline during the project, a work platform of sand and gravel was constructed on which the backhoe operated to load rocks over the pipeline and into railroad cars. The location of the work platform changed as the work progressed along the railroad tracks. When work initially began in April 1994, Hunz & Hunz covered an approximately 300-foot section of the pipeline with railroad ties, sand, and ballast material for protection.

After Hanousek took over responsibility for the project in May 1994, he concluded that no further sections of the pipeline along the 1,000-foot work site needed protection, with the exception of the movable backhoe work platform. That judgment, which appeared altogether reasonable at the time, would prove Hanousek's undoing.

On the evening of October 1, 1994, while Hanousek was off-duty away from the site, Shane Thoe, a Hunz & Hunz backhoe operator, used the backhoe on the work platform to load a train with rocks. After the train departed, Thoe noticed that some fallen rocks had caught the plow of the train as it departed and were located just off the tracks in the vicinity of the unprotected pipeline. Violating standing instructions not to move the backhoe off the work platform, Thoe drove it down alongside the tracks between 50 and 100 yards from the work platform. While using the backhoe bucket to sweep the rocks from the tracks, Thoe accidentally struck the pipeline, causing a rupture. The pipeline was carrying heating oil, and an estimated 1,000 to 5,000 gallons of oil were discharged over the course of many days into the adjacent Skagway River.

> **The Congressional Research Service cannot even accurately count the current number of federal crimes.**

Hanousek (not Thoe) was charged with two federal crimes: negligently discharging a pollutant into a waterway of the United States (a misdemeanor offense punishable by up to one year in prison) and making false statements for allegedly lying to the Coast Guardsmen investigating the incident. His superior, M. Paul Taylor, was charged with the same negligent discharge offense and with conspiracy to make false statements for his part in Hanousek's alleged cover-up. Prosecutors did not allege that either Hanousek or Taylor had directly caused the accident. The government's theory was rather that Hanousek and Taylor had failed to exercise the care required of a reasonable supervisor in their positions of authority. They had thus negligently failed to supervise Thoe and so contributed to the accident.

At trial, Taylor was acquitted of both charges, and Hanousek was acquitted of the more serious felony false statement charge. Hanousek was, however, convicted of the charge of negligence for his failure to supervise the construction project appropriately and was sentenced to six months imprisonment. His conviction was subsequently affirmed on appeal.

Regulatory Crimes in America Today

The law under which Hanousek was prosecuted is far from unique. Congress has exercised precious little self-restraint in expanding the reach of federal criminal laws to new regulatory areas.

Estimates of the current size of the body of federal criminal law vary. Professor John Baker, in a study published in 2007, estimated that it was in excess of 4,450 and that the number has been growing by roughly 500 new crimes every year.[3] For now, however, it is enough to know that the Congressional Research Service cannot even accurately count the current number of federal crimes.[4] The American Bar Association reported in 1998 that there were in excess of 3,300 separate criminal offenses.[5] More than 40 percent of these laws have been enacted in just the past 30 years as part of the growth of the regulatory state.[6] These laws are scattered in over 50 titles of the United States Code, encompassing roughly 27,000 pages.[7] By contrast, at the time of our Founding, the Constitution identified only three crimes: piracy, treason, and counterfeiting.

The first federal criminal statute created roughly 30 separate crimes.[8] Today, of course, the story is different:[9]

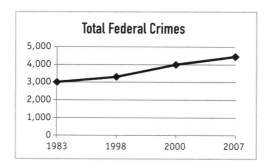

Total Federal Crimes

Worse yet, the statutory code sections often incorporate, by reference, the provisions and sanctions of administrative regulations promulgated by various regulatory agencies under congressional authorization. Estimates of how many such regulations exist are even less well settled, but the ABA thinks there are "[n]early 10,000."[10]

> More federal resources are invested in regulatory prosecutions than in the prosecution of murder, robbery, violent racketeering, and kidnapping combined.

The appetite for more federal criminal laws is driven principally by political considerations,[11] not by any consideration of whether particular laws are intrinsically federal in nature.[12] The growth of "public welfare" offenses will therefore be restrained (if at all) only by a public or a court system educated as to the need for restraint.

Nor is the growth in the number of federal criminal statutes merely an academic question without real-world effects. To the contrary, between March 2007 and March 2008 (the most recent year for which data are available), federal prosecutors commenced 68,582 cases involving 89,697 individual defendants.[13] More than 2,100 of these defendants were charged with "regulatory offenses," including violations of food and drug, antitrust, and migratory bird regulations. [14] This number exceeds the number of federal prosecutions during the same period for a host of common-law offense categories, including murder, robbery, embezzlement, and forgery. About the same number of defendants were prosecuted for all federal sex crimes.

Put another way, more federal resources are invested in regulatory prosecutions than in the prosecution of murder, robbery, violent racketeering, and kidnapping combined.[15]

The Changing Face of Criminal Law

The origin of modern criminal law can be traced to early feudal times. From its inception, the criminal law expressed both a moral and a practical judgment about the societal consequences of certain activity: To be guilty of a crime, the law required that an individual must both cause (or attempt to cause) a wrongful injury and do so with some form of malicious intent.

Classically, lawyers capture this insight in two principles: For there to be a crime, there must be both an *actus reus* (a bad act) and a culpable *mens rea* (a guilty mind). At its roots, the criminal law did not punish merely bad thoughts (intentions to act without any evil deed) or acts that achieved unwittingly wrongful ends but without the intent to do so. The former were for resolution by ecclesiastical authorities, and the latter were for amelioration in the tort system. As Hanousek's case and the others summarized in Part I demonstrate, this classical understanding of criminal law no longer holds.

To these fundamental changes in the nature of criminal liability one must also add significant changes in the subject matter of criminal law. At its inception, criminal law was directed at conduct that society recognized as inherently wrongful and, in some sense, immoral. These acts were wrongs in and of themselves (*malum in se*), such as murder, rape, and robbery. In recent times, the reach of the criminal law has been expanded so that it now addresses conduct that is wrongful not because of its intrinsic nature but because it is a prohibited wrong (*malum prohibitum*)—that is, a wrong created by a legislative body to serve some perceived public good. These essentially regulatory crimes have come to

> The law criminalizes conduct undertaken without any culpable intent.

be known as "public welfare" offenses. (The sociological origins of this phenomenon are outlined by Professor Baker in Chapter 14.)

Thus, the criminal law has strayed far from its historical roots. Where once the criminal law was an exclusively moral undertaking, it now has expanded to the point that it is principally utilitarian in nature. Many statutes punish those whose acts are wrongful only by virtue of legislative determination. In many instances, the law criminalizes conduct undertaken without any culpable intent. It also makes criminal the failure to act in conformance with a litany of imposed legal duties. This distortion of the classical criminal law has arisen for a variety of reasons, some of which may have been accompanied by benign motives.

Some have argued that the growth in the use of criminal sanctions is a response to the increasing industrialization of American economic activity and the difficulty of capturing within the classical construct of criminal law the "wrongs" done to society arising from such activity. For example, the Enron scandal and similar acts of intentional corporate fraud have led to overly broad reform proposals that may trap honest but unsophisticated corporate managers.[16] Others argue that public choice theories provide a better explanation.

Whatever the cause, however, the distortion is not without its consequences. The landscape of criminal law today is vastly different from what it was 100 years ago—so much so as to be almost unrecognizable.

The result in *United States v. Hanousek* thus captures three troubling trends in criminal law.

- It involves crimes within a regulated industry that, under any historical understanding, would not be perceived as inherently morally wrong;

- It involves the criminalization of simple negligence (that is, of acts commonly thought to be more appropriately addressed through lawsuits in the civil tort system); and

- It involves conviction of a manager for what was, in essence, his failure to manage the conduct of a subordinate.

These changes are especially significant given the gravity of the nature of criminal liability. Not only does the imposition of such liability give rise to public condemnation and fines, but it can also result in an individual's loss of personal liberty. Historically, this most severe of societal sanctions has been reserved for conduct most deserving of condemnation—a limitation that in the past 100 years has been significantly eroded.

This chapter outlines the scope and nature of this historical change. Only by understanding the source of these trends can these developments be fairly judged.

The Historical Meaning of *Actus Reus*

The concept of individual responsibility lies at the heart of the criminal law: "It is a fundamental principle of Anglo-Saxon jurisprudence that guilt is personal."[17] Traditionally, the law punishes individuals because they are responsible for certain criminal acts they have personally committed or because they are liable for the criminal acts of others with whom they have consciously associated themselves when those others engaged in criminal conduct. Thus, the requirement of an *actus reus* links two concepts:

the necessity for an act and the necessity for a relationship between the criminal act and the individual who is held criminally culpable for the act's performance.

The requirement of an actual act of some form is fundamental. As an initial premise, Anglo-American criminal law does not punish thought. For a crime to have been committed, there typically must be some act done in furtherance of the criminal purpose. As Blackstone said in discussing whether it would be a crime to imagine the death of the King: "[A]s this compassing or imagining is an act of the mind, it cannot possibly fall under any judicial cognizance, unless it be demonstrated by some open or overt act."[18]

> "It is a fundamental principle of Anglo-Saxon jurisprudence that guilt is personal."

This is not to say that the criminal law requires that an act be completed before a crime is committed; the King does not have to die for treason to occur. An attempt to commit a felony or a misdemeanor is itself a crime.[19] Ultimately, however, the common law has required some act bearing a causal link to the crime or the attempted crime.

More significantly, the law generally requires an association between a criminal *actus reus* and an individual accused of a crime. Those who do not act are not guilty of a crime. Put another way, mere acquiescence in the criminal conduct of another is not enough to impose criminal liability on an individual for the acts of a third party.[20] The simplest case, of course, is when the defendant personally engages in a voluntary act of some sort that is causally linked to a crime. In that situation, the requirement of a connection between the act and the actor is easily satisfied.[21]

The law has also long recognized the potential for criminal liability for the acts of others. Most typically, this

> Those who do not act are not guilty of a crime. Mere acquiescence in the criminal conduct of another is not enough to impose criminal liability on an individual.

arises because an individual has directly aided and abetted the commission of the crime in some way.[22] Thus, if one drives the getaway car for the bank robbery, one is equally guilty of the theft even though the confederate committed the actual robbery. So, too, one may cause a crime to occur through the acts of an innocent agent who is unaware of the criminality of the conduct.[23] And one may be guilty of joining in a conspiracy to commit a crime so long as one of the participants in the conspiracy does an act in furtherance of the conspiracy.[24]

Traditionally, these broad rules of liability for the acts of another have had limits. Those limits are illustrated well by an early English case, *Rex v. Huggins*.[25] The warden of a prison and his deputy were charged with the murder of a prisoner for keeping him in an "unwholesome place." On appeal, the deputy's conviction was affirmed, for it was the deputy who had taken up the victim, Arne, and imprisoned him, but the justices of the King's Bench were unanimously of the opinion that the warden could not be held criminally liable for his deputy's actions. As Lord Chief Justice Raymond wrote:

> So that if an act be done by an under-officer, unless it is done by the command or direction, or with the consent of the principal, the principal is not criminally punishable for it. In this case the fact was done by Barnes [the deputy]; and it no where appears in the special verdict that [the warden, Huggins] ever commanded, or directed, or consented to this duress of imprisonment, which was the cause of Arne's death. 1. No command or direction is found. And 2. It is not found that Huggins knew of it.[26]

The final piece of the historical puzzle lies in the concept of criminal liability for "negative acts"—that is, criminal liability for the failure to act. Historically, such liability has been rare, for the general rule is that "[s]tarting with a human act, we must next find a causal relation between the act and the harmful result; for in our law—and it is believed in any civilized law—liability cannot be imputed to a man unless it is in some degree a result of his act."[27]

> Criminal responsibility arises only where the defendant is in fact capable of performing the act he is called upon to perform and where the legal duty to act exists.

Nonetheless, the common law has recognized that in certain limited circumstances one may be held criminally liable without having done an affirmative act, precisely because the failure may be said to be a cause of the resulting harm. Historically, the hallmark of such liability is the existence of some legal duty on the part of the defendant to act. That duty has typically arisen through the common law, based upon some special legal relationship between the criminal defendant and the activity in question.

Thus, for example, parents may be held liable for failing to provide care or support for their children.[28] Similarly, a master of a vessel might be criminally liable for his failure to maintain a safe ship when that failure is the cause of the drowning of his passengers.[29] But criminal responsibility arises only where the defendant is in fact capable of performing the act he is called upon to perform[30] and where the legal duty to act exists.[31] It does not, for example, extend to impose criminal liability on a spouse for failing to summon medical aid for his competent adult spouse who has consciously chosen not to seek medical assistance.[32]

Contemporary Concepts of Managerial Liability

In the past 50 years, American law has drifted far from this traditional concept of criminal liability where a legal duty to act arises from the special nature of a relationship between the defendant and the victim of the crime (or the harm caused by the crime).[33] Social and legal obligations have come to be imposed by statute rather than through the common law. Early instances of this phenomenon continued to require some close relationship between the harm caused and the actor upon whom the duty was imposed. For example, the owners of cars were criminally liable for accidents caused while others were driving but only, apparently, if they were present in the car at the time of the accident.[34]

The law has now gone far from that model of liability for the failure to act and, in effect,

> Social and legal obligations have come to be imposed by statute rather than through the common law.

has begun to impose criminal liability for the acts of another based upon failures of supervision that are far different from the common law's doctrine of liability for negative acts. The trend was begun by the Supreme Court in 1943, in *United States v. Dotterweich*.[35] There, the Court addressed a provision of the Food and Drug Act making it a crime to introduce into commerce an adulterated or misbranded drug (that is, one not suitable for consumption or mislabeled).

Dotterweich was the president of a pharmaceutical company that indisputably had transported certain adulterated drugs in interstate commerce, but it was equally clear that there was "no evidence...of any personal guilt" on the part of Dotterweich; there was no proof that "he ever knew of the introduction into commerce of the adulterated drugs in question, much less that he actively participated in their introduction."[36]

Nonetheless, by a 5–4 vote, the Supreme Court determined that Dotterweich could be held criminally liable for his "responsible share in the furtherance of the transaction which the statute outlaws."[37] The Court reasoned that the purpose of the legislation "touches phases of the lives and health of people which, in the circumstances of modern industrialism are largely beyond self-production."[38] Thus, Congress

> **Guilt was "imputed to [Dotterweich] solely on the basis of his authority and responsibility as president and general manager of the corporation."**

could reasonably have determined to "penalize[] the transaction though consciousness of wrongdoing be totally wanting" because it

> preferred to place [the hardship] upon those who have at least the opportunity of informing themselves of the existence of conditions imposed for the protection of consumers before sharing in illicit commerce, rather than to throw the hazard on the innocent public who are wholly helpless.[39]

As a consequence, guilt was "imputed to [Dotterweich] solely on the basis of his authority and responsibility as president and general manager of the corporation."[40]

The prosecution of managers based upon theories of managerial liability has increased since *Dotterweich*. In one famous (perhaps notorious is a better word) case,[41] the president of Acme Food, John Park, was charged with violation of the Food and Drug Act. Park had been told of a rodent problem in a Baltimore warehouse. He worked in Philadelphia and delegated responsibility for responding to the rodent problem to the Acme Baltimore division vice president. When the problem was not resolved by the vice president's actions, Park was charged and convicted of a crime because he bore a "responsible relation to the situation even though he may not have participated in it personally."[42]

In short, Park was convicted "by virtue of [his] managerial position [and] relation to the actor" who actually committed the offense.[43] According to the U.S. Supreme Court, managers in Park's position have

> not only a positive duty to seek out and remedy violations when they occur but also, and primarily, a duty to implement measures that will insure that violations will not occur. The requirements of foresight and vigilance imposed on responsible corporate agents are beyond question demanding, and perhaps onerous, but they are no more stringent than the public has a right to expect of those who voluntarily assume positions of authority in business enterprises whose services and products affect the health and well-being of the public that supports them.[44]

In other words, it has now become common[45] in American society to enforce complex and often unclear regulatory obligations not through the law of tort and civil liability but through the stringent provisions of criminal law. Those who voluntarily choose to engage in productive economic conduct place themselves at risk of criminal sanction for their "felony failure to supervise." There is no better way to dissuade those who work to produce goods and services from continuing to do so than to criminalize their conduct without reference to whether or not they have personally acted in a culpable manner.[46]

One can readily see the consequences of this development of the law. Under current doctrine, Edward Hanousek was deemed liable for the conduct of Shane Thoe without any demonstration that Hanousek had deliberately or purposefully chosen to associate himself with Thoe's acts or that Hanousek had affirmatively acted in any way to cause the criminal injury involved: the rupture of the pipeline.

At the government's insistence, the court rejected Hanousek's request that the jury be instructed that he was "not responsible for and cannot be held criminally liable for any negligent acts or omissions by Shane Thoe or other Hunz & Hunz personnel." It also rejected his argument that he could not personally be deemed to have caused the accident if the actual result was not within the risk of which he was aware or should have been aware. Instead, the court said that Hanousek could be deemed guilty for, in essence, his managerial failings so long as he had a "direct and substantial" connection to the discharge and the jury concluded that the discharge would not have occurred "but for" Hanousek's actions.[47]

The Historical Meaning of *Mens Rea*

The origins of "intent" as a hallmark of responsibility lie as far back as Biblical times. The book of Numbers in the Old Testament defines murder as killing a person with "premeditated hostility" or in anger. Vengeance was permitted, but only against the blameworthy.

The first criminal law system to integrate a comprehensive theory of *mens rea* was apparently the Anglo-Saxon law of the 12th and 13th centuries. This was a direct result of the integration of canonical principles into a relatively uniform and maturing system of criminal law.

The writings of Lord Henry Bracton in the mid-13th century record that "a crime is not committed unless the intention to injure exists." Bracton, chancellor of Exeter Cathedral in addition to being a professional judge, pointed out that neither executioners nor soldiers were guilty of murder when they killed within the bounds of their profession. Likewise, infants and the insane could never be guilty of murder.

> The origins of "intent" as a hallmark of responsibility lie as far back as Biblical times.

In the first instance, there is presumed to be no criminal intent for such authorized killings. In the latter, the prospective perpetrators are presumed incapable of forming any criminal intent at all.

A good early example of the use of "intent" in criminal law is the case of *Regina v. Faulkner*.[48] Faulkner, a British sailor intent on stealing rum, ventured into the hold of his ship. He succeeded at boring a hole into a cask and drank his fill, but in the darkness of the bowels of the vessel, he had difficulty plugging the hole. In order to see, he lit a match. The flame quite unfortunately ignited the rum, which proceeded to conflagrate the ship.

Faulkner was put on trial for arson, which required the Crown to show that he had "unlawfully and maliciously" set the fire. The Crown argued that Faulkner's malicious intent to steal the rum was sufficient and won essentially a directed verdict. On appeal to the Court of Crown Cases, however, the conviction was overturned. Actual intent to burn the ship or reckless disregard of the risk of such a result was necessary for a conviction for arson.

Roscoe Pound summed up the connection between *mens rea* and the development of Anglo-American criminal law: "Historically, our substantive criminal law is based upon the theory of punishing the vicious will. It postulates a free agent confronted with a choice between doing right and doing wrong and choosing freely to do wrong."[49]

> "Even a dog distinguishes between being stumbled over and being kicked."

The development of criminal intent as part of the definition of criminality was neither accidental nor unique to some particular time or place. Rather, as Oliver Wendell Holmes said, it was the manifestation of the instinctive sense that just punishment presupposes some kind of wrongful intent: "Even a dog distinguishes between being stumbled over and being kicked."

Thus was developed the second fundamental precept of criminal law: the concept of *mens rea*, which must be joined with the illegal act. (*Mens rea* is Latin for "guilty mind"; lawyers use it as a shorthand for the concept of intent.) Historically, the law has required that before an individual is deemed a criminal, he must have acted with the intent to do wrong. Accidents and mistakes are not considered crimes: "It is a fundamental principle of Anglo-Saxon jurisprudence that guilt…is not lightly to be imputed to a citizen who…has no evil intention or consciousness of wrongdoing."[50]

In this area also, recent developments in the law have diverged far from that model.

Reduction and Elimination of the *Mens Rea* Requirement in Modern Times

In modern times, courts attempting to define the degree of intent (also sometimes called "scienter") that the government must prove for various criminal statutes have often written of the difficulty involved in determining what intent requirement the legislature adopted and in defining the terms that the legislature used. There is "variety, disparity and confusion" in the many judicial definitions of the "requisite but elusive mental element" of many criminal offenses.[51]

The requirement that a crime involve culpable purposeful intent has a solid historical grounding. As Justice Robert Jackson wrote:

> The contention that an injury can amount to a crime only when inflicted by intention is no provincial or transient notion. It is as universal and persistent in mature systems of law as belief in freedom of the human will and a consequent ability and duty of the normal individual to choose between good and evil. A relation between some mental element and punishment for a harmful act is almost as instinctive as the child's familiar exculpatory "But I didn't mean to," and has afforded the rational basis for a tardy and unfinished substitution of deterrence and reformation in place of retaliation and vengeance as the motivation for public prosecution. Unqualified acceptance of this doctrine by English common law was indicated by Blackstone's sweeping statement that to constitute any crime there must first be a "vicious will."[52]

Thus, the very earliest English common law recognized that one who intended to commit an act (for example, injuring a horse) and mistakenly committed a different crime (killing the horse) could not be said to have intended the graver crime of intentional killing of the animal.[53]

But this conception of intent (or what the Model Penal Code would call "purpose")[54]—that is, a conception necessitating proof that a defendant intended both to do the act that constituted the offense and to accomplish the particular harm prohibited—did not long survive even in the common law. English and American courts quickly came to the view that, in most legal contexts, a criminal actor who intends to engage in an act is liable for whatever harm eventuates, even if it is different from that which was within his original contemplation.[55] In the words of the Model Penal Code, one can act "knowingly" or with the general intent to do the acts that constitute the offense without regard to any specific intent to do a wrongful act or violate a law.[56]

This concept of "knowing" intent has also taken hold in the context of regulatory offenses. Building on the time-honored maxim that "ignorance of the law is no excuse," courts now routinely conclude that one can be convicted of a crime for having acted knowingly (that is, purposefully doing an act) without the additional requirement that the government prove that the defendant had a conscious desire to achieve a particular end or to violate a known legal duty (typically, one found in the form of a statutory or regulatory prohibition).

Justice Robert Jackson, who prosecuted the Nuremberg trials, knew that a guilty mind was the key to criminal conduct.

Thus, for example, violations of the Sherman Antitrust Act require only proof of deliberate business conduct without proof of intent to monopolize or intent to violate the law.[57]

The law also recognizes yet another culpable mental state with a further diminished aspect of purposefulness: One may be deemed guilty of a crime if one has acted with "criminal negligence." One common-law definition of "criminal negligence" (that is, negligence of such a substantial kind and degree as to warrant punishment) suggests the nature of the historical definition: "aggravated, culpable, gross or reckless [conduct], that is, the conduct of the accused must be such a departure from what would be the conduct of an ordinarily prudent or careful man under the same circumstances as to be incompatible with a proper regard for human life."[58] Under this standard, for example, chiropractic doctors who have recommended fasting as a treatment for tuberculosis have been convicted of culpably negligent manslaughter.[59]

One may be deemed guilty of a crime if one has acted with "criminal negligence."

Today, this type of "negligence" is more commonly called "recklessness"—that is, the awareness of a risk and disregard of the risk in circumstances that the law would consider unreasonable—but even this definition, in effect limiting "criminal negligence" to wanton recklessness, is no longer the rule. In many instances, the courts have allowed criminal convictions upon a showing of simple negligence—that is, a mere failure to exercise "reasonable care" that might normally give rise to civil tort liability. These cases, in contrast to those involving reckless conduct, concern situations where the actor was actually not aware of the risk involved, though perhaps he ought to have been.

Hanousek's case is one example of this trend. Hanousek had argued that criminally negligent conduct had to encompass some aspect of moral wrongdoing—in other words, a gross disregard of reasonable standards. He requested that the jury be instructed that the government had to prove that his negligence constituted "a gross deviation from the standard of care that a reasonable person would observe in the situation,"[60] a concept consistent with a traditional understanding of moral culpability. The court rejected that argument, concluding that the negligence standard for a criminal violation of law was identical to that for a civil violation: simple negligence for the failure to use reasonable care.[61]

In the area of regulatory crimes, even proof of negligent conduct is not always necessary; regrettably, the courts have accepted legislatures' increasing attempts to do away with the *mens rea* requirement altogether. In other words, a defendant may be found guilty of the crime even if he had no intention whatsoever that it occur and the *actus reus* arose, for example, as a result of an accident. Though the elimination of all *mens rea* requirements so that purely innocent conduct is punished criminally ought to be deemed a violation the Constitution, the courts have said that it is not.[62]

> A defendant may be found guilty of the crime even if he had no intention whatsoever that it occur and his acts were the result of an accident.

It is difficult, if not impossible, to identify when the first strict-liability offense entered the federal statute books. One scholar has concluded that it was no earlier than 1850 and that prior to that time all common-law crimes required proof of some form of *mens rea*.[63] An early example is *Regina v. Stephens*,[64] where the bed-ridden 80-year-old owner of a granite quarry had given management of the quarry to his children. Contrary to his direct orders (and those of his sons), workers at the quarry deposited rubbish in the River Tivy, thereby creating a nuisance. The owner, Stephens, was deemed strictly liable and convicted of the criminal offense.

Today, although rare, there are a number of criminal offenses that impose criminal liability without fault,[65] and where the doctrine was originally limited to misdemeanor

> One court held a company strictly liable for the death of certain migratory birds "even if the killing of the birds was accidental or unintentional."

criminal liability, it is now often imposed as part of felony prosecutions. For example, one court held a company strictly liable for the death of certain migratory birds "even if the killing of the birds was accidental or unintentional."[66] Similarly, courts have held strictly liable those whose conduct contravenes the laws relating to the sale of liquor and narcotics, foods, and possession of unregistered firearms, among others.[67]

Intent and Regulatory Offenses

However, this description of the *mens rea* requirements that have developed is incomplete. It does not fully make clear the extent to which actors in a highly regulated industry are subject to criminal liability for their acts. Though the law often requires that they have acted "knowingly"—a seeming protection from the imposition of strict liability—that requirement is but a parchment barrier to what is, in effect, the imposition of absolute liability.

At the urging of prosecutors, judges have interpreted many of the statutes that apply to regulated industries so that those who participate in the industry are presumed knowledgeable of all the arcane regulatory intricacies that govern their conduct.[68] As a consequence, the only requirement imposed by requiring proof that one has acted "knowingly" is that the government must demonstrate that the defendant has purposefully done the act constituting the offense. In the context of regulated economic conduct,

> Proof that one in fact lacked knowledge of the regulatory requirement at issue is no defense to the prosecution.

that showing is trivial. Moreover, proof that one in fact lacked knowledge of the regulatory requirement at issue is uniformly no defense to the prosecution.

Consider, for example, the crime of "knowingly filing a false monitoring report"[69] under the Clean Water Act. The law that defines what is false or misleading is part of a large regulatory scheme that also includes a regulation-imposed obligation on each individual to ensure the accuracy of any reports made. As a consequence, the only showing the government must make to the satisfaction of a jury is that the defendant has "knowingly filed" the report, irrespective of whether or not he actually knew it was false.

> What is particularly disturbing about the trend toward diminished intent requirements is that it is exacerbated by a trend toward significantly harsher penalties.

Since nobody files a report without doing so intentionally (reports do not get signed, sealed, and mailed by accident or mistake), the only showing necessary is the trivial showing that the defendant has actually put a letter in the mail on purpose. As Justice Potter Stewart noted: "As a practical matter, therefore, they are under a species of absolute liability for violation of the regulations despite the 'knowingly' requirement."[70]

What is particularly disturbing about the trend toward diminished intent requirements is that it is exacerbated by a trend toward significantly harsher penalties. Historically, when the courts first considered regulatory laws containing reduced intent requirements, the laws almost uniformly provided for very light penalties such as a fine or a very brief jail term, not imprisonment in a penitentiary.[71] As commentators noted, modest penalties are a logical complement to crimes that do not require specific intent.[72] Indeed, some courts questioned whether any imprisonment at all could be imposed in the absence of intent and culpability.[73]

This historical view has, of course, been lost. Regulatory laws with reduced *mens rea* requirements are often now felonies.[74] Even misdemeanor offenses, through the stacking of sentences, can result in substantial terms of incarceration.[75]

> "If we use prison to achieve social goals regardless of the moral innocence of those we incarcerate, then imprisonment loses its moral opprobrium and our criminal law becomes morally arbitrary."

In short, the history of changes in the *mens rea* requirements has been substantial. The criminal law today is far different from the criminal law of 100 years ago. For regulatory crimes, there is in effect a standard of near-absolute liability.

One is entitled to wonder whether contemporary legislators who have enacted regulatory statutes with increasingly onerous criminal penalties have lost sight of a fundamental truth: "If we use prison to achieve social goals regardless of the moral innocence of those we incarcerate, then imprisonment loses its moral opprobrium and our criminal law becomes morally arbitrary."[76] Or as the drafters of the Model Penal Code said:

> It has been argued, and the argument undoubtedly will be repeated, that strict liability is necessary for enforcement in a number of the areas where it obtains. But if practical enforcement precludes litigation of the culpability of alleged deviation from legal requirements, the enforcers cannot rightly demand the use of penal sanctions for the purpose. Crime does and should mean condemnation, and no court should have to pass that judgment unless it can declare that the defendant's act was culpable. This is too fundamental to be compromised.[77]

Due Process and the Public Welfare Offense Doctrine

The definition of the elements of a criminal offense—whether it requires an *actus reus* or a *mens rea*—is for the most part entrusted to the legislature. This is especially true for federal offenses, which are solely creatures of statute.[78] Also, as noted earlier, Congress itself has exercised precious little self-restraint in the creation of federal criminal regulatory offenses.

> Congress itself has exercised precious little self-restraint in the creation of federal criminal regulatory offenses.

The final question to consider, then, is whether there are any external limits on this trend. Does the Constitution restrict the extent to which the legislature may do away with traditional act and intent requirements?

One limit on the expansion of *malum prohibitum* crimes (that is, crimes that are crimes because the legislature says so, not because of their inherent criminal nature) lies in the interpretative methodology used by the courts. The courts can (and sometimes even do) read statutes narrowly—to require, for example, proof that a defendant knew of the law and regulations proscribing his alleged offense when "to interpret the statute otherwise would be to criminalize a broad range of apparently innocent conduct."[79]

Similarly, where a defendant engages in apparently innocent conduct (that is, where he is unaware of underlying predicate facts that place him on notice as to the existence of criminal regulation), the courts sometimes read the Due Process clause as imposing a modest limit on criminalizing the conduct; a defendant's contention that he was completely unaware of the underlying facts that put him on notice as to the existence of regulations is exculpatory.[80] Put another way, due process has sometimes (though rarely) been construed to require that defendants who engage in seemingly innocent conduct must be proven to have had knowledge of facts that put them on notice of the potential criminalization of their conduct.[81]

But this interpretive methodology has not yet been used aggressively by the courts to cabin legislative power. Rather, the courts have generally concluded that the due process requirements of the Constitution do not apply in the same way and with the same effect when the crime being addressed is a regulatory offense.

The doctrine of "public welfare" offenses has its origins early in the 20th century.[82] Though usually thought of as being limited to *malum prohibitum* crimes, it has come to comprise a category of criminal laws construed by the courts as lacking, or having diminished, *mens rea* requirements.[83] Thus, under this doctrine, criminal statutes that have diminished intent requirements (that is, that punish conduct that is not deliberate as, for example, when the law criminalizes conduct that is no more than simple negligence) are deemed not to violate the due process requirements of the Constitution. This, however, is exactly backwards: It is this class of intent-less crimes for which due process analysis is most appropriate.

> "In the interest of the larger good [the law] puts the burden of acting at hazard upon a person otherwise innocent but standing in responsible relation to a public danger."

The courts reason that Congress may render criminal "a type of conduct that a reasonable person should know is subject to stringent public regulation and may seriously threaten the community's health or safety."[84] In such circumstances, the law puts the burden of knowledge of the regulatory structure on those who act and presumes their knowledge of the law rather than requiring proof of that fact. "In the interest of the larger good [the law] puts the burden of acting at hazard upon a person otherwise innocent but standing in responsible relation to a public danger."[85]

Consider again the Hanousek case: Consistent with earlier decisions of the Ninth Circuit,[86] the government argued that the discharge of pollutants, prohibited by the Clean Water Act, was a "public welfare offense." Because Hanousek, according to the government, was working in a heavily regulated

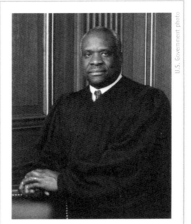

Justice Clarence Thomas objected to the Supreme Court's decision not to review Hanousek's case.

business that was a threat to community safety, he was presumed to know all of the obligations imposed upon him by the Clean Water Act and thus precluded from challenging his conviction on the ground that he did not know of his obligation not to act negligently.

When Hanousek asked the Supreme Court to review his case, the Court declined. Justices Clarence Thomas and Sandra Day O'Connor, however, thought that the expansive use of criminal sanctions in what was essentially a simple negligence tort merited review. As Justice Thomas wrote, rejecting the application of the public welfare offense doctrine to Hanousek's activity:

> [T]o determine as a threshold matter whether a particular statute defines a public welfare offense, a court must have in view some category of dangerous and deleterious devices that will be assumed to alert an individual that he stands in "responsible relation to a public danger."[87]

The lower courts' broader view of the appropriate scope of criminal law, as Justice Thomas recognized, "expose[s] countless numbers of construction workers and contractors to heightened criminal liability for using ordinary devices to engage in normal industrial operations."

Thus, Justice Thomas viewed the result in Hanousek as inconsistent with Supreme Court precedent, which had

> never held that any statute can be described as creating a public welfare offense so long as the statute regulates conduct that is known to be subject to extensive regulation and that may involve a risk to the community. Indeed, such a suggestion would extend this narrow doctrine to virtually any criminal statute applicable to industrial activities. I presume that in today's heavily regulated society, any person engaged in industry is aware that his activities are the object of sweeping regulation and that an industrial accident could threaten health or safety.[88]

Put another way, given the comprehensive nature of regulation in American society today, the growth of the public welfare offense doctrine has led, in effect, to the abandonment of any criminal intent requirement within virtually the entire range of commercial, social, and economic activity in the marketplace.

Disappearance of the Tort–Crime Distinction

One corollary to the growth of the public welfare offense doctrine is the disappearance of the distinction between tort and crime in American law.[89] The use of the public welfare offense doctrine to address social goals enlists the criminal law as an agent of social regulation and change.

> The use of the public welfare offense doctrine to address social goals enlists the criminal law as an agent of social regulation and change.

Historically, tort law has been a private mechanism for compensating for injuries. Affirmative civil enforcement by the government has been seen as a means of enforcing compliance with social norms through administrative procedures or civil litigation—the latter even having a component of punishment by virtue of the proliferation of punitive damages. These systems were once thought sufficient to require economic actors to internalize the costs of their conduct and avoid imposing those same costs on unwitting external actors.

While the traditional legal definition of a crime requires a wrongful act done with culpable intent, a civil law tort is simply a wrongful act. Thus, the mind is often all that distinguishes criminal from tortfeasor. The tortfeasor is liable for damages to recompense an injured party. The criminal can be convicted of a crime—the signet of a societies' moral condemnation— and can be punished. Punishment is not about compensating particular injured parties. While there

> Without a moral foundation, crime may be nothing more than the whim of legislatures.

are competing theories of what punishment is and what ends it serves, it certainly conveys moral approbation and aspires to eliminate particular criminal behaviors. Tort liability, on the other hand, seeks to regulate risky behaviors—such as maintaining a reservoir, operating a railroad, or selling coffee—at an efficient level.

Reducing or eliminating intent as a part of the definition of crime blurs the distinction between criminal and civil law. It confuses traditional criminal behavior that society seeks to eradicate and risky behavior that society seeks to regulate. This trend also erodes the moral foundation that underlies the traditional concept of crime. Without this foundation, crime may be nothing more than the whim of legislatures. The drift away from the *mens rea* requirement is reducing the effectiveness of both civil and criminal law. Collateral consequences range from economic inefficiencies to a reduced respect for law and law enforcement.

Nonetheless, today, the criminal law is being used in an avowedly instrumental capacity. Identically phrased statutes are often applicable to the same conduct, one authorizing a civil penalty and the other a criminal sanction.[90] In effect, the criminal law, through the public welfare offense doctrine, has become a tool of socialization, losing its historic character as a system for addressing wrongful conduct. Criminal sanctions for conduct affecting the public welfare have become a reflex answer. The result is a substitution of criminal law for more traditional

> Criminal law, through the public welfare offense doctrine, has become a tool of socialization, losing its historic character as a system for addressing wrongful conduct.

tort and civil law: There is a "more pervasive use of the criminal sanction, a use that intrudes further into the mainstream of American life and into the everyday life of its citizens than has ever been attempted before."[91]

What accounts for this change? We can only surmise that it arises from groups who view the very concept of criminal intent as a hindrance to the achievement of their particular policy objectives. As Professor Baker demonstrates in Chapter 14, a collection of academics, either misunderstanding or intentionally misconstruing the distinction between crimes and civil actions and regulatory enforcement, have argued that people in business—"the rich"—are just as "criminal" as those from lower socioeconomic strata. The white-collar crime argument suggests that concepts like *mens rea* function to protect those engaged in complex business "crimes" while offering little or no protection to traditional criminals like rapists or robbers. Columnist Christopher Byron has summed up this view, declaring that criminal intent is "nothing more than a ploy by which a quick-witted defendant can beat a rap."

The problem with this assumption is that it rests on a demonstrably false premise. When someone is charged with a crime, proving criminal intent has nothing to do with the wealth or poverty of the accused. It does have a lot to do with the particular charges. For crimes like armed robbery or forcible rape, proof of the criminal act is often essentially proof of *mens rea*. For other crimes, like shoplifting or tax evasion, proof of the act is not sufficient. Someone may have inadvertently walked out of the store without paying for an item or have forgotten to "carry the one" when adding columns on their IRS 1040 form.

It is certainly easier to prove *mens rea* for traditional crimes than it is for complex regulatory crimes, but it is also far more likely that someone actually did make a mistake regarding complex regulation. Thus, the very complexity of the underlying regulations calls for a stronger intent requirement, not a lesser one.

The Consequences of Judicial Inaction

In effect, then, the courts have deliberately chosen a limited, almost self-abnegating role in constraining the use of criminal sanctions. As it stands today, no effective judicial constraint limits the extent to which individual conduct that bears no causal relationship to a societal harm may be criminalized. Nor is there a limit on the extent to which, in the social and economic context, legislatures may dispense with the traditional conceptions of *mens rea*. The consequences of this are twofold: a patho-

logical legislative approach to criminal law and an excess of prosecutorial
discretion.

As Professor William Stuntz has
noted, American criminal law "covers
far more conduct than any jurisdiction

> The consequences are twofold: a pathological legislative approach to criminal law and an excess of prosecutorial discretion.

could possibly punish."[92] This wide span of American law is the product of
institutional pressures that draw legislators to laws with broader liability
rules and harsher sentences.[93] The reason is the dynamic of legislative consideration: When a legislator is faced with a choice on how to draw a new
criminal statute, either narrowly and potentially underinclusive or broadly
and potentially overinclusive, the politics of the situation naturally causes
the legislator to be overinclusive. Few, if any, groups regularly lobby legislators regarding criminal law. When such lobbying does occur, it usually
seeks harsher penalties and more rather than fewer criminal laws.

In addition, the political dynamic is exacerbated by the consideration
(usually implicit) of the costs associated with the criminal justice system.
Broad and overlapping statutes with minimum obstacles to criminalization and harsh penalties are easier to administer and reduce the costs of
the legal system. They induce guilty pleas and produce high conviction
rates, minimizing the costs of the cumbersome jury system and generally
producing outcomes popular with the public.[94]

The final piece of the equation is legislative reliance on the existence
of prosecutorial discretion. Broader and harsher statutes may produce bad
outcomes that the public dislikes, but blame for those outcomes will lie
with prosecutors who exercise their discretion poorly, not the legislators
who passed the underlying statute. As a consequence, every incentive exists for criminal legislation to be as
expansive as possible.

In the absence of any judicial
check on this legislative trend, the result is a wholesale transfer of power

> Every incentive exists for criminal legislation to be as expansive as possible.

from elected legislative officials to prosecutors who, in many instances, are
unelected and not responsible to the public. Where once the law had strict
limits on the capacity of the government to criminalize conduct, those limits have now evaporated. Society has come instead to rely on the "con-

science and circumspection in prosecuting officers."[95] Or, as the Supreme
Court said in *Dotterweich*, Americans are obliged to rely only on "the good
sense of prosecutors, the wise guidance of trial judges, and the ultimate
judgment of juries" to determine criminal conduct.[96] In effect, the legislative branch has transferred a substantial fraction of its authority to regulate
American social and economic conduct to those who have no expertise
in the matter: prosecutors, trial judges, and jurors who make decisions on
criminalizing conduct without the ability or responsibility to consider the
broader societal impacts of their decisions.

And so the criminal law has come to this odd and unusual point in its
development. Where once, to be a criminal, an individual had to do an
act (or attempt to do an act) with willful intent to violate the law or with
knowledge of the wrongful nature of his conduct, today it is possible to
be found criminally liable and imprisoned for a substantial term of years
for the failure to do an act required by law, without any actual knowledge
of the law's obligations and with no wrongful intent whatsoever. These
developments are advanced in the name of the "public welfare"—an express invocation of broader social
needs at the expense of individual
liberty and responsibility. It is,
ultimately, the triumph of a Ben-
thamite utilitarian conception of
the criminal law over the morally grounded understanding of criminal law
advanced by Blackstone with its origins in Biblical strictures.

Are broader social needs well served when individual liberty and responsibility suffer?

One may—and, indeed, one should—doubt the wisdom of such a
course. Given how the criminal law has developed, a free people are constrained to ask the question: Are broader social needs well served when
individual liberty and responsibility suffer?

CHAPTER 13

BLAMEWORTHINESS AND INTENT

Tim Lynch

On July 22, 2009, Tim Lynch appeared before the Subcommittee on Crime, Terrorism and Homeland Security of the House Committee on the Judiciary. The subject of the hearing (the same hearing at which Kirster Evertson testified) was "Over-Criminalization of Conduct/Over-Federalization of Criminal Law." Professor Lynch's testimony, reprinted here, analyzes several aspects of criminal law and the problem of overcriminalization, with a particular focus on the concept of blameworthiness, or intent, and how it has changed over time, echoing many of the themes outlined by Professor Rosenzweig in the previous chapter.

Although I believe the problems of Over-Criminalization of Conduct and Over-Federalization of Criminal Law are among the most serious problems facing the Congress today,[1] my role this afternoon, as I understand it, is to highlight a related trend in the law—and that is the drift away from the idea of blameworthiness as a first principle of American criminal justice. That is, too often the government seeks to deny the proposition that it is unjust to inflict criminal punishment on people who are not blameworthy. My remarks will focus on that subject.

Introduction and Background

My approach to the criminal law begins with three basic propositions.

First, the power that is wielded by police and prosecutors is truly immense. A dramatic raid, arrest, or indictment can bring enormous damage to a person's life—even before he or she has an opportunity to mount a defense in court.

Second, the term "criminal" carries a stigma. It implies that the culprit has done something that is blameworthy.

Third—and relatedly—it is important to keep a close eye on the manner in which the government creates and defines "criminal offenses." For as Harvard Law Professor Henry Hart once noted, "What sense does it make to insist upon procedural safeguards in criminal prosecutions if anything whatever can be made a crime in the first place?"[2]

In my view, all persons of goodwill ought to be disturbed by the fact that the government is now bypassing the procedural protections of the Bill of Rights and attaching the "criminal" label to people who are not truly blameworthy.

> "What sense does it make to insist upon procedural safeguards in criminal prosecutions if anything whatever can be made a crime in the first place?"

Let me begin by trying to clarify some terminology. In our law schools today, the terms "intent" and "*mens rea*" are commonly used in a very broad manner—as concepts that include a spectrum of mental states (ranging from purposeful conduct to strict or vicarious liability) to be defined in statutes by policymakers. But for purposes of my testimony today, I will be using those terms in a more narrow sense. As Justice Potter Stewart once observed, "Whether postulated as a problem of '*mens rea,*' of 'willfulness,' of 'criminal responsibility,' or of 'scienter,' the infliction of criminal punishment upon the unaware has long troubled the fair administration of justice."[3]

Today, I want to advance the claim that it is wrong to criminally punish those who were "unaware" of the facts or rules that made their conduct unlawful. The remainder of my testimony will pinpoint the areas of our law where this problem is especially acute.

The Problem Areas

Ignorance of the Law Is No Excuse

The sheer volume of modern law makes it impossible for an ordinary American household to stay informed. And yet, prosecutors vigorously defend the old legal maxim that "ignorance of the law is no excuse."[4] That maxim may have been appropriate for a society that simply criminalized inherently evil conduct, such as murder, rape, and theft, but it is wholly inappropriate in a labyrinthine regulatory regime that criminalizes activities that

> It is wrong to criminally punish those who were "unaware" of the facts or rules that made their conduct unlawful.

are morally neutral. As Professor Henry M. Hart opined, "In no respect is contemporary law subject to greater reproach than for its obtuseness to this fact."[5]

To illustrate the rank injustice that can and does occur, take the case of Carlton Wilson, who was prosecuted because he possessed a firearm. Wilson's purchase of the firearm was perfectly legal, but years later, he didn't know that he had to give it up after a judge issued a restraining order during his divorce proceedings. When Wilson protested that the judge never informed him of that obligation and that the restraining order itself said nothing about firearms, prosecutors shrugged, "ignorance of the law is no excuse."[6] Although the courts upheld Wilson's conviction, Judge Richard Posner filed a dissent:

> We want people to familiarize themselves with the laws bearing on their activities. But a reasonable opportunity doesn't mean being able to go to the local law library and read Title 18. It would be preposterous to suppose that someone from Wilson's milieu is able to take advantage of such an opportunity.[7]

Judge Posner noted that Wilson would serve more than three years in a federal penitentiary for an omission that he "could not have suspected was a crime or even a civil wrong."[8]

It is simply outrageous for the government to impose a legal duty on every citizen to "know" all of the mind-boggling rules and regulations that have been promulgated over the years. Policymakers

> It is simply outrageous for the government to impose a legal duty on every citizen to "know" all of the mind–boggling rules and regulations that have been promulgated over the years.

can and should discard the "ignorance-is-no-excuse" maxim by enacting a law that would require prosecutors to prove that regulatory violations are "willful" or, in the alternative, that would permit a good-faith belief in the legality of one's conduct to be pleaded and proved as a defense. The former rule is already in place for our complicated tax laws—but it should also shield unwary Americans from all of the laws and regulations as well.[9]

Vague Statutes

Even if there were but a few crimes on the books, the terms of such laws need to be drafted with precision. There is precious little difference between a secret law and a published regulation that cannot be understood.

History is filled with examples of oppressive governments that persecuted unpopular groups and innocent individuals by keeping the law's requirements from the people. For example, the Roman emperor Caligula posted new laws high on the columns of buildings so that ordinary citizens could not study them. Such abominable policies were discarded during the Age of Enlightenment, and a new set of principles—known generally as the "rule of law"—took hold. Those principles included the requirements of legality and specificity.

> History is filled with examples of oppressive governments that persecuted unpopular groups and innocent individuals by keeping the law's requirements from the people.

"Legality" means a regularized process, ideally rooted in moral principle, by which crimes are designated and prosecuted by the government. The Enlightenment philosophy was expressed by the maxim *nullum crimen sine lege* (there is no crime without a law). In other words, people can be punished only for conduct previously prohibited by law. That principle is clearly enunciated in the Ex Post Facto Clause of the U.S. Constitution (Article I, Section 9). But the purpose of the Ex Post Facto Clause can be subverted if the legislature can enact a criminal law that condemns conduct in general terms, such as "dangerous and harmful" behavior. Such a law would not give people fair warning of the prohibited conduct. To guard against the risk of arbitrary enforcement, the Supreme Court has said that the law must be clear:

> A criminal statute cannot rest upon an uncertain foundation. The crime, and the elements constituting it, must be so clearly expressed that the ordinary person can intelligently choose, in advance, what course it is lawful for him to pursue. Penal statutes prohibiting the doing of certain things, and providing a punishment for their

violation, should not admit of such a double meaning that the citizen may act upon the one conception of its requirements and the courts upon another.[10]

The principles of legality and specificity operate together to reduce the likelihood of arbitrary and discriminatory application of the law by keeping policy matters away from police officers, administrative bureaucrats, prosecutors, judges, and members of juries, who would have to resolve ambiguities on an *ad hoc* and subjective basis.

Although the legality and specificity requirements are supposed to be among the first principles of American criminal law, a "regulatory" exception has crept into modern jurisprudence.

Although the legality and specificity requirements are supposed to be among the first principles of American criminal law, a "regulatory" exception has crept into modern jurisprudence. The Supreme Court has unfortunately allowed "greater leeway" in regulatory matters because the practicalities of modern governance supposedly limit "the specificity with which legislators can spell out prohibitions."[11] During the past 50 years, fuzzy legal standards, such as "unreasonable," "unusual," and "excessive," have withstood constitutional challenge.

The Framers of the American Constitution understood that democracy alone was no guarantor of justice. As James Madison noted:

More than 200 years ago, James Madison warned of "voluminous" and "incoherent" laws.

The White House Historical Association photo

> It will be of little avail to the people that the laws are made by men of their own choice if the laws be so voluminous that they cannot be read, or so incoherent that they cannot be understood; if they be repealed or revised before they are promulgated, or undergo such incessant changes that no man, who knows what the law is today, can guess what it will be tomorrow.[12]

Unfortunately, Madison's vision of unbridled lawmaking is an apt description of our modern regulatory state.[13] For example, the Environmental Protection Agency received so many queries about the meaning of the Resource Conservation and Recovery Act that it set up a special hotline for questions. Note, however, that the "EPA itself does not guarantee that its answers are correct, and reliance on wrong information given over the RCRA hotline is no defense to an enforcement action."[14]

Legal uncertainties should be resolved in favor of private individuals and organizations, not the government.

The situation is so bad that even many prosecutors are acknowledging that there is simply too much uncertainty in criminal law. Former Massachusetts Attorney General Scott Harshbarger concedes, "One thing we haven't done well in government is make it very clear, with bright lines, what kinds of activity will subject you to...criminal or civil prosecution."[15]

The first step toward addressing the problem of vague and ambiguous criminal laws would be for the Congress to direct the courts to follow the rule of lenity in all criminal cases.[16] Legal uncertainties should be resolved in favor of private individuals and organizations, not the government.

Strict Liability

Two basic premises that undergird Anglo-American criminal law are the requirements of *mens rea* (guilty mind) and *actus reus* (guilty act).[17] The first requirement says that for an act to constitute a crime, there must be "bad intent."

Dean Roscoe Pound of Harvard Law School writes, "Historically, our substantive criminal law is based upon a theory of punishing the vicious will. It postulates a free agent confronted with a choice between doing right and doing wrong and choosing freely to do wrong."[18] According to that view, a man could not be prosecuted for leaving an airport with the luggage of another if he mistakenly believed that he owned the luggage. As the Utah Supreme Court noted in *State v. Blue* (1898), *mens rea* was considered an indispensable element of a criminal offense. "To prevent the punishment of the innocent, there has been ingrafted into our system of jurisprudence, as presumably in every other, the principle that the wrongful or criminal intent is the essence of crime, without which it cannot exist."[19]

By the same token, bad thoughts alone do not constitute a crime if there is no "bad act." If a police officer discovers a diary that someone mistakenly left behind in a coffee shop and the contents include references to wanting to steal the possessions of another, the author cannot be prosecuted for a crime. Even if an off-duty police officer overhears two men in a tavern discussing their hatred of the police and their desire to kill a cop, no lawful arrest can be made if the men do not take action to further their cop-killing scheme. The basic idea, of course, is that the government should not be in the business of punishing "bad thoughts."

> The government should not be in the business of punishing "bad thoughts."

When *mens rea* and *actus reus* were fundamental prerequisites for criminal activity, no person could be branded a "criminal" until a prosecutor could persuade a jury that the accused possessed "an evil-meaning mind with an evil-doing hand."[20] That understanding of crime—as a compound concept—was firmly entrenched in the English common law at the time of the American Revolution.

Over the years, however, the moral underpinnings of the Anglo-American view of criminal law fell into disfavor. The *mens rea* and *actus reus* requirements came to be viewed as burdensome restraints on well-meaning lawmakers who wanted to solve social problems through administrative regulations. As Professor Richard G. Singer has written, "Criminal law… has come to be seen as merely one more method used by society to achieve social control."[21]

The change began innocently enough. To protect young girls, statutory rape laws were enacted that flatly prohibited sex with girls under the age of legal consent. Those groundbreaking laws applied even if the girl lied about her age and consented to sex and if the man reasonably believed the girl to be over the age of consent. Once the courts accepted that exception to the

> "Criminal law… has come to be seen as merely one more method used by society to achieve social control."

mens rea principle, legislators began to identify other activities that had to be stamped out—even at the cost of convicting innocent-minded people.

The number of strict-liability criminal offenses grew during the 20th century as legislators created scores of "public welfare offenses" relating to health and safety. Each time a person sought to prove an innocent state of mind, the Supreme Court responded that there is "wide latitude" in the legislative power to create offenses and "to exclude elements of knowledge and diligence from [their] definition."[22] Those strict-liability rulings have been sharply criticized by legal commentators. Professor Herbert Packer argues that the creation of strict-liability crimes is both inefficacious and unjust.

> It is inefficacious because conduct unaccompanied by an awareness of the factors making it criminal does not mark the actor as one who needs to be subjected to punishment in order to deter him or others from behaving similarly in the future, nor does it single him out as a socially dangerous individual who needs to be incapacitated or reformed. It is unjust because the actor is subjected to the stigma of a criminal conviction without being morally blameworthy. Consequently, on either a preventative or retributive theory of criminal punishment, the criminal sanction is inappropriate in the absence of mens rea.[23]

A dramatic illustration of the problem was presented in *Thorpe v. Florida* (1979).[24] John Thorpe was confronted by a thief who brandished a gun. Thorpe got into a scuffle with the thief and wrested the gun away from him. When the police arrived on the scene, Thorpe was arrested and prosecuted under a law that made it illegal for any felon to possess a firearm. Thorpe tried to challenge the application of that law by pointing to the extenuating circumstances of his case. The appellate court acknowledged the "harsh result" but noted that the law did not require a vicious will or criminal intent. Thus, self-defense was not "available as a defense to the crime."[25]

Strict-liability laws should be abolished because their very purpose is to divorce a person's intentions from his actions.

True, *Thorpe* was a case from 1979. The point here is simply to show the drift of our law. As Judge Benjamin Cardozo once quipped, once a principle or precedent gets established, it is usually taken to the "limit of its logic." For a more recent federal case, consider what happened to Dane Allen Yirkovsky. Yirkovsky was convicted of possessing one round of .22 caliber ammunition, and for that he received the minimum mandatory *15-year sentence*.[26] Here are the reported circumstances surrounding his "crime."

In late fall or early winter of 1998, Yirkovsky was living with Edith Turkington at her home in Cedar Rapids,
Iowa. Instead of paying rent, Yirkovsky agreed to remodel a bathroom at the home and to lay new carpeting
in the living room and hallway. While in the process of
removing the old carpet, Yirkovsky found a Winchester
.22 caliber, super x, round. Yirkovsky put the round in a
small box and kept it in the room in which he was living
in Turkington's house.

Subsequently, Yirkovsky's ex-girlfriend filed a complaint
alleging that Yirkovsky had some of her property in his
possession. A police detective spoke to Yirkovsky regarding the ex-girlfriend's property, and Yirkovsky granted
him permission to search his room in Turkington's house.
During this search, the detective located the .22 round.
Yirkovsky admitted to police that he had placed the round
where it was found by the detective.[27]

The appellate court found the penalty to be "extreme" but affirmed
Yirkovsky's sentence as consistent with existing law.[28]

Strict-liability laws should be abolished because their very purpose is
to divorce a person's intentions from his actions. But if the criminal sanction imports blame—and it does—it is a perversion to apply that sanction
to self-defense and other acts that are not blameworthy. Our criminal law
should reflect the old Latin maxim, *actus not facit reum nisi mens sit rea*
(an act does not make one guilty unless his mind is guilty).[29]

Vicarious Liability

Everyone agrees with the proposition that if a person commands, pays,
or induces another to commit a crime on that person's behalf, the person should be treated as having
committed the act.[30] Thus, if a
husband hires a man to kill his
wife, the husband is also guilty
of murder. But it is another mat-
ter entirely to hold one person criminally responsible for the *unauthorized*
acts of another. "Vicarious liability," the legal doctrine under which a per-

> It is another matter entirely to hold one
> person criminally responsible for the
> *unauthorized* acts of another.

son may be held responsible for the criminal acts of another, was once "repugnant to every instinct of the criminal jurist."[31] Alas, the modern trend in American criminal law is to embrace vicarious criminal liability.

Vicarious liability initially crept into regulations that were deemed necessary to control business enterprises. One of the key cases was *United States v. Park* (1975).[32] As detailed in the previous chapter, John Park was the president of Acme Markets Inc., a large national food chain. When the Food and Drug Administration found unsanitary conditions at a warehouse in April 1970, it sent Park a letter demanding corrective action. Park referred the matter to Acme's vice president for legal affairs. When Park was informed that the regional vice president was investigating the situation and would take corrective action, Park thought that was the end of the matter. But when unsanitary warehouse conditions were found on a subsequent inspection, prosecutors indicted both Acme and Park for violations of the Federal Food, Drug and Cosmetic Act.

An appellate court overturned Park's conviction because it found that the trial court's legal instructions could have "left the jury with the erroneous impression that [Park] could be found guilty in the absence of 'wrongful action' on his part" and that proof of that element was constitutionally mandated by due process.[33] The Supreme Court, however, reversed the appellate ruling. Chief Justice Warren Burger opined that the legislature could impose criminal liability on "those who voluntarily assume positions of authority in business enterprises" because such people have a duty "to devise whatever measures [are] necessary to ensure compliance" with regulations.[34] Thus, under the rationale of *Park*, an honest executive can be branded a criminal if a low-level employee in a different city disobeys a supervisor's instructions and violates a regulation—even if the violation causes no harm whatsoever.[35]

> Under the rationale of *Park*, an honest executive can be branded a criminal if a low-level employee in a different city disobeys a supervisor's instructions and violates a regulation—even if the violation causes no harm whatsoever.

Likewise, consider again the case of Edward Hanousek (also discussed in Chapter 12 of this book). In 1994, Hanousek was employed as a roadmaster for a railroad company. In that capacity, Hanousek supervised a rock quarrying project near an Alaska river. During rock removal operations, a backhoe operator accidentally ruptured a pipeline—and that mistake led to an oil spill into the nearby river. Hanousek was prosecuted under the Clean Water

> To crack down on the drug trade, Congress enacted a law that was so strict that tenants could be evicted if one of their household members or guests used drugs.

Act even though he was off duty and at home when the accident occurred. The case prompted Justice Clarence Thomas to express alarm at the direction of the law: "I think we should be hesitant to expose countless numbers of construction workers and contractors to heightened criminal liability for using ordinary devices to engage in normal industrial operations."[36]

Note that vicarious liability has *not* been confined to the commercial regulation context.[37] Tina Bennis lost her car to the police because of the actions of her husband. The police found him in the vehicle with a prostitute.[38] Pearlie Rucker was evicted from her apartment in a public housing complex because her daughter was involved with illicit drugs. To crack down on the drug trade, Congress enacted a law that was so strict that tenants could be evicted if one of their household members or guests used drugs. The eviction could proceed even if the drug activity took place outside the residence. Also under that federal law, it did not matter if the tenant was totally *unaware* of the drug activity.[39] Further, in some jurisdictions, the drivers of vehicles are exposed to criminal liability if any passenger brings contraband—such as a marijuana joint—into an automobile even if there is no proof that the driver was aware of the contraband's existence.[40]

This is true vicarious liability.

Conclusion

The federal criminal code has become so voluminous that it bewilders not only the average citizen, but also the most able attorney. Our courthouses have become so clogged that there is no longer adequate time for trials. And our penitentiaries are now operating well beyond their design capacity—many are simply overflowing with inmates.

> The federal criminal code has become so voluminous that it bewilders not only the average citizen, but also the most able attorney.

These developments evince a criminal law that is adrift. To get our federal system back "on track," Congress should take the following actions:

- ***Discard the old maxim that "ignorance of the law is no excuse."*** Given the enormous body of law presently on the books, this doctrine no longer makes any sense.

- ***Minimize the injustice of vaguely written rules*** by restoring traditional legal defenses such as diligence, good faith, and actual knowledge.

- ***Restore the rule of lenity for criminal cases*** by enacting a statute that will explicitly provide for the "strict construction" of federal criminal laws.

- ***Abolish the doctrine of strict criminal liability as well as the doctrine of vicarious liability.*** Those theories of criminal liability are inconsistent with the Anglo-American tradition and have no place in a free society.

These reform measures should be only the beginning of a fundamental reexamination of the role of the federal government, as well as the role of the criminal sanction, in American law.

CHAPTER 14

THE SOCIOLOGICAL ORIGINS OF "WHITE-COLLAR CRIME"

John S. Baker, Jr.[1]

Are millions of middle-class Americans really white-collar criminals? The unauthorized importation of prescription drugs from a foreign country is a federal crime. So is "sharing" copyrighted material without permission. Assisting someone in the commission of a federal crime is also a federal crime. Countless American seniors purchase prescription drugs from Mexican and Canadian pharmacies. Millions of Americans, including teens using family computers, share copyrighted music without paying for it.

According to the Department of Justice, "White-collar offenses shall constitute those classes of non-violent illegal activities which principally involve traditional notions of deceit, deception, concealment, manipulation, breach of trust, subterfuge or illegal circumvention." Under that definition, the illegal purchase of prescriptions and pirating music clearly qualify. The Justice Department has recently promoted the idea that enforcement of federal crimes should be uniform. Nevertheless, it is highly unlikely that federal prosecutors will hand down millions (or any) indictments of seniors, parents, and children for these crimes.

Despite the rhetoric, the decision to prosecute is unavoidably discretionary. How do prosecutors determine whom to prosecute? All too often, the choice reflects contemporary politics—and today's criminal *du jour* is the "white-collar" crook. Yet when most people talk about vigorously prosecuting white-collar crime, they don't mean locking up those who purchase medicine from neighboring countries or pirate music over the Internet, despite the fact that such crimes defraud pharmaceutical and music corporations (and thus their shareholders) of billions of dollars.

What accounts for the difference in treatment? The Justice Department's formal definition of white-collar crime disregards class or economic status, but the truth is that in white-collar cases, such distinctions often influence decisions about whether or not to prosecute. Government prosecutors are far more likely to indict the "upper-class" businessman who works for Tyco—or the faceless Arthur Andersen partnership—than a middle-class grandmother who buys medications in Canada. This, at least in part, reflects the socialist origin of the "white-collar crime" concept. The war against white-collar crime stems from and unwittingly embraces a class-based sociological concept of crime—one that may well see a resurgence in the current economic climate.

> The war against white-collar crime stems from and unwittingly embraces a class-based sociological concept of crime— one that may well see a resurgence in the current economic climate.

"White-Collar Crime"

The terms "white-collar crime" and its offshoot, "organized crime," reflect a half-century-old movement to remake the very definition of crime. All of this traces back to the work of Professor Edwin Sutherland, a sociologist who coined the term "white-collar crime" and disagreed with certain basic substantive and procedural principles of criminal law.

In his landmark book, *White Collar Crime*,[2] first published in 1949, Sutherland dismisses the traditional *mens rea* requirement and the presumption of innocence.[3] He claims that the "rules of criminal intent and presumption of innocence…are not required in all prosecution in criminal courts and the number of exceptions authorized by statutes is increasing."[4] If nothing else, such flippant disregard for age-old foundational principles of criminal law should cast doubt on the balance of Sutherland's work.

Sutherland goes on to construct a class-based definition of "white-collar crime." He is concerned with who the alleged perpetrator was more than he is with what that person might have done. "White collar crime," says Sutherland, is "crime committed by a person of respectability and high social status in the course of his occupation."[5] This reorganization of criminal law according to the socioeconomic status of the defendant struck at the very meaning of criminality and the criminal law. In effect, Suther-

> Flippant disregard for age-old foundational principles of criminal law should cast doubt on the work of sociologist Edwin Sutherland, who coined the term "white-collar crime."

land attempted to drain the word "crime" of its very meaning. He subordinated distinctions based on act and intent to those based on the status of the accused.[6] Professor Sutherland's supporters have stated:

> The term white-collar crime served to focus attention on the social position of the perpetrators and added a bite to commentaries about the illegal acts of businessmen, professionals, and politicians that is notably absent in the blander designations, such as "occupational crime" and "economic crime," that sometimes are employed to refer to the same kinds of lawbreaking....[7]

Even his friends acknowledged that Professor Sutherland was "intent upon...pressing a political viewpoint" and that he did so in a "tone...reminiscent of the preaching of outraged biblical prophets."[8]

A Presumption of Guilt

Sutherland claimed that both corporate and individual defendants are routinely deprived of the presumption of innocence in criminal proceedings.[9] To Sutherland, proof of culpability is unimportant. He justifies his mislabeling by alleging that the powerful—despite the lack of criminal procedure protection that he recognizes and celebrates—receive preferential treatment in the legal system.[10] Sutherland's updated 1983 treatise on white-collar crime explains:

> The thesis of this book, stated positively, is that persons of the upper socioeconomic class engage in much criminal behavior; that this criminal behavior differs from the criminal behavior of the lower socioeconomic class principally in the administrative procedures which are used in dealing with the offenders; and that variations in administrative procedures are not significant from the point of view of causation of crime....[11]

> [M]any of the defendants in usual criminal cases, being in relative poverty, do not get good defense and consequently secure little benefit from these rules; on the other hand, the commissions [that enforce certain commercial regulations] come close to observing these rules of proof and evidence although they are not required to do so.[12]

Sutherland intended to provide a basis for facilitating more criminal punishment of executives and corporations by reconceptualizing crime through the term "white-collar crime." He began by equating the "adverse decisions" of regulatory agencies with criminal convictions.[13] As to people involved in business, Sutherland sought to deemphasize the presumption of innocence and the *mens rea* requirement to facilitate establishing their criminal liability.[14]

What Sutherland called a crime was often in truth a regulatory violation.

Yet what Professor Sutherland called a crime was often in truth a regulatory violation. Intent is not normally considered in such enforcement actions; thus, many of Sutherland's "crimes" may have been inadvertent, unintended acts.[15] Nevertheless, Sutherland was determined to classify such acts as crimes.

Stigma Without Sin

Often, when convinced that a person or class of persons is guilty of a crime, people become impatient with legal niceties. Sutherland and others who assume the guilt of much of the business world believe that the ordinary protections of the law need not apply to persons involved in business.[16] When such attempts at prejudgment are directed at any other group—even at terrorists—civil libertarians cry "tyranny." Yet a civil libertarian outcry in defense of corporate defendants appears most unlikely.

Concluding that those engaged in business do not deserve the presumption of innocence, Professor Sutherland dispensed with the essential (and often most difficult to prove) element of crime: a guilty mind.[17] Although it would be unconstitutional to eliminate the presumption of innocence,[18] Sutherland tried to circumvent this by eliminating the mental element requirement.

Sutherland dismissed the most fundamental principles of criminal law in service to his belief that the law unfairly stigmatizes the poor while it does not stigmatize the rich and powerful enough.[19] Claiming that the law should treat the two classes more equally, he wrote:

> Seventy five percent of the persons committed to state prisons are probably not, aside from their un-esteemed cultural attainments, "criminals in the usual sense of the word." It may be excellent policy to eliminate the stigma of crime from violations of law by both the upper and the lower classes, but we are not here concerned with policy.[20]

Sutherland did not seek to eliminate the stigma of crime (although dispensing with the intent requirement should theoretically achieve this goal). Rather, he sought to expand it. The concept of "white-collar crime" has ensured that, in the quest for greater egalitarianism, the stigma of crime has been applied against much of corporate America; but before society stigmatizes and punishes a criminal defendant, the rule of law requires that reliable procedures determine the defendant's culpability. Although some academics might wish it were so, it is not a crime simply to be wealthy or powerful.

> Although some academics might wish it were so, it is not a crime simply to be wealthy or powerful.

By disregarding culpability, Sutherland sought to apply the stigma usually associated with criminal convictions to businesspeople and corporations in non-criminal regulatory proceedings.[21] His book charged that "70 corporations [discussed in his book] committed crimes according to 779 adverse decisions [although] the criminality of their behavior was… blurred and concealed by special procedures."[22]

In Sutherland's view, the complexity of business transactions may make it more difficult to prove criminal activity. But it is equally possible that this complexity was evidence that, in a particular case, no criminal conduct occurred. Without requiring proof beyond a reasonable doubt of a cognizable criminal intent, there is no basis for distinguishing guilty from innocent actions. When prosecutors indict corporations or their executives for federal crimes, relaxed standards for proving criminal intent result in convictions where actual innocence has been "blurred and concealed."[23]

Traditionally, and for good reason, the stigma of crime attaches only to individuals proven to have been "morally culpable" by virtue of having acted with a guilty state of mind.[24] In Sutherland's view, this traditional protection is an antiquated technicality. Rather, culpability should involve an externalized standard of whether a defendant's acts violated the "moral sentiments" of the people.[25] Of course, as the Supreme Court has forcefully stated, the most basic "moral sentiment" is that society not stigmatize persons as criminals unless they are proven to have a guilty mind.

> Culpability should involve an externalized standard of whether a defendant's acts violated the "moral sentiments" of the people.

The contention that an injury can amount to a crime only when inflicted by intention is no provincial or transient notion. It is as universal and persistent in mature systems of law as belief in freedom of the human will and a consequent ability and duty of the normal individual to choose between good and evil. A relation between some mental element and punishment for a harmful act is almost as instinctive as the child's familiar exculpatory "But I didn't mean to."[26]

White-Collar's Sociological Echoes Today

Sutherland and his successors remain deeply influential today, albeit often buried in the subconscious of lawmakers. They have greatly expanded the scope of crime by shifting the focus from particular acts done with specified intents to corporations and individuals in the upper socioeconomic classes.[27]

A lawyer-sociologist critic of Sutherland's work, Paul W. Tappan, long ago noted that Sutherland's definition of crime departed from the legal definition.[28] Tappan charged that this development was a "seductive movement to revolutionize the concepts of crime and [the] criminal...."[29] According to Tappan, Professor Sutherland's definition of "white-collar crime" includes "a boor, a sinner, a moral leper or the devil incarnate but he does not become a criminal through sociological name-calling."[30]

Sutherland's influence is clearly evident in the contemporary substance and practice of federal criminal law. Many federal offenses prosecuted under the label of "white-collar crime" are regulatory or public welfare offenses rather than traditional crimes.[31] The principal architect of the U.S. Sentencing Commission's guidelines for sentencing organizations cites Professor Sutherland's "social science research," among that of others, to explain the need for the guidelines: namely, the "evidence of preferential treatment for white collar offenders."[32]

Indeed, the term "white-collar crime" has expanded even further to include such an array of possible crimes that it has become too amorphous for analysis.[33] Some sociologists, finding even Sutherland's very loose definition "too restrictive,"[34] "have dropped the class of the offender as a relevant element."[35] Thus, "white-collar" crime has now become a division of organizational crime.[36]

One example is the Justice Department's effort to force corporations to waive their privileges of attorney–client confidentiality (as discussed in a later chapter of this book). This is consistent with and sociologically derived from Sutherland's thesis that "white-collar" criminals are not entitled to the same constitutional protections af-

> Many federal offenses prosecuted under the label of "white-collar crime" are regulatory or public welfare offenses rather than traditional crimes.

forded other defendants. Recently and rather remarkably, the Justice Department espoused an essentially class-based view of the law in requesting that the Sentencing Commission disallow departures from the sentencing guidelines for "white collar criminal defendants, who typically have sophisticated counsel."[37]

In short, Sutherland's influence continues to thrive. Indeed, compared to contemporary theoreticians, Sutherland might seem to have been a veritable cheerleader for corporate America. Although mentored by a protégé of socialist Thorstein Veblen,[38] Sutherland "fundamentally was an advocate of free enterprise," albeit a highly regulated form thereof.[39] At the conclusion of his book, he said that the upper class commit many crimes, but he could not say whether "the upper class is more criminal or less criminal than the lower class, for the evidence is not sufficiently precise to justify comparisons and common standards and definitions are not available."[40]

By contrast, and despite a lack of evidence, Sutherland's own protégé, Donald Cressey, has repeatedly preached to college students in his standard college text on criminology that "the people of the business world are probably more criminalistic than the people of the slums."[41] Cressey's views are influential. He was instrumental in the creation of the "enterprise" concept at the core of the Racketeer Influenced Corrupt Organizations (RICO) Act.[42] Supposedly designed to target "organized crime," this statute has been used by prosecutors to indict all kinds of corporations, and private parties have used it to sue most major corporations as well as the Catholic Church.[43] All have been labeled "organized criminals."[44]

And thus, Sutherland's legacy continues to echo today.

––––––––

The origin of the "white-collar crime" concept derives from a socialist, anti-business viewpoint that defines the term by the class of those it stigmatizes. In coining the phrase, Sutherland initiated a political movement within the legal system. This meddling in the law perverts the justice system into a mere tool for achieving narrow political ends. As the movement expands today, those who champion it would be wise to recall its origins, for those origins reflect contemporary misuses made of criminal law: the criminalization of productive social and economic conduct not because of its wrongful nature but, ultimately, because of fidelity to a long-discredited class-based view of society.

> The origin of the "white-collar crime" concept derives from a socialist, anti-business viewpoint that defines the term by the class of those it stigmatizes.

CHAPTER 15

WHAT'S WRONG—AND RIGHT— WITH NEW YORK CRIMINAL LAW

James R. Copland

The growth in criminalization is not limited to the federal government. After all, substantially more than 90 percent of all criminal prosecutions are brought by state and local authorities. We would not expect state legislators and elected state prosecutors to be immune from the siren call of overcriminalization—nor have they been. But it would be impossible in this short volume to survey the overcriminalization efforts in every one of the 50 states, so we have chosen a single state, New York, as an exemplary illustration.

In many respects, New York has followed the national trend in overextending the reach of its criminal law. Its legislature has added new laws and sanctions to the books, many of which do not comport with traditional common-law principles. Included among these new crimes are hosts of regulatory offenses that lie outside the bounds of the state's penal code. The state legislature's actions have not been unilaterally expansive in growing the criminal law—most notably, the legislature earlier this year relaxed the state's Rockefeller drug laws—but the general trend has been to criminalize more conduct.

While the legislative branch has expanded the statutory bounds of what constitutes a crime in New York, the executive branch has leveraged its criminal prosecution powers to regulate, *ad hoc*, vast swaths of business conduct in actions that have national economic implications. Most notoriously, former Attorney General Eliot Spitzer leveraged the state's broad, ambiguous, long-standing Martin Act to threaten the prosecution of investment banks, insurers, and mutual funds.

City of New York photo

Even as the legislature and executive branch have expanded the scope of criminal law, old-fashioned violent and property crimes—some would say "real" crimes—have continued to fall in the Empire State. Driven by precipitous declines in New York City, the number of major crimes reported statewide has fallen every year since 1990, with murders down 71 percent, robberies down 74 percent, and car thefts down 86 percent over the 17-year period ending in 2007.[1] New York today is the safest large state in the nation, with a crime rate roughly one-third lower than that in Illinois and California and half that in Florida and Texas. If the criminal law in New York has outgrown its proper bounds, as this chapter argues, we must approach reform cognizant of the real improvements brought about by reducing violence in the streets, since the state's well-being and future are integrally linked to its decline in violent crime.[2]

The decline in violent crime in New York is attributable to better policing techniques and enforcement. The proliferation of regulatory crimes and enforcement actions threatens rather than enhances the state's ability to sustain positive law-enforcement trends. This chapter first examines the expanded criminal law, both in and out of the penal code, and discusses a few recent changes in the

> The proliferation of regulatory crimes and enforcement actions threatens rather than enhances the state's ability to sustain the decline in violent crime in New York.

state's criminal law. Next, it describes and assesses the state attorney general's regulatory prosecutions of businesses. Then it briefly assesses the recent crime reductions in New York City, which have been driven largely by improved policing techniques. The chapter concludes with proposals for reform.

Legislative Expansions and Contractions of Criminal Law

The Expansiveness of New York Criminal Law

New York has long been a national leader in codifying its criminal law. In 1865, lawyer David Dudley Field submitted to the legislature what would become the state's penal code. Field's code was enacted into law in 1881 and served the state until 1967, when the principles of the Modern Penal Code were codified in the New York Penal Law.[3]

Of late, however, the number of crimes on the state's ledgers has multiplied, both within and outside the penal code. The penal code expressly provides for strict-liability offenses lacking *mens rea*, as well as offenses of omission lacking *actus rea*:

> The minimal requirement for criminal liability is the performance by a person of conduct which includes a voluntary act or the omission to perform an act which he is physically capable of performing. If such conduct is all that is required for commission of a particular offense, or if an offense or some material element thereof does not require a culpable mental state on the part of the actor, such offense is one of "strict liability."[4]

Fortunately, the code does at least establish a default against strict liability unless expressly called for by a statute.[5] Unfortunately, however, strict-liability crimes have proliferated, for offenses ranging from felonies to violations, throughout the New York laws. These crimes are hardly limited to the penal code itself and span both the consolidated and unconsolidated laws. In total, a mind-boggling 65 areas of the consolidated laws outside the penal codes contain criminal offenses,[6] as do at least eight areas of the unconsolidated laws.[7]

> Unfortunately, strict-liability crimes have proliferated, for offenses ranging from felonies to violations, throughout the New York laws.

Some of these laws contain "catch-all" provisions making any breach of the voluminous regulations a criminal offense. For instance, the Environmental Conservation Law contains a provision stipulating that "a person who violates any provision of the environmental conservation law, or any rule, regulation or order promulgated pursuant thereto, or the terms or conditions of any permit issued thereunder, shall be guilty of a violation" punishable by 15 days in prison for *each day* a violation occurred: An individual in breach of a regulation for a year, in other words, could face up to 15 years in jail.[8] The Agricultural and Markets Law, Insurance Law, and Labor Law similarly make any breach of any of their provisions at least a misdemeanor.[9]

As if criminalizing the vast expanse of regulations were not problematic enough, New York also empowers municipalities and regulatory agencies—ranging from the Department of Environmental Conservation to the Department of Health to the Department of Transportation—with criminal rule-making authority. In New York today, it is essentially impossible to be on notice for crimes one might be committing, and everyone is likely guilty of some criminal infraction on a regular basis.

The notice problem is not, however, limited to the proliferation of criminal penalties. Many criminal statutes in New York are themselves so ambiguous as to make it essentially impossible for anyone to know *ex ante* whether he is committing a crime even if fully aware of the statute's existence and prohibitions.

For example, New York's infamous Martin Act, the provision of the General Business Law employed by Eliot Spitzer to prosecute Wall Street's financial titans, criminalizes not only false statements, but also any "promise or representation as to the future which is beyond reasonable expectation or unwarranted by existing circumstances"[10]—a prohibition so meaningless and subject to hindsight bias as to make it enforceable against almost any business executive making public statements that turn out to be false after the fact. Unlike the federal securities laws, the Martin Act has no requirement of an intent to defraud, no requirement that anyone relied on the alleged fraud, no requirement that anyone was injured by the fraud, and no requirement that any securities transaction took place.

> In New York today, everyone is likely guilty of some criminal infraction on a regular basis.

New York's criminal law also gives prosecutors heavy clubs through ill-defined crimes that add penalties when paired with other overlapping violations. Examples are the "enterprise corruption" portion of the Penal Law[11]— New York's analogue to the federal Racketeer Influenced and Corrupt Organizations (RICO)

> New York's criminal law also gives prosecutors heavy clubs through ill-defined crimes that add penalties when paired with other overlapping violations.

Act—and the Penal Law's money-laundering provisions,[12] also similar to federal statutes. Each creates felony offenses. While these laws are lumped under "organized crime" and were intended to and have been used to prosecute mob activity, they are sufficiently vague as to permit prosecutions of ordinary business activities deemed fraudulent, and prosecutors have used them to go after stock brokerages and executives such as Tyco's Dennis Kozlowski. Even if some of these targets were guilty of a crime, the stretching of anti-mob statutes to prosecute such activities gives government prosecutors substantially more leverage than they would have if limited to the underlying, predicate offenses.

Recent Legislative Activity

In recent years, New York's legislature has continued to expand the reach of the criminal law by adding new offenses, expanding existing offenses to include new conduct, heightening penalties for various crimes, and lengthening or eliminating statutes of limitation. In 2008, the legislature passed 41 acts generally expanding the Penal Law.[13] New additions to the penal code principally toughened criminal sanctions for real offenses, coming down hard against sex offenders and child abductors, those who defrauded the elderly, and those committing other frauds, including mortgage fraud. Some of the new laws, however, were questionable at best.

For example, the legislature expanded the state's already problematic "hate crimes" statutes to include electronic media like compact discs and DVDs.[14] Although there is no principled reason that such media should not be treated like traditional written communication generally, the state's hate-crime laws remain deeply troubling.

New York's criminal offense of "aggravated harassment" subjects someone to potential imprisonment if he "communicates with a person, anonymously or otherwise…in a manner likely to cause annoyance or alarm."[15]

> New York's criminal offense of "aggravated harassment" subjects someone to potential imprisonment if he "communicates with a person, anonymously or otherwise...in a manner likely to cause annoyance or alarm."

Obviously, "annoying speech" is protected under the First Amendment, but that did not deter the legislation's sponsor, Assemblyman Mike Spano (D–Yonkers), who remarked, "Causing fear and annoyance to anyone should be illegal, and this legislation provides some solace to those who are the subject or target of hate and discrimination."[16] Thankfully, New York's courts have failed to apply the aggravated-harassment statute to cases of mere annoyance on constitutional grounds,[17] but the statute as written is so plainly problematic and subject to prosecutorial whim that it should be subjected to a strong challenge to its facial unconstitutionality.

First Amendment concerns also afflicted recent video-game legislation supported by the governor, which passed the State Assembly but failed to move through the Senate. The legislation, A8696, would make it a Class E felony—punishable by as much as four years in prison—to distribute video games to minors that include "depictions of depraved violence and indecent images." As the New York City Bar Association argued in a letter to the legislative committee considering an earlier version of the bill, the requirements are almost certainly unconstitutional.[18]

Another law intending to protect minors did pass in 2007, however, and is at least as problematic as the video-game bill. Chapter 8 of the 2007 laws (A2012/S748) amended a pre-existing statute to criminalize the dissemination of "words or images [of] actual or simulated nudity" to a minor.[19] While the law has an intent requirement, it is ambiguous as to whether the sender has to have knowledge or reason to believe that the recipient is a minor. Thus, the

> One who failed to store a weapon according to the law's provisions could face up to seven years in prison.

law on its face potentially criminalizes dissemination of non-obscene images protected under the First Amendment, though not appropriate for minors, even when the sender thinks that an unknown Internet recipient is an adult.

A 2008 bill that passed the Assembly but not the Senate would take crimes of "possession" to a new level: The so-called Children's Weapon

Accident Protection Act (A76.A) would criminalize storage of an otherwise legal weapon—by someone legally entitled to possess it—if the weapon was not stored according to the law's specifications. One who failed to store a weapon according to this legislation's provisions could face up to seven years in prison. In addition to obvious notice problems, the bill would likely have Second Amendment issues, assuming the Supreme Court decides to extend its recent decision on the scope of the Second Amendment to bind the states.[20]

Notwithstanding the legislative expansion of criminal law in general, the most noteworthy change in New York's criminal laws in the past few years is a dramatic reduction in criminal liability through the overhaul of the 36-year-old Rockefeller Drug Laws. Enacted to combat the perceived growth in drug abuse in the late 1960s and early '70s and named for Governor Nelson Rockefeller, the laws established punishments for possessing a small amount of narcotics that are the equivalent of those for second-degree murder: 20 years to life.[21] Correction Department data show that "[d]rug offenders as a percentage of New York's prison population surged from 11% in 1973 to a peak of 35% in 1994"[22] even as violent crime rates soared. Over time, critics from the left and right alike began to question the wisdom of lengthy incarcerations for non-violent addicts.[23]

After piecemeal changes in the Rockefeller Laws in 2004 and 2005, in April 2009, New York governor David Patterson signed into law a comprehensive reform of New York's harsh drug-law regime.[24] The reforms were designed to facilitate drug treatment for non-violent addicts without other

Under Governor Nelson Rockefeller, New York enacted harsh anti-drug laws in the 1970s.

criminal histories, under special drug court judges, while maintaining stiff sentences for drug offenders who are also involved in other serious crimes.[25] If these reforms work as intended, they will free resources—police, prosecution, and prison—needed to enforce the laws against violent and property crimes while reducing recidivism among incarcerated drug offenders.[26]

Even if New York's overall legislative trend has been toward overcriminalization, the Rockefeller Drug Law reform represents a significant shift away from expanded prosecution of non-violent crimes.

Prosecutorial Abuse Under the Martin Act

Regrettably, many laws remain on the books in New York that exceed the proper bounds of the criminal law. Foremost among them is the now-infamous Martin Act, used as a bludgeon against companies by former Attorney General Eliot Spitzer in his role as the "Sheriff of Wall Street."

In the 1910s and 1920s, at a time when no federal securities fraud law existed, states around the country passed laws intended to combat fraudulent stock brokers who sold unwitting consumers equity in fictitious companies that had no genuine operating business and thus consisted of no more than "the blue sky above." New York's Martin Act, named for legislative sponsor Louis Martin, was one such blue-sky law. The 1933 and 1934 securities laws specifically left these state laws intact, in part because Congress was unsure that its new laws would survive judicial review since the Supreme Court at the time was overturning many pieces of New Deal legislation on constitutional grounds.

Many laws remain on the books in New York that exceed the proper bounds of the criminal law.

New York's original Martin Act was one of the weakest of its kind: Firms under investigation by the attorney general received immunity when they testified or answered questions. In 1925, Attorney General Albert Ottinger successfully pushed the legislature to amend the law to remove the immunity provision. "Spitzer's forebear in many ways, Ottinger sought out high-profile fraud cases and used the Martin Act to shut down the Consolidated Stock Exchange, a lowbrow offshoot of the New York Stock Exchange."[27]

Business groups challenged Ottinger in court, but he won victories that broadened the Martin Act's scope. In *People v. Federated Radio Corp.*,[28] the New York Court of Appeals interpreted the Act's "words 'fraud' and 'fraudulent practices'" very broadly "so as to include all acts, although not originating in any actual evil design or contrivance to perpetrate fraud or injury upon others, which do by their tendency to deceive or mislead the purchasing public come within the purpose of the law." Subsequently:

> [Courts] liberally interpreted every important term in the act—including "security," "material," "public offering," and "fraud"—and have declared that they don't have the authority to review the attorney general's discretion under the act because he is the state's chief law enforcement officer.[29]

The Martin Act got a further "upgrade"—including the addition of criminal as well as civil enforcement powers—in 1955, under Attorney General Jacob Javits. Based in part on broadly worded federal mail-fraud statutes, the "new" Martin Act criminalized misstatements even when no individual had ever been defrauded—or, indeed, when no security had ever been sold. Combining broad civil subpoena powers with real criminal penalties, the Act's almost limitless language invited New York's attorney general to overstep the proper boundaries of law enforcement.

For decades, attorneys general resisted this temptation. Shortly after the revisions of the Martin Act were passed, Jacob Javits headed to the U.S. Senate, and the law had fallen into desuetude until Spitzer dusted it off and fashioned it into his weapon of choice. The Martin Act would become a powerful weapon indeed for Spitzer.

Given the severity of the collateral consequences that attach to a criminal conviction, or even an indictment, prosecutors generally have vast power to coerce behavioral changes in their corporate criminal targets. Corporate executives, often fearful of their own potential criminal liability as individuals, can be placed in a situation that inherently conflicts with their shareholders' interests. Directors, themselves fearful of criminal liability as well as the shareholders' interest in resolving criminal disputes without an actual prosecution, can be placed in a position adverse to a corpora-

> Combining broad civil subpoena powers with real criminal penalties, the Martin Act's almost limitless language invited New York's attorney general to overstep the proper boundaries of law enforcement.

tion's management team. Thus, prosecutors are regularly able to extract meaningful concessions from management and corporate directors in reaction to their prosecutorial inquiries.

With the open-ended Martin Act, Spitzer assumed vast powers to tax and regulate national financial and commercial activity. Spitzer's first targets under the Martin Act were New York's investment banks. As the dotcom bubble burst, Spitzer sought a scapegoat, and he found them in the banks' "sell side" research shops. Some internal documents suggested that banks' client and investment-banking relationships had driven analysts' sunny forecasts for now-busted tech companies, exposing a conflict of interest between the companies' stock analysis and banking divisions.

Rather than steadily and quietly building a case against the banks, Spitzer made his fight public: He directly confronted Merrill Lynch star analyst Henry Blodget on CNBC. Spitzer understood that the Martin Act's vast powers meant Merrill Lynch could put up little resistance, especially with the bank's stock price plummeting. Spitzer not only was able to realize a large financial settlement—he

> With the open-ended Martin Act, Attorney General Spitzer assumed vast powers to tax and regulate national financial and commercial activity.

ultimately took down over $1.4 billion in settlements from New York's 10 biggest investment firms[30]—but also was able to reshape the investment banks' analyst businesses entirely by forcing the banks to adopt firewalls between their research shops and fee-based banking.

Emboldened by this success, Spitzer in 2003 targeted mutual funds for offering trading advantages to bigger clients by allowing hedge funds to trade late—illegally—after the closing bell and by allowing larger investors to get premium execution on trades through "market timing." Spitzer ultimately extracted some $1 billion from the mutual-fund industry in addition to strengthening late-trading prohibitions.

In October 2004, Spitzer announced that he was pursuing civil action—and threatening criminal indictment—against the Marsh & McLennan Companies, a risk and insurance brokerage. Coincident with the civil action, Spitzer announced that two AIG executives had pleaded guilty to a first-degree felony "scheme to defraud."[31] Spitzer had uncovered evidence of bid-rigging, wherein certain individuals had conspired to manufacture fake insurance bids to throw business to a favored customer without actually soliciting competitive bids.

Upon Spitzer's announcement, Marsh's stock dropped 24 percent and AIG's over 10 percent. Within weeks, Marsh's CEO, Jeffrey Greenberg, had resigned. In March 2005, Spitzer extracted an $850 million civil settlement from Marsh, a sum that constituted more than twice the company's net income.

The attorney general then brazenly announced, "The insurance industry needs to take a long, hard look at itself. If the practices identified in our suit are as widespread as they appear to be, then the industry's fundamental business model needs major corrective action and reform."[32] What Spitzer perceived to be a major conflict of interest in the insurance industry was the standard practice of paying commercial insurance brokers "contingent commissions" wherein their commission fee on each sale was based in part on the fees paid to the brokerage firm. Spitzer apparently viewed contingent commissions as central to the incentive structure that precipitated the bid-rigging scam: Because Marsh's brokers were paid in part contingent on the ultimate fee generated to the brokerage house, they had an extra incentive to steer its customers toward AIG's higher-bid insurance offerings.

While Spitzer was correct that brokers being paid a contingent commission do have an incentive to deliver a higher-priced bid to a buying customer, the same is true for any broker operating on a flat commission who similarly has an incentive to maximize sale price—an incentive notably adverse to the interests of the buyer. Spitzer argued, however, that unlike standard flat commissions, the contingent commissions were not transparent to the customer, even though Marsh claimed that they were fully disclosed. Although Spitzer apparently viewed contingent commissions as the insurance industry's analogue to the conflicts of interests he claimed to have found in Wall Street brokerages' research analyst departments, it is worth noting that Marsh's high-end, specialized brokerage mostly served corporate and institutional clients, none of whom seemed concerned with the contingent commission practice.

> The attorney general brazenly announced, "The insurance industry needs to take a long, hard look at itself."

In any event, Spitzer ultimately targeted the company whose employees were involved in the alleged bid-rigging scheme, AIG, and specifically Hank Greenberg, the company's chairman and CEO dating back to the late 1960s. Some of the allegations Spitzer hurled at Greenberg in his media campaign bordered on the bizarre, including inquiries into Greenberg's management *in the early 1970s* of the Starr Foundation, the charity established by AIG's founder that Greenberg manages. Ultimately, charges centered on alleged sham reinsurance transactions entered into between AIG and General Re, a reinsurer owned by Warren Buffett's Berkshire Hathaway.

Long before the criminal laws ensnared him, New York Attorney General Eliot Spitzer used the Martin Act to criminalize any misstatement, even if no victims were harmed.

In March 2005, under pressure from Spitzer, the AIG board forced Greenberg to resign. In 2008, four former employees of General Re and one former employee of AIG were convicted in a federal prosecution covering the alleged sham transactions, and these transactions also formed the substantive basis for the Securities and Exchange Commission's later settlement with Greenberg—though, notably, they made out no case of civil let alone criminal fraud against the former CEO.

All told, the Spitzer prosecutions under the Martin Act—and those recounted here are only among the largest and most prominent examples—exacted quite a toll. Some of the conduct Spitzer investigated was indeed worthy of inquiry. For instance, if insurance companies submitted "phantom bids" intended to price-fix the market, as Spitzer alleged, such actions warrant prosecution. But the attorney general's visible, public, frontal assault on Wall Street, while in his own political self-interest, did his constituents little good: The very Wall Street companies that Spitzer targeted represented the lifeblood of the state's economy, perhaps to a fault: By 2007, the securities industry accounted for 3 percent of the state's employment but 9 percent of its economy and 20 percent of its tax revenues.[33]

Moreover, the process through which Spitzer reached his ultimate regulatory end subverted the rule of law. As Professor Henry Manne, a founder of the law and economics movement, opined in *The Wall Street Journal*:

> Mr. Spitzer has introduced the world to yet a new form of regulation, the use of the criminal law as an in terrorem weapon to force acceptance of industry-wide regulations. These rules are not vetted through normal authoritative channels, are not reviewable by any administrative process, and are not subject to even the minimal due-process requirements our courts require for normal administrative rule making. The whole process bears no resemblance to a rule of law; it is a reign of force.[34]

Even in cases in which Spitzer identified actual criminal misconduct, there is little reason to be confident that the changes he coercively imposed—adjusting actual business practices and replacing CEOs—did not, in at least some cases, severely compromise the economic model of the business or industry he targeted and perhaps the customers of the firms he was theoretically trying to protect.

Take, for instance, contingent commissions. Purchasers of insurance have many interests apart from minimizing their premium price, including the terms of the contract and the creditworthiness of the insurer. Contingent commissions can serve as a proxy—a useful non-price sorting mechanism—for capturing precisely such non-price concerns.[35] As a result of Spitzer's investigations, contingent commissions have now been eliminated from the insurance brokerage industry, but it is far from clear that such brokerages' customers are better off as a result.

> The process through which Spitzer reached his ultimate regulatory end subverted the rule of law.

Similarly, it is somewhat ironic that many of the businesses Spitzer targeted in his investigations and settlements ultimately imploded in the 2008 financial crisis. One explanation of this outcome would redound to Spitzer's credit: The managements of the companies Spitzer targeted were dishonest, so it is hardly surprising that they took excessively risky gambles with their shareholders' money.

The problem with this explanation is that Spitzer in many cases effected a change of corporate management—sometimes directly—in his role as businesses' heavy-handed "sheriff." There is some reason to believe that by encouraging corporate boards to replace seasoned, results-oriented managers with leaders more focused on regulatory compliance—and on placating the attorney general—Spitzer may have contributed inadvertently to companies' waning risk-management practices.

Consider AIG. Greenberg's successor, Martin Sullivan, admits that upon taking the company's reins, he "focused on other priorities including repairing AIG's standing with customers and regulators [and] cooperating with several government probes."[36] Over the nine-month period after Greenberg departed, the company wrote as many credit-default swaps as it had in the previous seven years combined, and that position ultimately forced the company to the brink of bankruptcy and into government receivership. While it is certainly possible that AIG would have amassed the same large derivative position had Greenberg remained at the helm, the long-serving CEO had a proven track record of monitoring the financial-products group's risk.

> **Spitzer may have contributed inadvertently to companies' waning risk-management practices.**

David Havens, a credit analyst with UBS, insists, "Had Hank Greenberg still been running the company, I think it's pretty safe to say the situation wouldn't even be close to what is now."[37]

The risks of a statute like the Martin Act have proven themselves too much to bear. Spitzer's successor, Andrew Cuomo, has continued to pursue Martin Act investigations, albeit with more discretion and care rather than as a public spectacle.[38] Still, as Cuomo issues subpoenas to executives from the latest crisis, like Bank of America CEO Ken Lewis,[39] it is still an open question how far the current attorney general will use the Martin Act's vast powers.

A Record of Real Crime-Fighting Success

The most salient change in criminal law in New York over the past 15 years is neither the proliferation of statutory offenses nor the abusive Martin Act prosecutions by the attorney general's office. Instead, the remarkable, precipitous drop in violent and property crime in the state—well beyond crime declines nationally or any other large city—is cause for both celebration and analysis. Before we look to pare back criminal laws and tie prosecutors' hands, we must assure ourselves that the project we undertake

The NYPD has developed a new, more successful model of crime fighting.

will not undo the real progress made in reversing crime trends that had made New York City virtually unlivable.

Although it is not plausible to link New York's declines in violent crimes with Spitzer's Martin Act prosecutions, which followed much of the drop in crime rates and were wholly unrelated to violent crime itself, we cannot reject out of hand the hypothesis that the statutory expansion of criminal law is somehow linked to New York's amazing crime record. The evidence, however, belies such a theory.

From 1990 to 2007, all major violent and property crimes—murder, rape, robbery assault, larceny, burglary, and auto theft—fell dramatically in New York State.[40] All told, these crimes fell from 6,364 per 100,000 residents in 1990 to 2,393 per 100,000 residents in 2007, a drop of 62 percent.[41] Critically, however, this state-wide decline has been driven exclusively by declines in New York City: "violent crime within New York City has decreased by 71% since 1990 while violent crime outside of New York City has not changed significantly."[42]

> "Violent crime within New York City has decreased by 71% since 1990 while violent crime outside of New York City has not changed significantly." The difference is policing.

If New York State's expansion of crimes on the books contributed materially to the drop in statewide crime rates, we would expect the results of the statutory crime expansion to be felt statewide, not merely in the state's large metropolis. The data can only lead to a conclusion that my colleague Heather Mac Donald is correct: The difference is policing.[43]

The New York Police Department's record of success owes to two main factors. First, under the leadership of Chief William Bratton and Mayor Rudy Giuliani, the department embraced an idea posited by George Kelling and Catherine Coles: "fixing broken windows."[44] It may seem odd for a critic of overcriminalization to extol the virtues of enforcing petty crimes like vandalism, public urination, and jumping subway turnstiles, but enforcing "quality of life" criminal offenses is not the same as criminalizing regulatory offenses, engaging in harassing pursuit of corporate enterprises, or throwing hefty sentences on non-violent offenses.

> Breaking a window and skipping a subway fare are universally understood to be criminal, if petty. Enforcing such rules not only has the benefit of creating a climate of lawfulness, but also helps capture more hardened criminals.

Breaking someone else's window and skipping a subway fare are universally understood to be criminal, if petty. Enforcing such rules not only has the benefit of creating a climate of lawfulness, but also helps capture more hardened criminals. Virtually everyone is guilty of breaking one of thousands of state and federal offenses, but not everyone breaks windows. It turns out that those who commit petty crimes are much more likely to be those who commit serious crimes, and by curbing petty crimes, police apprehend suspects for more serious offenses.

The second major policing innovation employed by the NYPD is Compstat, New York's data-driven crime-fighting brain trust that crunches numbers to understand how best to allocate resources and measure results:

> For each week's session, Compstat analysts pore over every statistic in the precinct scheduled for review—outstanding warrants and wanted cards, fingerprint hits, parolees in the area.... Compstat is an unmatched mechanism for disseminating the department's cumulative knowledge about tactics and for evaluating what does and doesn't work.[45]

In a sense, the NYPD's success with Compstat is a shining example of importing private sector–style measures—data and accountability—to make government work more efficiently. When violent and property crimes fall as much, as consistently, and over such a period as they have in New York City, the program is working well.

Conclusion and Recommendations

The NYPD's success in curbing New York City crime offers a template for tackling the issue statewide. Rather than adding hosts of new crimes to already convoluted statutes—and pursuing open-ended Martin Act and enterprise corruption prosecutions against businesses—New York State should work vigorously to import the city's police program to other communities.

New York's Finest has already successfully exported its diaspora: NYPD alumni have helped to clean up Los Angeles; Philadelphia; Lawrence, Massachusetts; Raleigh, North Carolina; East Orange and Newark, New Jersey; and satellites to the city's north like White Plains, Mount Vernon, and Yonkers. Not only have the NYPD's approaches traveled well, but they have met with some extraordinary results: From 2003 to 2007, major crimes fell in East Orange by 67 percent, including a 68 percent drop in homicides.[46]

> As New York increases its pursuit of real criminals, it should pare back, simplify, and integrate its criminal law to conserve resources and preserve individual liberty.

As New York increases its pursuit of real criminals, it should pare back, simplify, and integrate its criminal law to conserve resources and preserve individual liberty. Reforming the Rockefeller Drug Laws is a good start, but the state should seriously consider other reforms as well:

- *Consolidate all crimes within the Penal Code.* Both the Model Penal Code and New York's version constrain lawmakers to contemplate how a new crime fits within the totality of the criminal law. Hosts of duplicative, overlapping, vague, and illogical crimes scattered throughout the consolidated and unconsolidated laws—not to mention the regulations of localities and regulatory agencies—frustrate rather than facilitate the criminal law's ends.

- *Eliminate "default" criminal rules.* Too many New York laws outside the Penal Code have "default" criminal provisions converting any regulatory violation into a crime. By and large, such violations should be civil, not criminal, and the legislature should have to decide expressly to make an action criminal. Default criminality for large, complex regulatory schemes not only spreads scarce resources too thin, but also ensures that essentially everyone is a criminal and thus vests too much discretion in prosecutors' hands.

- **Subject all new crimes to rigorous vagueness and constitutional review.** The legislature is passing too many crimes that give inadequate notice to offenders and run afoul of constitutional norms. All new laws, but particularly crimes, should be subjected to more thorough review.

- **Amend the Martin Act and Enterprise Corruption Laws.** Many laws in New York are vague and expansive, but the Martin Act has proven uniquely susceptible to abuse. The legislature should scale back the Act's provisions and, in particular, sharply limit the scope of criminality under the Act. In addition, the enterprise corruption laws should be limited to their original purpose: targeting organized crime.

- **Constrain the attorney general and other prosecutors.** Prosecutors should build their case before they launch it rather than launching a public attack to generate leverage over their targets, who may be guilty of no criminal wrongdoing. The legislature should adopt clear rules of conduct to constrain prosecutorial abuse.

CHAPTER 16

RECENT OVERCRIMINALIZATION DEVELOPMENTS IN TEXAS

Marc A. Levin

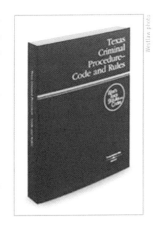

In Texas, criminal law is not just for criminals anymore—at least not criminals as they have been traditionally defined. There are currently 779 Texas statutes that contain the word "misdemeanor," but only 64 of these instances are in the Penal Code or Code of Criminal Procedure. Likewise, the word "felony" appears 418 times in Texas statutes, but only 64 of these occurrences are in the Penal Code or Code of Criminal Procedure. The vast majority of the remaining 1,069 references to felonies or misdemeanors involve the existence of criminal offenses in areas such as agriculture, health care, natural resources, and insurance.

The blurring of civil and criminal law is not a novel development in Texas, but rather part of a national trend. More than 18 years ago, in 1991, Columbia University Law Professor John Coffee observed, "The dominant development in substantive federal criminal law over the last decade has been the disappearance of any clearly definable line between civil and criminal law."[1] Coffee added, "[T]his blurring of the border between tort and crime predictably will result in injustice, and ultimately will weaken the efficacy of the criminal law as an instrument of social control."

In the most recent three Texas legislative sessions, many new proposals emerged for criminalizing conduct traditionally addressed through the free

market or civil law. Proposed legislation would have criminalized everything from failure to recycle any piece of electronics equipment to placing
a business sign on a rural road and even leaving a dog tethered to a tree for
a total of eight hours in a 24-hour
period. Other bills would have increased the criminal penalties for
existing offenses. For example,
legislation would inexplicably make unscrupulous business practices relating to construction or repair of homes a state jail felony, while such
practices would remain a misdemeanor in all other industries.

> If you don't register Fido with Texas, you're now a crook.

Fortunately, all of these measures were defeated. However, the legislature did enact a statute authorizing the Texas Animal Health Commission
to implement the National Animal Identification System (NAIS) being
forced upon states by the U.S. Department of Agriculture and creating a
Class C misdemeanor for failure to comply. If you don't register Fido with
Texas, you're now a crook.

Despite the usual slew of bills that would expand criminal law, the 79th
Legislature commendably acted to rein in overcriminalization by prohibiting local strict-liability criminal ordinances (that is, crimes without any
criminal intent) if punishable by more than a $500 fine. Also laudably,
the legislature reformed the public school zero-tolerance law to allow a
child's intent to be considered in deciding whether expulsion is appropriate and limiting the use of city nuisance laws to criminalize law-abiding
businesses that are victimized by crime.

The Distinction Between Civil and Criminal Law in Texas

In many ways, civil law is a scalpel and criminal law is an anvil. Civil
law, commonly referred to as tort law, seeks to balance the benefits and
costs of the conduct at issue, while criminal law passes moral judgment
and therefore generally eschews
any such balancing. Because it
is based on moral condemnation rather than a balancing of
interests, criminal law tends to
be an overly blunt instrument

> In many ways, civil law is a scalpel and criminal law is an anvil. Criminal law tends to be an overly blunt instrument for regulating business activities.

for regulating business activities, particularly activities not done with intent to defraud.

Texas Criminal Offenses
Texas Penal Code, Title III, Ch. XII

Offense Level	Maximum Penalty
Capital Felony	Death
First Degree Felony	Life in Prison, $10,000 Fine
Second Degree Felony	20 Years in Prison, $10,000 Fine
Third Degree Felony	10 Years in Prison, $10,000 Fine
State Jail Felony	2 Years in State Jail, $2,000 Fine
Class A Misdemeanor	One Year in County Jail, $4,000 Fine
Class B Misdemeanor	180 Days in County Jail, $2,000 Fine
Class C Misdemeanor	$500 Fine

Although the modern trend toward punitive damages has injected a punitive component into civil law, the centrality of punishment remains a distinguishing feature of criminal law. The most notable form this punishment takes is, of course, incarceration. While incarceration is traditionally associated with violent crime, half of all Texans behind bars are there for non-violent offenses. The Texas Court of Criminal Appeals recently noted that Class C misdemeanors "are still crimes, and the fact is the person charged can be arrested on warrant like any ordinary criminal, forced to travel a long distance to attend the court, remanded in custody and imprisoned in default of payment of the fine."[2] Moreover, conviction for a criminal offense other than a speeding ticket also exacts punishment by pinning a scarlet letter on the offender, which often makes it difficult for the individual to obtain employment, housing, and other benefits.

Another distinction between the two systems of law is that criminal law, because it is enforced entirely by state prosecution, tends to minimize the importance of the harm to the victim. In contrast, the victim

> Another distinction between criminal and civil law is that criminal law tends to minimize the importance of the harm to the victim.

plays a much larger role in civil law because enforcement often comes through administrative complaints or lawsuits filed by affected individuals. As a result, criminal laws may be enforced less frequently because enforcement is entirely dependent on the discretion of local prosecutors. And that discretion may be exercised in ways that few Texans are aware

The dome of the Lone Star State capitol building.

of; for example, one Texas legislator recently noted that, despite a few high-profile cases, local prosecutors have a general policy of not enforcing criminal violations of Texas election laws.[3]

Traditionally, civil and criminal law have also been distinguished by the requirement that a criminal must have a guilty state of mind, expressed in the Latin term *mens rea*. As one court explained, "[T]he concept of *mens rea* can be traced to Plato and, since the Middle Ages, has been an integral part of the fabric of the English common law from which we have drawn our own criminal and constitutional analysis."[4] Legal scholar Henry Hart has demonstrated that America's Founders were influenced by the writings of Blackstone in their belief that individual blameworthiness is a prerequisite for the application of criminal law.[5]

Another traditional difference between civil and criminal law is the role of *respondeat superior* in civil law. Under this principle, a corporation or supervisor can be held liable for conduct committed by an employee in the scope of his employment. While the U.S. Supreme Court has extended this concept to strict-liability criminal laws (e.g., public welfare offenses), it remains inapplicable to most criminal law violations by employees.[6] Consequently, criminal laws affecting small businesses are more likely than civil penalties to have the often unintended effect of punishing rank-and-file employees while letting the business and its executives, who may the most responsible, off the hook.

Legislative Alternatives to Criminal Law

As the Texas legislature considers new criminal laws, it often neglects to consider better, more efficient alternatives. A review of the legislative debates finds, sadly, precious little consideration of these factors:

> The Texas legislature often neglects to consider better, more efficient alternatives to new criminal laws.

- Is a state law necessary at all? Or is regulation of the subject best left to the free market or local entities? For example, the market has developed various institutions and mechanisms for protecting consumers from deceptive trade practices, including voluntary certification regimes such as Underwriters Laboratories for electronics and local Better Business Bureaus. Some residential activities, such as those involving noise, ambient light, and burning refuse, may be better addressed by local governments or deed restrictions.

- Can an administrative process be used to impose a fine instead of creating criminal misdemeanors? This approach is likely to be more efficient for the state to enforce. Unlike a criminal charge that always requires a prosecution to be brought in court, agencies can impose civil fines through an administrative proceeding. The respondent can appeal to a hearings examiner, to an administrative judge, and finally to state district court, but because none of these appeals are pursued in most cases, the state can achieve significant savings and clear the dockets of state courts so that they can hear more serious matters without protracted delays.

- Can the state utilize other civil penalties to enforce civil laws? Among the most effective are suspension or forfeiture of a state license or permit. When the conduct at issue involves an occupation or activity for which such a license or permit is required, this approach is particularly useful.

- Finally, for some activities that are criminalized or for which criminal penalties are being considered, would creation of a private civil cause of action be appropriate to provide a remedy for someone who is truly being harmed unjustifiably by the activity at issue? One advantage of this approach is that it empowers the victims of the conduct at issue to seek enforcement of the law rather than simply relying on police and prosecutors.[7]

Overcriminalization in the Texas Legislature

The Texas legislature seems little interested in these possibilities. Instead, as recent developments indicate, the trend toward overcriminalization continues almost unabated. Fortunately, in Texas (unlike many other states), a number of overcriminalization efforts have failed, most likely as a result of traditional Texan suspicion of government. A review of these recent developments can be divided into the following categories:

> **Fortunately, in Texas (unlike many other states), a number of overcriminalization efforts have failed, most likely as a result of traditional Texan suspicion of government.**

- General Business Activities;
- Alcohol, Fireworks, and Other Regulated Business Activities;
- Occupational Licensing;
- Non-Economic Activities;
- School Discipline; and
- Penalties for Different Offense Classes.

General Business Activities

A number of legislative proposals have been made to create a criminal offense, or adjust existing criminal penalties, for various business activities. For example, House Bill 3, the omnibus tax bill in the 79th legislative session that ended in May 2005, would have created a Class A misdemeanor for businesses that deduct from employee wages the new payroll tax created in the legislation. Aside from the question of whether it is good tax policy to mandate that businesses hide the tax burden that the government is imposing on workers, the bill failed to define "deduction." Thus, it is possible a court could determine that a decline in wages, or in the rate of increase in wages, was a deduction even if it was not explicitly indicated as such on an employee's pay stub. Funds are fungible, and many businesses would have had no choice but to scale back their budgets in many areas, particularly labor since that is what is being taxed, in order to maintain profitability. Moreover, because this bill also includes civil penalties for deducting the tax from wages, the criminal penalty was arguably unnecessary.

Another failed bill in the 79th session, House Bill 33, would have made a deceptive business practice relating to construction or repair of homes a state jail felony, while similar offenses in other areas would remain Class C misdemeanors. The difference is significant. While a Class C misdemeanor is punishable by a maximum $500 fine, a state jail felony results in up to two years in a state jail. Deceptive business practices are broadly defined in Texas and would include misstating the composition of a material used in building or repairing a home or its geographical origin. While

> While discouraging misleading business sales tactics is a laudable goal, sending offenders to jail is a draconian remedy.

discouraging misleading business sales tactics is a laudable goal, sending offenders to jail is a draconian remedy, especially since the Texas Deceptive Trade Practices Act generally does not require that the consumer prove that the defendant intentionally or knowingly committed a violation.

House Bill 891, which also failed in the 79th session, would have made auto sellers, even private-party sellers of used cars, subject to a Class A misdemeanor (and a third or second degree felony for multiple offenses) for failure to provide a written statement to purchasers stating whether an air bag had inflated. This penalty would have applied without regard to whether or not the airbag had in fact previously inflated, whether it was defective as a result, or whether such defect compromises future occupant protection in any actual collision. The legislation also failed to consider that a seller may have no way of reliably determining whether an airbag had deployed while the vehicle was driven by another owner.

Farmers and ranchers face criminal penalties under House Bill 1361, passed in the 79th session, if they fail to register their premises and all of their animals with the state. This legislation, which is now law, created a Class C misdemeanor (and a Class B misdemeanor for multiple offenses) for failure to register a premises or an animal. The bill empowers the Texas

Animal Health Commission to create and implement a registration program consistent with the National Animal Identification System (NAIS). Legislators explained that they had no choice but to implement an animal identification program in Texas, since otherwise the federal government would impose its own regime, which stems from fears of mad-cow disease and bioterrorism.

The new law is a nightmare for small farmers and ranchers, who must tag and register every animal.

Compliance is a nightmare for small farmers and ranchers, who must register their premises and tag and register every animal. Moreover, they must report within 24 hours any missing animal, any missing tag, the sale of an animal, the death of an animal, the slaughter of an animal, the purchase of an animal, the movement of an animal off the farm or homestead, or the movement of an animal onto the farm or homestead. After a torrent of criticism from small farmers and ranchers, the Texas Animal Health Commission decided in April 2006 to postpone consideration of the program until 2007.

As this book goes to press, the program is still awaiting implementation, and the federal government is trying to bribe Texas to implement the program by offering a subsidy. Whether the NAIS program becomes a re-

Soon it may be a crime if you fail to register your cattle in Texas.

ality remains very much an open question. The threat of a criminal record for failure to get with the program remains, however, very real.

House Bill 599 in the 79th session would have created a misdemeanor for individuals who post business signs on rural roads without a permit, in addition to existing civil penalties and the ability of the state to obtain injunctive relief. The bill was defeated on the Senate floor.

Some bills that would have created new criminal penalties seemed like nothing more than an attempt to protect a certain industry or occupation. House Bill 1200 in the 79th session would have made it a Class C misdemeanor for distributors of soft drinks and cigarettes to enter into a promotional agreement with retailers for a special advertising or distribution service. Similarly, House Bill 1500 and Senate Bill 246 would have created a Class C misdemeanor for selling tickets to an event for more than the face value unless the person's primary occupation is as a ticket broker. All three of these bills failed; perhaps no legislator could explain why scalping tickets should be a crime only if the scalper does not do it for a living.

In the 79th session, legislators also rejected House Bill 1359 and its companion Senate Bill 564, both of which would have created a Class C misdemeanor for a person who disposes of any electronic equipment in a landfill.

Unlike most bills in this category that target business, House Bill 3052 would have created a sliding scale of criminal penalties—up to a state jail felony for amounts over $1,500—on buyers who avoid payment on a retail installment transaction. While consumers should pay their bills, creditors already have recourse against debtors through the civil justice system.

Amidst the many bills that would have worsened the overcriminalization problem, a major bright spot in the 79th session was House Bill 1690,

> While consumers should pay their bills, creditors already have recourse against debtors through the civil justice system.

which reined in the power of cities to criminally charge business owners with maintaining a public nuisance. The bill, sponsored by Representative Terry Keel and signed into law by Governor Rick Perry, came in response to complaints by business owners that the City of Dallas had abused its public nuisance law, which, like most nuisance laws, had both civil and criminal components. The Dallas law enabled the city to fine the property owner $500 for each day while the nuisance exists, remove the nuisance by police action if not abated, and place a lien on the real estate.

Representative Keel told *The Quorum Report* that Dallas has used the law to punish local businesses simply because they happened to be located in high-crime areas such as the Stemmons Freeway corridor and that the ordinance was being used by Dallas as a revenue enhancement tool. Representative Terri Hodge spoke of a case in her district where a car wash in a low-income neighborhood was targeted even though those running the car wash had nothing to do with the criminal activity.

Many business owners testified before the legislature about their own experiences. One hotel owner said Dallas police officers told him his problems with the nuisance abatement law would "go away" if the hotel owner were to hire off-duty police officers rather than a private security company and suggested that a business contribute to an elected official's "birthday fund." A hotel owner was told by another officer to perform constitutionally suspect pat-down searches of employees and run criminal background checks on hotel guests.

A hotel owner was told by an officer to perform constitutionally suspect pat-down searches of employees and run criminal background checks on hotel guests.

Keel's bill made several changes in the state law that authorizes local governments to enact public nuisance ordinances.

First, and perhaps most important, it altered the standard for conviction from "knowingly maintaining" a place where crime occurs to "knowingly tolerating criminal activity." In other words, the owner must affirmatively know of and sanction the criminal conduct.

Second, it provided that police calls and other affirmative steps taken by property owners to combat crime cannot be used against them. Some business owners testified that the City of Dallas used their police calls against them in municipal court as evidence that they were aware of the criminal activity.

Finally, House Bill 1690 clarified that only managers of condominiums can be held liable, not all individual residents of complexes, since they lack authority to take anti-crime measures.

Despite vigorous opposition from Dallas Mayor Laura Miller, House Bill 1690 is now law, and the House Criminal Jurisprudence Committee and House General Investigating Committee have published a joint interim report on the bill and the abuses under the Dallas nuisance law that it was designed to remedy.[8]

In the 80th legislative session that concluded in May 2007, the legislature rejected House Bill 553, which would have created a second degree felony (up to 20 years in prison) for a person working at an electric utility that is found to have engaged in "market power abuses." Another bill that failed in the 80th session, House Bill 617, would have required counties to enact construction and remodeling codes. Unlike state regulations governing homebuilders, this proposal would have applied to individuals who remodel their own residence.

The legislature also enacted Senate Bill 1154, which imposed a slew of regulations on metal sellers, including a Class B misdemeanor if a person solicits the purchase of regulated material at a location other than a business location at which the material is produced as a byproduct in the ordinary course of that business. So scrap metal purchase and sale now may become a crime in Texas under certain circumstances.

In the 81st legislative session that ended in May 2009, lawmakers wisely rejected House Bill 1118, which would have allowed populous counties to regulate development and impose criminal penalties. This legislation would have adversely affected property developers. Another proposal

> Scrap metal purchase and sale now may become a crime in Texas under certain circumstances.

that failed in 2009 was House Bill 1234, which would have imposed criminal penalties on sellers of aerosol paint when the can is subsequently used for graffiti—as if they could know how the cans would have been used.

Finally, the legislature rejected Senate Bill 204, which would have banned the serving of foods with transfats and imposed a criminal penalty. Remarkably, 23 of the 30 Senators who cast their votes voted for the bill, but it was not considered by the House of Representatives.

Alcohol, Fireworks, and Other Regulated Business Activities

Criminal penalties applying to regulated business activities are more common and are justified as less objectionable because businesses and individuals involved in these industries might be expected to know that they are subject to extensive state regulation. Moreover, for offenses relating to gambling and obscenity, the majority of Texans may believe that the moral condemnation function of criminal law is an appropriate means to enforce widely shared societal values. Nonetheless, even criminal penalties affecting regulated business activities should be scrutinized to determine whether they are excessive in their scope or degree of punishment and whether civil penalties would be more appropriate.

Sellers of alcohol were the targets of several proposed increases in criminal penalties. House Bill 13 would have increased the penalty for multiple offenses of selling alcohol to a minor from a Class A misdemeanor to a state jail felony. Due to the resulting increase in incarceration, the bill has a fiscal cost of over $1 million, which likely contributed to its failure. Although restricting alcohol sales to minors is a legitimate goal, other sanctions, such as civil fines and revocation of state liquor licenses, might be equally effective as and less costly than incarceration.

> If it had not been defeated, a bill would have created a Class A misdemeanor for the holder of an alcoholic beverage permit to sell a drink with more than one-half an ounce of absolute alcohol in it.

Two other bills imposing criminal penalties on alcohol sellers also failed. In an effort to crack down on Bacchanalian 21st birthday celebrations, House Bill 36 would have made it a Class A misdemeanor to sell alcohol to a minor on his 21st birthday. House Bill 38 would have created a Class A misdemeanor for the holder of an alcoholic beverage permit to sell a drink with more than one-half an ounce of absolute alcohol in it. This would effectively ban king-size beer cans, as these contain more than 12 ounces of beer, which is about 4 percent alcohol by volume. Larger glasses of mixed drinks would also have been prohibited. This bill did not provide a level of culpability for the offense, which means that under Texas Penal Code Section 6.02, the default minimum of criminal negligence would have applied.

These bills would have burdened bars and restaurants, and their employees, with making on-the-spot determinations about the age of the purchaser and the amount of absolute alcohol in a glass, subjecting them to possible jail time should they make a mistake. Finally, the legislature also rejected House Bill 193, which would have created a statewide keg registration system with an accompanying Class C misdemeanor for possessing a keg without a sticker.

The legislature also decided against imposing new obligations and criminal penalties on sellers of fireworks, another highly regulated industry. House Bill 1454 would have created a Class C misdemeanor for selling fireworks to an intoxicated person if the seller does not make a reasonable effort, through breath analysis test or otherwise, to determine whether the buyer is intoxicated. With most fireworks sold at small roadside stands, it would seem unreasonable to ask such sellers to purchase the equipment to conduct a breath analysis test, obtain training for employees to conduct this test, and then properly administer such a test to each buyer—or face a criminal penalty.

In addition to weighing whether to expand state-sponsored gambling in the form of video lottery terminals and casinos, the legislature considered House Bill 103, which would have increased the penalty for possession of gambling paraphernalia from a Class C misdemeanor to state jail felony. The bill had a negative fiscal note of approximately $400,000 due to the resulting increased incarceration costs. While the intent of this bill was to stop the proliferation of illegal eight-liner machines, the existing statute defines gambling paraphernalia to include even a betting slip or other writing. Therefore, as it was written, this bill would have relied upon prosecutorial discretion to avoid sending to jail two friends and sports fans who write down their bets on football games. Legislators decided this was a bad bet, as House Bill 103 was left pending in a House committee.

Another bill would have relied upon prosecutorial discretion to avoid sending to jail two friends and sports fans who write down their bets on football games.

Occupational Licensing

Several bills filed in the past few years would have expanded state occupational licensing to cover additional occupations and subjected those who fail to obtain such licenses to criminal penalties. Government licensing of doctors, lawyers, and other professionals has been justified on the grounds of the special training and expertise required, the knowledge asymmetry between the professional and the consumer of services, and the deleterious consequences of an incompetent provider of such services.

In extending occupational licensing to new areas, legislators must first ask, before even considering the appropriate penalty, whether these same justifications apply to the occupations at issue or whether licensure would simply create a barrier to entry, increasing costs for consumers. If licensing is extended to occupations for which it traditionally has not been a requirement, many individuals in these fields may be unaware of the new law and therefore fail to obtain a license.

House Bill 577 garnered considerable press attention. It would have created a Class C misdemeanor for labeling oneself a meteorologist without meeting certain training criteria set forth in the bill.

The legislature also decided against making residential property managers and interior designers licensed occupations. Senate Bill 926 would have imposed a Class B misdemeanor for failing to register as a residential property manager with the state under the new licensing scheme in the bill. Similarly, House Bill 1649 and its companion Senate Bill 339 would have imposed a Class C misdemeanor for working as an interior designer without a state license.

> Legislators found it challenging to define who is an interior designer, since this occupation falls somewhere in between architects, who are licensed, and interior decorators, who are not.

Legislators found it challenging to define who is an interior designer, since this occupation falls somewhere in between architects, who are licensed, and interior decorators, who are not.

The legislature also rejected bills that would have licensed real estate self-financiers (HB 1042) and roofing contractors (HB 3304) and established criminal penalties.

In the 80th session, completed in May of 2007, the legislature enacted House Bill 463, which creates a licensing and regulatory scheme for air conditioning and refrigeration contractors, with criminal penalties. The legislature also rejected several other proposals.

- House Bill 689 would have created a licensing and regulatory scheme for landmen;

- House Bill 703 would have created a licensing and regulatory scheme for lactation consultants;

- House Bill 1281 would have created a licensing and regulatory scheme for certain journeymen and apprentice sheet metal workers, including requiring 8,000 hours of work experience and authorizing a detailed state written exam with questions on federal air quality standards;

- House Bill 2211 and Senate Bill 1120 would have created a licensing and regulatory scheme for automotive shops, automotive technicians, and automotive service writers, advisers, and estimators;

- House Bill 2764 would have enacted a licensing and regulatory scheme for swimming pool and spa installers; and

- House Bill 1985 and Senate Bill 832 would have created a licensing and regulatory scheme for interior designers, including a fine of up to a $5,000 per day for each day a violation of state rules occurs.

In the 81st session in 2009, fewer occupational licensing bills were filed. One bill, House Bill 1854, would have imposed a licensing scheme and criminal penalties on roofers. Had this legislation passed, roofers would have been required to carry $250,000 in insurance, likely putting some of them out of business.

Non-Economic Activities

Several proposed bills in the 79th session would have criminalized non-economic personal activities not normally associated with a business purpose. While animal cruelty is already appropriately a criminal offense under Section 42.09 of the Penal Code, House Bill 521 would have created a Class A misdemeanor, as well as a state jail felony for multiple offenses, for tethering a dog to a tree or other stationary object on a leash less than 10 feet in length for eight or more hours in a 24-hour period. Though jail time may be appropriate for animal torture, legislators evidently concluded that this well-intentioned bill to protect dogs barked up the wrong tree.

> Though jail time may be appropriate for animal torture, legislators evidently concluded that a well-intentioned bill to protect dogs barked up the wrong tree.

On the other hand, it is the misbehavior of pets, not their owners, that was the subject of House Bill 1096 and its companion, Senate Bill 1111. These bills, which would have applied only to Harris County (the state's largest county, which contains Houston), created a Class A misdemeanor and third degree felony for the owner of a dog that attacks someone if the victim is seriously injured or killed. In so doing, these bills would have dispensed with any level of culpability and, unlike the current law, apply whether or not the dog is categorically dangerous. Moreover, these bills would not have exempted a situation where a burglar or other unauthorized person trespasses an owner's property and is bitten by his dog.

These bills also would have created a Class C misdemeanor and a Class B misdemeanor for owners who escort their dogs without a leash on property other than their own, including that of family members and friends. The overly broad language and excessive criminal penalties in these bills, as well as their limited applicability to one county, suggests that their aims might be better accomplished through locally enacted regulations.

Finally, high school registrars, of all people, were targeted by a criminal penalty under House Bill 2056. This bill would have created a Class C misdemeanor if a high school registrar fails to distribute a voter registration card to each graduating senior who is or will turn 18, as well as a Class A misdemeanor if the registrar's failure to do so was intentional. In this instance, a reprimand from that registrar's supervisor would seem more appropriate than a personal criminal offense for a registrar's failure to perform a new job responsibility mandated by the state.

School Discipline

As detailed in an earlier chapter of this book, school discipline is, for several reasons, an important aspect of the overcriminalization problem. The traditional requirement of *mens rea* is particularly critical in this context, as children, because they are not fully mature, are more prone than adults to making honest mistakes. Furthermore, children are more impressionable than adults, so excessively punishing a child who is not blameworthy can have serious long-term effects on the child's development.

> Children are more impressionable than adults, so excessively punishing a child who is not blameworthy can have serious long-term effects on the child's development.

Finally, from a political standpoint, this issue provides an opportunity to build non-traditional alliances based on shared principles in different contexts, as the legislators most concerned with guarding against overcriminalization in the school disciplinary context are sometimes not as instinctively sympathetic to businesses that face similarly problematic criminal statutes.

In 1995, the legislature passed the zero-tolerance Safe Schools Act, which required the expulsion of students who possess weapons, including any kind of knife, or prescription drugs without school approval. School officials interpreted the law as not providing them with the discretion to apply a lighter punishment to a student who had no culpable mental state.

> The legislature heard testimony about the expulsion of a child because he took Celebrex for his broken knee at lunch.

For example, the legislature heard testimony recently from parents of a student who was expelled for unknowingly bringing a pocketknife to school because it was in the pocket of the same jacket he took to go hunting on the weekend. Another parent testified about the expulsion of her child because he took Celebrex for his broken knee at lunch. These students were removed from their schools by police and banished to Juvenile Justice Alternative Education Programs (JJAEPs), some of which are military-style boot camps.

In the 79th legislative session, House Bill 603 was passed to reform the zero-tolerance law. The legislation, which was signed by Governor Rick Perry, expressly allows school districts to consider whether a student had a culpable state of mind and a prior disciplinary history before imposing a mandatory expulsion. While HB 603 was a step in the right direction, its sponsor, Representative Rob Eissler (R–The Woodlands), continues to hear from parents in his district who say that schools continue to impose zero-tolerance policies without regard to the student's intent or disciplinary history. Eissler, a former school board member, is looking at strengthening this legislation.

Another important bill to rein in zero-tolerance abuses—House Bill 1688, introduced by Representative Harold Dutton—did not pass. It would have changed state law so that a school disciplinary infraction is not automatically a crime if it is not otherwise a violation of any law. The Education Code currently allows school districts to classify any violation of a school district policy, such as a rule in the student code of conduct, as a Class C misdemeanor. As a result, Texas courts are being deluged with thousands of cases involving violations of a student code of conduct that are not otherwise criminal offenses, such as chewing gum or dressing improperly at school. Representative Dutton, a lawyer, defended an eight-year-old girl in municipal court who was issued a Class C misdemeanor by school police for chewing gum.[9]

> Texas courts are being deluged with thousands of cases involving violations of a student code of conduct that are not otherwise criminal offenses, such as chewing gum or dressing improperly at school.

In 2009, the legislature went further, enacting House Bill 171, which requires school districts to take into account the intent of a student, or lack thereof, before suspending or expelling the student.

Penalties for Different Offense Classes

Several bills related to overcriminalization did not address a specific offense but proposed altering the penalties for one or more existing offense classes.

Most significantly, House Bill 970, filed in the 79th session by Representative Terry Keel and now law, prevents cities and counties from enacting Class C misdemeanors that both dispense with any level of culpability and impose a harsher penalty than the $500 maximum fine set by the Penal Code. The default level of culpability in the Penal Code is criminal negligence,[10] but cities and counties are increasingly adopting criminal statutes that explicitly disavow any state-of-mind requirement.

For example, the City of Austin imposes fines of $2,000 for certain Class C Misdemeanors with no culpable mental state required for conviction. At a hearing before the Criminal Jurisprudence Committee, Representative Keel cited a small business that was repeatedly being fined thousands of dollars by the City of Austin because a neighbor's animals, unbeknownst to that business owner, were entering the property. In October 2005, U.S. District Judge Sam Sparks relied upon House Bill 970 in reducing the penalty for violating the City of Austin ordinance banning smoking in bars from $2,000 to $500.

On the other end of the spectrum, House Bill 1762, also filed in the 79th session, would have increased the penalty for all misdemeanors to the next highest level of offense if a conviction is the second or more for the same offense, unless otherwise specified in the statute creating the offense. Had it passed, this bill would have resulted in many misdemeanors becoming felonies upon multiple offenses and would have created either the option or requirement of jail or prison time when it was never intended for the offense in question.

> Decisions regarding enhanced penalties for multiple transgressions are better made as to each specific offense rather than as part of an across-the-board approach that may result in unintended consequences.

Many offenses already include enhanced penalties for multiple transgressions, and where they do not, there may be a good reason for not doing so. This decision is better made as to each specific offense rather than as part of an across-the-board approach that may result in unintended consequences.

The Texas legislature has had a mixed record in the past few years, enacting some laws that exacerbate overcriminalization but also passing some laws that rein in abusive city nuisance laws, reform zero tolerance, and limit local ordinances creating strict criminal liability offenses. Despite these successes, those who are concerned with overcriminalization must remain vigilant, as many failed proposals return in successive legislative sessions.

In debates on legislation, it seems that the penalty portion is often the least scrutinized. When legislators ask the Texas Legislative Council to draft a new law to prohibit some activity or practice, the default approach appears to be the imposition of a criminal penalty. Texas would be better served by the use of specific criteria to determine whether civil or criminal law is a better instrument for addressing the problem.

If criminal law is to be invoked, legislators should carefully consider whether a culpable mental state should be required and, if so, what level of punishment is most appropriate. Criminal statutes must be drafted with precision so that they are not unconstitutionally vague or overbroad and do not cover conduct the legislature may not intend to outlaw.

CHAPTER 17

OVERCRIMINALIZATION AND THE NEED FOR LEGISLATIVE REFORM

Dick Thornburgh[1]

On July 22, 2009, Dick Thornburgh also appeared before the Subcommittee on Crime, Terrorism and Homeland Security of the House Committee on the Judiciary to discuss the topic of "Over-Criminalization of Conduct/Over-Federalization of Criminal Law." Thornburgh is a former Attorney General of the United States and a former governor of Pennsylvania. His testimony, reprinted here, examines the need for legislative reform of criminalization trends.

I have served on both sides of the federal criminal aisle, as a federal prosecutor for many years and currently as a defense attorney involved in proceedings adverse to the Department of Justice. I believe I have a balanced view of the issues before the Committee and hope I can provide some insight and suggest some ideas to deal with the current phenomenon of overcriminalization.

The problem of overcriminalization is truly one of those issues upon which a wide variety of constituencies can agree—witness the broad and strong support from such varied groups as The Heritage Foundation, the Washington Legal Foundation, the National Association of Criminal Defense Lawyers, the ABA, the Cato Institute, the Federalist Society, and the ACLU.

These groups share a common goal: to have criminal statutes that punish *actual criminal acts* and do not seek to criminalize conduct that is better dealt with by the seeking of civil and regulatory remedies. The criminal sanction is a unique one in American law, and the stigma, public condemnation, and potential deprivation of liberty that go along with that sanction demand that it should be utilized only when specific mental states and behaviors are present.[2]

By way of background, let me briefly remind you of some fundamentals of the criminal law. Traditional criminal law encompasses various acts, which may or may not cause results, and mental states, which indicate volition or awareness on the part of the actor. These factors are commonly known as the requirements of *mens rea* and *actus reus*, or an "evil-meaning mind [and] an evil-doing hand."[3]

With respect to what has now become known as "overcriminalization," objections are focused on those offenses that go beyond these traditional, fundamental principles and are grounded more on what were historically civil or regulatory offenses without the mental states required for criminal convictions.

[Other chapters of this book discuss] the *mens rea* requirement for federal crimes and the need to reform statutes that lack such a requirement. Without a clear *mens rea* requirement, citizens are not able to govern themselves in a way that assures them of following the law, and many actors are held criminally responsible for actions that do not require a wrongful intent. Indeed, a recent Federalist Society report states that federal statutes provide for over 100 separate

Although many scholars and the Department of Justice have tried to count the total number of federal crimes, only rough estimates have emerged.

terms to denote the required mental state with which an offense may be committed,[4] and The Heritage Foundation issued a report stating that 17 of the 91 federal criminal offenses enacted between 2000 and 2007 *had no mens rea requirement at all.*[5] This trend cannot continue, and suggested legislative reform in the nature of a default *mens rea* requirement when a statute does not require it is worthy of consideration.[6]

Although many scholars and the Department of Justice have tried to count the total number of federal crimes, only rough estimates have emerged. The current "estimate" is a staggering 4,450 crimes on the books. If legal scholars and researchers and the Department of Justice itself cannot accurately count the number of federal crimes, how do we expect ordinary American citizens to be able to be aware of them?[7] One criminal law expert stated that we can no longer say with confidence the long-standing legal maxim that "ignorance of the law is no excuse," because the average American citizen cannot actually know how many criminal laws there actually are.[8]

We can't show you a picture of Woodsy Owl. Using it without authorization from the federal government is a crime.

Although I could probably spend my whole panel time citing you the often-mentioned, truly absurd examples of overcriminalization, such as using the character of "Woodsy Owl" or the slogan "Give a Hoot, Don't Pollute" without authorization, mixing two kinds of turpentine, or wearing a postal uniform in a theatrical production that discredits the postal service, the dangers of overcriminalization for more serious offenses are real and impact real people such as the individuals before you today and corporations, which I will discuss later in these remarks.

Make no mistake: When individuals commit crimes, they should be held responsible and punished accordingly. The line has become blurred, however, on what conduct constitutes a crime, particularly in corporate criminal cases, and this line needs to be redrawn and reclarified. The unfortunate reality is that Congress has effectively delegated some of its important authority to regulate crime

> The line has become blurred on what conduct constitutes a crime, particularly in corporate criminal cases, and this line needs to be redrawn and reclarified.

in this country to federal prosecutors, who are given an immense amount of latitude and discretion to construe federal crimes, and not always with the clearest motives or intentions.[9]

A striking example of this is the "honest services" mail and wire fraud statute, 18 U.S.C. §1346. That statute has been subject to scrutiny because of its expansion from traditional public corruption cases to private acts in business or industry that are deemed to be criminal almost exclusively at the whim of the individual prosecutor who is investigating the case.

Indeed, in a recent dissenting opinion on a denial of a writ of certiorari in the Supreme Court in an honest services case, Justice Scalia stated that the state of the law for honest services fraud was "chaos" and stated the practical reality of the statute as currently applied:

> Without some coherent limiting principle to define what "the intangible right of honest services" is, whence it derives, and how it is violated, this expansive phrase invites abuse by headline-grabbing prosecutors in pursuit of local officials, state legislators, and corporate CEO's who engage in any manner of unappealing or ethically questionable conduct.[10]

This overbreadth leads to a near paranoid corporate culture that is constantly looking over its shoulder for the "long arm of the law" and wondering whether a good-faith business decision will be interpreted by an ambitious prosecutor as a crime. Perhaps even more significant is the impact on corporate innovation: If an idea or concept is novel or beyond prior models, a corporation may stifle it if they are concerned about potential criminal penalties. This stifling may render some corporations unable to compete in a global marketplace just to ensure compliance with the laws—certainly a "cutting off one's nose to spite the corporate face."

"[I]t is simply not fair to prosecute someone for a crime that has not been defined until the judicial decision that sends him to jail."

Justice Scalia further stated in his dissent that "*[i]t is simply not fair to prosecute someone for a crime that has not been defined until the judicial decision that sends him to jail.*"[11] I couldn't agree more. This type of overbroad, arbitrary use of a federal criminal law demonstrates the dangers of overcriminalization and simply must be remedied.[12]

As noted, the issue of overcriminalization is especially poignant in corporate crime. A corporation is an "artificial entity." The legal persona of a corporation is wholly dependent on the laws that formed it. Thus, a corporation is a stable being separate and distinct from the human beings that perform its functions. The corporation is, in the eyes of the law, very much an *entity*.

Nevertheless, in 1909, the Supreme Court held in a railroad regulation case that a corporation could be held criminally liable for the acts of its agents under a theory of what is known as *"respondeat superior,"* or, in non-legalese, "the superior must answer," or an employer is responsible for the actions of employees performed within the course of their employment.[13]

> In the case of Arthur Andersen, a business entity received effectively a death sentence based on the acts of isolated employees over a limited period of time.

Since 1909, corporations have routinely been held criminally liable for the acts of their employees. In recent history, one of the more significant cases is Arthur Andersen, a case of which the Committee is no doubt aware, in which a business entity received effectively a death sentence based on the acts of isolated employees over a limited period of time. As this case illustrates, this is not a partisan issue—Arthur Andersen was prosecuted under a Republican Administration.

I gave a speech at the Georgetown Law Center in 2007 regarding overcriminalization,[14] and mentioned the Arthur Andersen case and referenced a political cartoon that was published after the Supreme Court reversed the company's conviction in which a man in a judicial robe was standing by the tombstone for Arthur Andersen and said, *"Oops. Sorry."*[15] That apology didn't put the tens of thousands of partners and employees of that firm back to work. This simply cannot be repeated, and reform is needed to make sure there are no future abuses.

What can be done to curb future abuses?

First, I have advocated for many years that we adopt a true Federal Criminal Code. While this may not be the first thing that comes to mind when analyzing the issues of concern in the criminal justice system, it is an important one that should be undertaken without delay. As I mentioned, there are now some 4,450 or more separate statutes—a hodgepodge without a coherent sense of organization. There is a template in existence, the Model Penal Code, that can act as a sensible start to an organized criminal code and has formed the basis for many efforts to establish state criminal codes in this country. What is needed is a clear, integrated compendium of the totality of the federal criminal law, combining general provisions, all serious forms of penal offenses, and closely related administrative provisions into an orderly structure, which would be, in short, a true Federal Criminal Code.[16]

A Commission should be constituted, perhaps in connection with Senator Webb's National Criminal Justice Commission Act, to review the federal criminal code, collect all similar criminal offenses in a single chapter of the United States Code, consolidate overlapping provisions, revise those with unclear or unstated *mens rea* requirements, and consider overcriminalization issues.[17] This is not a new idea: Congress has tried in the past to reform the federal criminal code, most notably through the efforts of the "Brown Commission" in 1971.[18] The legislative initiatives based on that Commission's work failed despite widespread recognition of its worth. It is incumbent on this Congress to seek to make sense out of our laws and make sure that average ordinary citizens can be familiar with what conduct actually constitutes a crime in this country.

> **A Commission should be constituted to review the federal criminal code and consider overcriminalization issues, among other goals.**

Second, Congress needs to rein in the continuing proliferation of criminal regulatory offenses. Regulatory agencies routinely promulgate rules that impose criminal penalties that are not enacted by Congress.[19] Indeed, criminalization of new regulatory provisions has become seemingly mechanical. One estimate is that there are a staggering *300,000* criminal regulatory offenses created by agencies.

This tendency, together with the lack of any congressional requirement that the legislation pass through the judiciary committees—which are responsible for keeping an eye on the rationality of the traditional criminal offenses—has led to an evolution of a new and troublesome catalogue of criminal offenses. Congress should not delegate such an important function to agencies. Indeed, in remedial legislation introduced in 2005 entitled the "Congressional Responsibility Act of 2005," the bill sought to ensure that federal regulations would not take effect unless passed by a majority of the members of the Senate and House and signed by the President.[20] Thus, the bill sought to "end the practice whereby Congress delegates its responsibility for making laws to unelected, unaccountable officials of the executive branch and requires that regulations proposed by agencies of the ex-

> Congress needs to rein in the continuing proliferation of criminal regulatory offenses. One estimate is that there are a staggering 300,000 such offenses created by agencies.

ecutive branch be affirmatively enacted by Congress before they become effective."[21] This type of legislation deserves reconsideration.

In this area, one solution that a renowned expert and former colleague from the Department of Justice, Ronald Gainer, has advocated is to enact a general statute providing administrative procedures and sanctions for all regulatory breaches.[22] It would be accompanied by a general provision removing all criminal penalties from regulatory violations, notwithstanding the language of the regulatory statues, except in two instances. The first exception would encompass conduct involving significant harm to persons, property interests, and institutions designed to protect persons and property interests—the traditional reach of criminal law. The second exception would permit criminal prosecution, not for breach of the remaining regulatory provisions, but for a pattern of intentional, repeated breaches. This relatively simple reform could provide a much sounder foundation for the American approach to regulatory crime than previously has existed.

Third, Congress should also consider whether it is time to address whether "*respondeat superior*" should be the standard for holding companies criminally responsible for acts of their employees. As the Committee is certainly aware, the Department of Justice has issued a succession of memoranda from Deputy Attorneys General during the past 10 years, from one issued by current Attorney General Holder in 1999, to the Thompson Memorandum in 2003 by former Deputy Attorney General Larry D. Thompson, to the McNulty Memorandum in 2006 by former Deputy Attorney General Paul J. McNulty, to the most recent Filip Memorandum authored by former Deputy Attorney General Mark Filip. Although these memoranda have evolved over time and addressed critical issues regarding charging corporations, particularly regarding the protection of the attorney–client privilege, the current guidelines may not be sufficient because they continue to vest an unacceptable amount of discretion in federal prosecutors.[23]

A law is needed to ensure uniformity in this critical area so that the guidelines and standards do not continue to change at the rate of four times in 10 years. Indeed, if an employee was truly a "rogue" or acting in violation of corporate policies and procedures, Congress can protect a well-intentioned and otherwise law-abiding corporation by enacting a law that holds the individual rather than the corporation responsible for the criminal conduct without subjecting the corporation to the whims of any particular federal prosecutor.

Ensuring uniformity is needed in this critical area so that the guidelines and standards do not continue to change at the rate of four times in 10 years.

Before I close, I wanted to commend Chairman Scott and other members of this Subcommittee for your role in securing passage of the Attorney–Client Privilege Act of 2007 in November 2007. The privilege is one that goes back to Elizabethan times, and the preservation of that privilege is something about which I have expressed concern for many years. Mr. Chairman, your recognition of the issue and legislation to stop "coercive waivers" and overreaching to gain access to privileged communications is precisely the type of legislation needed to protect this important privilege.[24]

With respect to the problem of overcriminalization, let me report that reform is needed. True crimes should be met with true punishment. While we must be "tough on crime," we must also be intellectually honest. Those acts that are not criminal should be countered with civil or administrative penalties to ensure that true criminality retains its importance and value in the legal system.

CHAPTER 18

PRINCIPLED, NONPARTISAN STEPS FORWARD

Brian W. Walsh

The earlier chapters of this book have shown us some of the personal horrors of overcriminalization and demonstrated some of the fundamental problems in contemporary criminal law and procedure that cause over-criminalization. The question that naturally arises is "What can be done?" The answer, fortunately, is much—and most of it is not complicated.

There is no substitute for getting back to the basics of a just criminal law. Criminal offenses, with exceedingly few exceptions, should cover conduct that is truly wrongful and should include a meaningful criminal intent requirement that protects from punishment those who engage in that conduct with no intent to do anything wrongful. The number of criminal offenses should be small and knowable by the average person covered by them. The legal rights, procedures, and other protections that were in place in America at the time the Bill of Rights was adopted should be respected, preserved, and enforced.

These basics form the guideposts for successful reform and highlight the need for specific reforms that would restore the sound fundamentals of criminal justice that prevailed before overcriminalization became rampant.

A Principled, Nonpartisan Approach to Criminal Justice

The path that we take to achieve reform of the criminal justice system is at least as important as having the "right" or "best" reform proposals.

In large part, American criminal justice and the federal criminal justice system in particular reached their current distorted and dangerous state because of unfounded theories about the nature and morality of crime and punishment that implicitly or explicitly rejected the development and wisdom of centuries of Anglo-American law.

Despite, for example, the centuries-old criminal intent requirement, which the Supreme Court has described "as universal and persistent in mature systems of law as belief in the freedom of the human will," legislators and interest groups in the middle of the 20th century began agitating for new criminal offenses that included no meaningful criminal intent requirement. Similar thinking also held that criminal law was an apt tool for shaping socially and economically beneficial conduct that certain interest groups, such as environmentalists, claimed were harmful, often without needing to present sufficient evidence to demonstrate such harm.

> In large part, American criminal justice and the federal criminal justice system in particular reached their current distorted and dangerous state because of unfounded theories about the nature and morality of crime and punishment.

Similarly, judges and Supreme Court justices who from the 1950s through 1970s effectively reduced punishments for some violent offenders and made it more difficult for law enforcement to obtain and use valid evidence laid the groundwork for a popular backlash in the 1980s and 1990s that toughened criminal laws and criminal sentences across the board and led to the overcriminalization explosion. Activist trial court judges who adopted novel theories of crime and punishment frequently imposed short, token, or even probationary sentences on violent offenders, even violent sexual offenders. These judges applied criminology theories that blamed "society" for most crimes (especially those committed by individuals coming from disadvantaged backgrounds) and theorized that punishment was an archaic, unprincipled response to crime.

Activist judges, led by the U.S. Supreme Court during Earl Warren's tenure as Chief Justice, fashioned elaborate procedural hurdles that ostensibly implemented the protections of the Bill of Rights and served as prophylactic measures to prevent law enforcement from violating those rights. The exclusionary rule that the Warren Court applied to the 50 states required courts to throw out strong evidence of guilt and overturn convictions based on that evidence when it was obtained in violation of the Court's arcane vision of the Fourth Amendment right against unreasonable searches and seizures.

Both the trial judges who turned convicted criminals out onto the streets with what the public considered to be a slap on the wrist and the Supreme Court justices whose innovative "constitutional" rulings resulted in overturned convictions of some confessed murderers and other violent criminals set the stage for a backlash against these criminal-friendly procedures and punishments. Not only were these

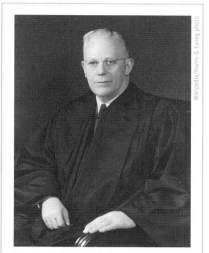

Justice Earl Warren led the Supreme Court to expand many criminal procedural rules.

decisions by the judiciary ill advised and unfounded, but they lacked support from conservatives and others on the political right as well as many members of law enforcement who are otherwise strong supporters of increased law and order.

As a result, it became easy to castigate anyone in favor of legal reforms and anyone who considered themselves to be "tough on crime." Public safety is one of the chief ends of government, and the American people did not take it lightly when the rules regarding who is punished and for how long were changed unilaterally and without their political consent by unelected, unaccountable judges.

> It became easy to castigate anyone in favor of legal reforms and anyone who considered themselves to be "tough on crime."

When these theories led to an increased crime rate and gave recidivists the opportunity to commit more crimes after little or no real punishment, something had to give. And so a new political analysis of federal criminal law was born into the vacuum that the innovators' theories left after they had dismantled the Anglo-American common-law traditions, which had worked well for centuries. The dynamics of the current, post-deconstruction system for determining the desirability of any proposal for new criminalization has devolved into just the sort of trivialized, polarizing dichotomy that finds itself welcome in today's instant news cycle and sound-bite world of the mainstream media: If a member of Congress or a state legislature votes against a criminalization proposal, someone in the media or a political opponent will use that particular vote to label him "soft on crime."

The "soft on crime" label comes fraught with baggage. It strongly suggests that its bearer would set confirmed pedophiles free to attack again or remove every legal impediment to corporate executives' ransacking their own companies and plundering their investors so that they can take a few more rides in the corporate jet and build bigger houses in St. Moritz (or wherever the "in" place now happens to be). This is true even, and sometimes especially, if the proposal against which the legislature voted criminalizes conduct that is already properly criminalized, fully enforced, and harshly punished by the states, the federal government, or both. In general, the "soft on crime" label or stigma is no longer based on sound analysis.

If a legislator votes against a criminalization proposal, he risks being labeled "soft on crime." But the "soft on crime" label is no longer based on sound analysis.

Being labeled "soft on crime" is only one-half of the simplistic media-enforced picture of criminal justice policy. Today, there is a "soft on crime"–"tough on crime" dichotomy where being "tough on crime" counts for about as much politically as being "soft on crime" counts negatively. Since the deconstruction of traditional criminal justice theory, the public has no principles to guide its decisions about what is and should be punished criminally—and how severely. Thus, support for policies that treat any crime problem harshly is likely to garner political support.

If media reports begin to emphasize the specter of marauding gangsters ruling city streets or conscience-less corporate criminals plundering Wall Street, any policy or legislation that proposes to increase the criminalization covering those real or perceived problems will be received favorably. It makes no difference, and hardly ever enters into media reports or public debate, that the conduct may already be criminalized, or whether those who are actually committing crimes are being identified and prosecuted, or whether the punishment the run-of-the-mill perpetrator is receiving is already far out of proportion to his crime's wrongfulness and severity or to the harm, if any, that it caused. It makes little or no difference in media reports if the proposal is for new criminalization on the federal level, yet the wrongful conduct is already criminalized and harshly punished by the states and is outside the proper reach of the federal government's constitutional powers.

In essence, then, with the erosion of traditional views of the proper scope of criminal law, the public has been left with three highly simplistic principles by which it now assesses the desirability and wisdom of any new criminal justice reform proposal:

1. It is always better to be "tough on crime" than "soft on crime."

2. When "bad things" happen, whether or not what caused them falls into the category of intentional criminal conduct, the best thing to do is to criminalize a broad range of conduct related to those bad things.

3. If those same "bad things" continue to happen after being criminalized, the solution is to criminalize an even broader range of related conduct, make it easier for the government to gain convictions, and make the punishments harsher.

A corollary to the third simplistic principle is that if criminalizing something at the state level is good, criminalizing it at the federal level must be even better. A state-level response is presumed to be inadequate, and only the heavy hand of federal intervention will suffice—a result directly contrary to our founding principles of federalism.

Given this political landscape, an indispensable component of the proper principled, nonpartisan approach to criminal justice reform is to change the public dialogue about crime and punishment. It is in the interest of all who believe that the criminal justice system is essentially broken and that its proper theoretical and principled moorings are in great

> It is a simplistic principle that if criminalizing something at the state level is good, criminalizing it at the federal level must be even better.

disrepair to work to restore in the public mind, in the public debate, an understanding of the principles of sound criminal law and criminal justice. As Rachel Brand, the former Assistant Attorney General for Legal Policy at the Justice Department, has written, the public needs to know about the practical benefits of constitutional limitations on criminal procedure and punishment and on government officials' power to enforce the laws. As initially modest reforms are implemented step by step, "airing their practical benefits and constitutional virtues in the public debate will begin to set the foundation for the more significant reforms that are needed."

It is similarly essential that the public begins to understand that average Americans just like themselves—individuals such as Kay Leibrand, George Norris, and Krister Evertson—are vulnerable to arrest, conviction, and prosecution under any number of the tens or hundreds of thousands of criminal offenses that are strewn about the federal statute books, federal regulatory code, state statutes and regulations, and even local and municipal ordinances and regulations. Due to the irresponsibility and political expedience of legislatures and courts, the average American is at the mercy of police, investigators, and prosecutors who have innumerable criminal laws and procedures at their disposal to exact criminal punishment—or at least a devastating investigation and prosecution—on almost anyone they choose. As Lavrentiy Beria, the thug who headed the Soviet Union's internal intelligence organization that preceded the KGB, reputedly said, "Show me the man, and I'll find you the crime."[1]

> The public needs to know about the practical benefits of constitutional limitations on criminal procedure and punishment and on government officials' power to enforce the laws.

Fortunately, the vast majority of U.S. federal and state prosecutors have a well-developed sense of justice and do not want to abuse their great power, but a single hyperaggressive, ambitious, vindictive, or politically motivated prosecutor can ruin almost anyone's life. This must be illustrated for the public, using examples that Americans can understand that involve victims of overcriminalization with whom they can identify.

The initial reforms must be nonpartisan as well. This approach will build a coalition of individuals and organizations who have learned to trust one another's proposals, as well as state and federal legislators on both sides of the aisle who have identified and share core criminal justice policies. Nonpartisan reforms will also inspire the public's confidence and trust in the criminal justice system and facilitate their ability to recognize

Fotolia photo

Congress needs to institute internal controls to prevent rampant overcriminalization.

sound criminal justice policy that may be derived from the expressions of interest-group politics. Only in this way can we create a political dynamic for change as legislators in Congress and the 50 states learn that they can derive political support both from the public's enhanced understanding and from the coalition of individuals and organizations combating overcriminalization.

What is also essential is that the reform undertaken to reverse the overcriminalization trend be reform that benefits all Americans equally. The American public, not to mention the mainstream media, has grown cynical in its view of criminal justice policy. For several decades, it has been used to favor or disfavor one constituency or interest group over another and trivialized to the "soft on crime"–"tough on crime" dichotomy for crass political gain. Such reforms will enable those who are attacked by the media and by their political opponents for being "soft on crime" because they vote against overcriminalization to rely on a broad, nonpartisan political constituency to refute and defend against these simplistic, dichotomized arguments.

While it remains to be seen whether President Barack Obama's over-arching criminal justice policy will conform to his promise, initial signs are mixed. The President has featured as a criminal justice policy an encouraging statement he made during his campaign about the even-handed application of criminal justice. At an address at Howard University, he made the following promise: "As President, I will...work every day to ensure that this country has a criminal justice system that inspires trust and confidence in every American, regardless of age, or race, or background." This statement was featured as the most prominent criminal justice policy statement on Mr. Obama's Web site for both his campaign and the post-election period.

This promise is vital and encouraging because it fits perfectly with the analysis of the problems and solutions of overcriminalization. Criminal punishment is the greatest power that government routinely uses against its own people.[2] Every expansion of the federal criminal law beyond its proper bounds and every unjust federal criminal offense is an exercise of raw governmental power that undermines Americans' trust and confidence in the justice system.

> The President promised to "work every day to ensure that this country has a criminal justice system that inspires trust and confidence in every American, regardless of age, or race, or background."

Despite this encouraging rhetoric, the Obama Administration has focused on constituent-rewarding reforms that would bring about benefits for certain classes of actual offenders or that would use the criminal law to promote a social engineering agenda. In the 1980s, members of many minority communities who saw the havoc crack cocaine was wreaking on their neighborhoods began lobbying for stricter federal punishment for relatively small amounts of crack cocaine possession. Never mind that this was already criminalized at the state level and that the possessory amounts had no true connection to Congress's alleged power to criminalize such conduct: its power under the Constitution's Commerce Clause to regulate interstate commerce. This political pressure resulted in the imposition of stiff federal sentences.

Now that the affected communities and their representatives in Congress have seen the effects of this overfederalization of crime, they are focused on eliminating the disparity between the amount of crack and the amount of powder cocaine that will trigger the same stiff sentence. This has been one of the highest

> There are indications that the Administration is moving in the wrong direction.

legislative priorities for criminal justice reform in this Administration, yet it benefits only an isolated class of offenders and does nothing to benefit Americans such as Krister Evertson and George Norris who are being subjected to federal criminal punishment for conduct that the average American would not consider criminal. If the Obama Administration is serious about even-handed criminal justice policy, reducing or eliminating the crack–powder disparity is something that should be part of a larger criminal-justice reform package, the components of which benefit all Americans equally.

Indeed, there are indications that the Obama Administration is moving in the wrong direction. Despite what should have been learned about the problems of federalizing truly local crime from the federal crack offenses, the Administration made a federal "hate crime" bill that epitomizes the problem its first legislative priority for criminal justice. The new law makes almost any violent crime—i.e., wrongful conduct that is truly local in nature and has always been criminalized in all states—a federal crime if it has even a tenuous connection to a person who belongs to one of several favored groups singled out for special protections.

Attorney General Eric Holder testified in June 2009 that the new federalization of crime was necessary to send a message to those who engage in violent crimes that such conduct will not be tolerated by the federal government when it involves a member of a protected group. In a Senate Judiciary Committee hearing in June 2009, a representative of one of the groups supporting the "hate crimes" bill reaffirmed that the purpose of the bill was to allow the federal government to engage in "selective prosecutions."[3]

> Whatever the political dynamics and benefits of the "hate crimes" law may be, it is bad criminal justice policy.

Whatever the political dynamics and benefits of the "hate crimes" law may be, it is bad criminal justice policy. Selective prosecutions necessarily and obviously do great damage to the public's confidence that justice is blind and will be applied even-handedly. They evoke echoes of Beria's approach to criminal "justice," where the goal is to make an example of a particular person by punishing him criminally and the law is merely a convenient tool to accomplish that political goal.

There is no reason for the federal government to add to the over 4,400 statutory criminal offenses and tens of thousands of regulatory criminal offenses where there is no showing of need. On the contrary, in response to direct questioning, Holder admitted that he was aware of no regular or systematic failure on the part of any state to enforce its laws against violent crimes on an even-handed basis, including when the victims were members of one of the protected groups. He further admitted that he was aware of no "hate crimes" that had gone unprosecuted.

Opponents of overcriminalization should hope that these two policies are aberrations and that the Obama Administration will begin to fulfill the promise of even-handed criminal justice policy for all that candidate Obama made to the students at Howard University. Because they respect and restore basic principles on which all criminal law should rest, proposals for criminal law reform such as those outlined below and in the rest of this book have broad support across the political and ideological spectrums. Nonpartisan coalitions are already in place to pursue and promote these reforms, and President Obama and his successors in the White House should work with these Left–Right coalitions to implement them.

> It is time for Americans of both parties to join together behind a reform agenda that returns criminal law to its historical foundations.

Further, these principle-based reforms benefit all Americans who are suspected of or charged with a crime. They are thus not as susceptible to the politicization that has infected most criminal justice policy. Implementing them would fulfill the promise that candidate Obama made to inspire Americans' trust and confidence in the federal criminal justice system.

In short, the political dynamic needs to change. Today, there are few who publicly oppose the ever-increasing ambit of criminal law. The great weight of political pressure is for expansion—and often for expansion on behalf of special-interest groups. It is long past time for Americans to reclaim their heritage of a just and fair criminal law by making it impolitic to support overcriminalization. It is time for Americans of both parties to join together behind a reform agenda that returns criminal law to its historical foundations.

The question, then, is: How do we start?

A sound reform strategy will rest on three pillars: restoring traditional criminal law concepts, reinvigorating constitutional rights, and reforming Congress. Each of these projects supports a transformative overall reform objective.

Restoring Traditional Criminal Law

Nothing is more essential to a just criminal law than making sure that the average American cannot become a criminal accidentally or inadvertently without intending to do anything unlawful or otherwise wrongful. Today, at any moment, a person can find himself facing the business end of a criminal investigation and prosecution because he has merely:

- Chosen to start a small businesses and not properly filled out some paperwork required by a confusing web of federal and international law,

- Not added the right sticker to an otherwise properly shipped UPS package,

- Failed to comply with unreasonable bureaucratic interpretations of city landscaping requirements,

- Not known that it was a federal crime to cut down a certain tree on his own residential property, or

- Eaten a French fry in a public place.

No one is really safe from grave injustice committed under the banner of the criminal justice system.

For centuries, the Anglo-American legal system has defined a crime to require both a guilty act (*actus reus*) and a guilty mind (*mens rea*). The latter is commonly referred to as a criminal intent requirement: To win a conviction, the government must prove beyond a reasonable doubt that the accused acted with criminal intent. Today, how-

> No one is really safe from grave injustice committed under the banner of the criminal justice system.

ever, Congress and state legislatures increasingly fail to include an adequate criminal intent requirement in new criminal offenses that they enact.[4] Without a meaningful criminal intent requirement, Americans who never intended to commit a crime—even those who violated a prohibition by accident—may nonetheless be convicted and punished as criminals.

The safeguard is to ensure that, in order to secure a conviction and impose criminal punishment on someone, the government must prove beyond a reasonable doubt that he acted with intent to do something unlawful or otherwise wrongful. Some exceptions exist, but they are rare. They include, for example, extraordinarily dangerous activities, such as making it a strict-liability crime to work with anthrax even if it is undisputed that a researcher's only goal is to develop a more effective vaccine. Some crimes involving minors as victims also do not and should not require prosecutors to prove that the perpetrator knew that the victim was in fact a minor. The burden is placed on the perpetrator to know the age of the victim. But the types of wrongful conduct that fall into these categories are few and limited, and the number of criminal offenses that lack an adequate criminal intent requirement should be decidedly rare.

Several reforms would redirect American criminal justice, especially at the federal level, back down the path of ensuring that no one becomes a criminal unless he intended to do something unlawful or otherwise wrongful.

Guiding Courts and Constraining Aggressive Prosecutors with Default Mens Rea Rules

To protect innocent Americans, new provisions should be added to federal law specifically directing federal courts to grant a criminal defendant the benefit of the doubt when Congress fails to speak clearly in its definition of criminal offenses and penalties. The American Law Institute's Model Penal Code includes key provisions standardizing how courts interpret criminal statutes that have unclear or non-existent criminal intent requirements. Federal law should include similar provisions. One such provision would apply a default criminal intent requirement to criminal statutes that lack any such requirement. If Congress is not explicit, the background law should provide a criminal intent requirement as a matter of course.

A second provision would mandate that unless Congress specifically determines otherwise, any introductory or blanket criminal intent requirement be applied to all elements of the offense. In other words, if the statute says that a crime consists of "knowingly transporting a hazardous substance in violation of a regulation," the crime would be committed only if someone knew (a) that he was engaged in the act of transportation; (b) that the substance was a hazardous one (in a commonsense understanding of hazardous); and (c) that the substance was regulated. This type of provision would reduce the likelihood of innocent Americans being ensnared (as Krister Evertson was) by their own honestly mistaken beliefs.

> If Congress is not explicit, the background law should provide a criminal intent requirement as a matter of course.

Although it would be unwise to do so, Congress would remain free to enact criminal offenses without meaningful criminal intent requirements, but Congress would have to make this purpose clear in the text of the statute. This reform would thus enable law-abiding Americans to know which conduct carries an unavoidable risk of criminal punishment (i.e., is act-at-your-peril conduct) and which conduct they may safely engage in as long as they have every intention of following the law.

A related reform would be to codify the common-law rule of lenity. The rule protects defendants from conviction under expansive interpretations of criminal provisions. It generally provides that ambiguities in a criminal statute (i.e., when it can reasonably be interpreted to define either a broader or a narrower offense) are to be resolved in favor of the defendant. The rule is based on the commonsense notion of justice that no one "should…languish[] in prison unless the lawmaker has clearly said they should."[5]

Passing a statute that makes the rule of lenity a law would reduce uncertainty in federal criminal law; narrow the scope of legal issues that the parties must litigate, both at trial and in the federal appellate courts; and require that Congress be clear when it defines a criminal offense. Americans are entitled to no less protection of their liberty.

Eliminating Vicarious Criminal Liability for Businesses

Business organizations, such as corporations, are persons only insofar as the law treats them as persons for limited purposes. Nevertheless, the U.S. Supreme Court, in a decision that broke with Anglo-American common-law tradition, held 100 years ago that a corporation could be prosecuted criminally.[6] The fact that the Supreme Court held that prosecuting business organizations criminally is permissible does not mean that it is wise, fair, or necessary to do so. Nothing compels Congress to pass any law making corporations criminally liable, and nothing prevents Congress from enacting more rational provisions directing that corporations may no longer be prosecuted criminally.

> The fact that the Supreme Court held that prosecuting business organizations criminally is permissible does not mean that it is wise, fair, or necessary to do so.

Particularly since the failures of Enron and Worldcom and the highly publicized investigations and prosecutions or Enron's Andrew Fastow, Ken Lay, and Jeffrey Skilling and Worldcom's Bernie Ebbers, the number of corporations that have come under criminal investigation by federal authorities has been on the increase. In response to widespread political and media pressure, the Bush Administration created the Justice Department's Corporate Fraud Task Force (CFTF) to focus on prosecuting businesses and their employees. Both the task force's mandate and powers to find and root out fraud and corruption are sweeping, for it has at its disposal some of the broadest criminal offenses to be found in the criminal law. These include the federal mail and wire fraud statutes and the vague, amorphous extension of the mail and wire fraud statutes that Congress passed in 1988, called "honest services fraud" (under which any action in violation of your terms of employment is potentially criminal because it deprives your employer of your honest services).

With these tools and the benefit of similarly broad enforcement powers of federal agencies such as the Securities and Exchange Commission, which have the authority to refer subjects of their investigations to the Justice Department for criminal prosecution, few corporations have been immune from investigations that could culminate in criminal charges.

The specious theory that allows the government to circumvent the traditional criminal intent requirement is that corporations are vicariously liable for the crimes of their employees. The standard is so low that a *Fortune* 500 corporation may be charged criminally for the wrongdoing of a single employee even if that employee was specifically instructed not to engage in the wrongful conduct. All that is required is that the employee act in a way that, however tenuous, benefits the company.

Congress should enact legislation eliminating vicarious criminal liability for business organizations (except, of course, for those that are specifically or-

Congress should enact legislation eliminating vicarious criminal liability for business organizations.

ganized to commit crime). This reform may not be immediately viable politically, especially after all of the misleading rhetoric about who caused the subprime mortgage meltdown and resulting worldwide financial crisis, but the consensus among academics on the left and right is growing and leading to compelling analyses of the injustices and irrationality of almost all criminal prosecutions of business organizations.

Two truths are at the heart of the problem. First, criminal offenses and criminal convictions that are truly just should require the government to prove that the defendant acted with criminal intent; yet it is only a legal fiction that a business organization is a person who can have criminal intent. An organization is merely an administrative and conceptual collection of a number of individual persons. Thus, ambitious prosecutors have had to invent numerous legal doctrines to get courts and juries to accept the idea that a business organization has acted with criminal intent.

As typically happens when law enforcement circumvents criminal intent requirements, injustices have resulted. Probably the most prominent recent injustice was the ultimately failed prosecution of international accounting firm Arthur Andersen. The Supreme Court reversed the firm's conviction because federal prosecutors had promoted and induced the trial court to adopt a specious reading of an obstruction of justice statute that circumvented the statute's criminal intent requirement. The reversal came too late to help Arthur Andersen or its 85,000 employees worldwide, for the indict-

As typically happens when law enforcement circumvents criminal intent requirements, injustices have resulted.

ment caused the firm to fail well before the trial even started. Like most companies, Arthur Andersen's success was based on its reputation for trustworthiness and quality products and services. Essentially no one would contract for its accounting services after it was under federal indictment.

Arthur Andersen's extreme vulnerability to mere criminal indictment, even though the firm would ultimately be vindicated by the Supreme Court, highlights the second problem at the heart of the injustice caused by prosecuting legitimate business organizations. By and large, business organizations—nonprofits, sole proprietorships, small and large partnerships, and corporations of all sizes—are far more vulnerable to "mere" indictment than are individuals. This vulnerability shifts the balance of power dramatically in favor of the government. Until a case goes to trial, law enforcement is largely in control of the criminal justice process. Only when a judge and jury are able to intervene at trial as neutral third parties to determine the strength and propriety of the government's evidence does law enforcement face a substantial check on its case. A trial of a business organization often does not commence until many months, or even several years, after the organization is indicted. Thus, any defendant who is likely to be destroyed by the indictment is essentially at the mercy of prosecutors and other law enforcement officials.

> By and large, business organizations—nonprofits, sole proprietorships, small and large partnerships, and corporations of all sizes—are far more vulnerable to "mere" indictment than are individuals.

As a result, business organizations have learned that from the moment they become aware of a criminal investigation, they must in effect agree to serve as confidential informants against themselves and their own employees, searching internally for evidence of wrongdoing and turning any such evidence they find—regardless of how vaguely or ambiguously that evidence might suggest the company's involvement in allegedly wrongful conduct—over to law enforcement. The goal is to curry favor with federal prosecutors in the form of "cooperation credit." The company hopes that it can satisfy the prosecution team's subjective criteria for awarding "cooperation credit" so that they in turn will agree to focus all of their criminal charges on the company's officers and employees and not charge the organization itself.

Since 1999, when Attorney General (then-Deputy Attorney General) Eric Holder established a set of open-ended factors for Justice Department prosecutors to consider in their subjective assessments of whether a business organization deserves "cooperation credit," companies in a mad scramble to save themselves from Arthur Andersen's fate have routinely had their in-house and outside legal counsel develop any and all evidence that might implicate specific employees of whatever wrongdoing the company allegedly committed. These "designated-go-to-jail" employees find once they are indicted that the company has developed and provided to the prosecution a "road map" for their prosecution.

As of 2008, the number of individuals against whom the CFTF had secured convictions, sometimes through trials but generally through guilty pleas, was nearly 1,300. Contrary to what one is led to expect by media reports, however, less than one-third of those individuals convicted were CEOs, CFOs, executive vice presidents, chief legal officers, or similar executives and high-ranking company officials. Fully two-thirds of those convictions were of employees whose positions could range anywhere from mid-level managers to line supervisors to low-level employees who had no supervisory responsibility whatsoever. The "prosecution's" case against a majority of these 800 employees is likely to have been developed largely by lawyers for companies whose very survival depended on shifting blame away from the company and onto the convicted employees.

The alternative to prosecuting business organizations criminally is *not* simply allowing them to engage in wrongdoing with impunity. This fallacious argument is often set up by law enforcement and by commentators who are hostile to corporations to support maintaining the status quo. The reality is that,

> Employees, if they violate the law and act with criminal intent, should be prosecuted to the full extent of the law.

regardless of whether business organizations are subject to vicarious criminal liability, they have been and will remain subject to extensive administrative regulations and civil penalties.

After Congress eliminates vicarious criminal liability for business organizations, each and every individual involved in corporate wrongdoing will remain subject to criminal liability. Individual wrongdoers can be prosecuted and punished criminally for conduct in the business context no less than individuals who engage in violent and drug conduct on street corners. Employees, if they violate the law and act with criminal intent, should be prosecuted to the full extent of the law.

The primary difference will be that the government will have to develop its own case without relying on the unfair advantage it has over a corporation subject to vicarious criminal liability. Before the explosion of overcriminalization, sound criminal justice policy was always based on the premise that it was government's responsibility to investigate and develop its own cases for prosecution. Individuals were not required to tes-

bill prohibits federal prosecutors from requesting, let alone demanding, that any company waive its attorney–client privilege or its work-product protections. The bill also forbids prosecutors from factoring a company's waiver—or refusal to waive—into the government's determination of whether to indict the company itself for the alleged wrongdoing of one or more of its employees. Short of eliminating altogether the irrational doctrine of vicarious criminal liability for business organizations, this prohibition against rewarding a company that waives or punishing a company that does not waive should prove to be one of the most effective safeguards against turning companies into agents of the Justice Department that will help investigate and prosecute their own employees.

Although the Attorney–Client Privilege Protection Act passed the House with broad bipartisan support, it has not enjoyed the support of one or two key members of the current majority party in the Senate Judiciary Committee. Thus, the attempts by organizations across the political and ideological spectrums to secure a legislative solution for the ever-expanding violation of employees' rights and fundamental legal protections has been stalled by that committee since the legislation was first introduced by Senator Arlen Specter in December 2006.

Senators should be reminded of the unfairness of the Holder Memorandum policies, which have resulted in constitutional violations of employees' rights,[7] until legislation is enacted that includes protective provisions like those in the Attorney–Client Privilege Protection Act. In the meantime, opponents of overcriminalization should work with the Obama Administration to secure an executive order that would make the improvements in the Justice Department's policies that former Deputy Attorney General Mark Filip put in place apply to every federal department and agency and to every federal investigation, whether criminal or civil.

Restoring the Protective Function of the Right to Indictment by a Grand Jury

As the U.S. Supreme Court has repeatedly explained, the grand jury is supposed to serve as a "protector of citizens against arbitrary and oppressive governmental action."[8] For this reason, the Founders enshrined in the Fifth Amendment the guarantee of a right to be indicted by a grand jury. The federal grand jury, however, no longer provides the protections that made it worthy of inclusion in the Bill of Rights as a bulwark against the tyranny of unjust criminal prosecutions. As a result, innocent individuals can find their lives being dismantled by a federal prosecution without ever having been given the benefit of adequate protection by the grand jury process.

> The federal grand jury no longer provides the protections that made it worthy of inclusion in the Bill of Rights as a bulwark against the tyranny of unjust criminal prosecutions.

Even if an individual is cleared of all charges and found not guilty, federal indictment by itself often works severe and irreparable damage to his career and reputation. President Reagan's Secretary of Labor, Raymond J. Donovan, famously captured the destructive effect of mere indictment, regardless of how unfounded the charges may be. After a jury acquitted him and each of his co-defendants of charges that federal prosecutors based on a tenuous theory of criminal culpability, Donovan asked, "Which office do I go to, to get my reputation back?"[9]

Entire business organizations can be destroyed by a federal indictment even if the U.S. Supreme Court later determines that the legal theory on which federal prosecutors based their charges was erroneous. That is what happened to international accounting firm Arthur Andersen, which, after 85 years in business, was destroyed by a federal indictment even though the U.S. Supreme Court later threw out Andersen's conviction. Defending against an unjust indictment can easily wipe out all of an individual's or company's financial resources.

Today, however, the federal system lacks important rights for grand jury targets and suspects, and it no longer serves as

> Defending against an unjust indictment can easily wipe out all of an individual's or company's financial resources.

the bulwark against unjust prosecution that it did when the Fifth Amendment was adopted. The former chief judge for the federal judicial district in Chicago, for example, said, "The grand jury is the total captive of the prosecutor, who, if he is candid, will concede that he can indict anybody, at any time, for almost anything before any grand jury."[10] This statement may include some hyperbole, and no one would suggest that most prosecutors abuse their power before the grand jury or do not attempt to achieve a just result. But many former federal prosecutors will admit in candid conver-

violent, drug, firearms, and immigration offenses had been included in the study, the total number of criminal offenses proposed by a single Congress would have been far higher.

Congress must throttle down the rate of its criminalization, but this must start with an acknowledgment that the proliferation of criminal offenses lacking a meaningful criminal intent requirement is a threat to every American's civil liberties. Debate and oversight of proposed legislation in the Senate and House Judiciary Committees provides legal and linguistic clarity to, and otherwise strengthens the criminal intent requirements of, criminal offenses in bills moving through Congress. The respective Judiciary Committees have special expertise and jurisdiction governing criminal law. Indeed, only the two Judiciary Committees have been granted express jurisdiction over criminal law and punishment. In addition, the Senate Judiciary Committee has primary responsibility for overseeing the confirmation process for presidentially appointed officials in the Justice Department, Federal Bureau of Investigation, and other federal law enforcement agencies.

> Members of Congress have apparently grown accustomed to thinking of criminal offenses as if they were monetary appropriations: merely a feature that any good bill should include.

Yet Congress as a whole is neglecting the special expertise and jurisdiction of the Judiciary Committees when crafting criminal offenses. Congressional rules and procedure should be changed to ensure that the Judiciary Committees are given automatic sequential referral over every bill that adds or modifies criminal offenses or penalties. As an initial matter, this recommendation is sensible because the Judiciary Committees alone have the special competence and expertise required to properly craft well-designed criminal law.

Members of Congress have apparently grown accustomed to thinking of criminal offenses as if they were monetary appropriations: merely a feature that any good bill should include. But ensuring that a proposed criminal offense is properly drafted and merits consideration by the entire chamber is no more a job for a generalist than is the task of ensuring that new provisions on nuclear energy policy are feasible and promote the proper ends. The two Judiciary Committees are by far in the best position to understand, for example:

- Whether one of the other criminal offenses among the 4,450 already in federal law already covers the same conduct;

- Whether federal law enforcement has the resources to enforce the new law or, on the other hand, whether enforcing it would detract from other, more important goals; and

- Whether the new offense is consistent with the Constitution, including constitutional federalism's reservation of a general or plenary police power to the states.

Requiring sequential referral to the respective Judiciary Committees of all bills with criminal provisions would also increase Congress's accountability for new criminalization and help prioritize and reduce overcriminalization. As it now stands, no single committee can take overall responsibility for reducing the proliferation of new (and often unwarranted, ill-conceived, and unconstitutional) criminal offenses or for ensuring that adequate *mens rea* requirements are a feature of all new and modified criminal offenses.

Once the Judiciary Committees take responsibility for all new criminal provisions, it will be clear to every Member of Congress and the public to whom they should address their interests and concerns about those new provisions. Indeed, because the Judiciary Committees have limited time and resources, as well as the best information about the level and allocation of federal law enforcement's available resources, they will be well positioned to prioritize all new criminalization, thus reducing the proliferation of federal criminal offenses, the unwarranted and unconstitutional federalization of inherently local crime, and other forms of overcriminalization.

Mandatory Reporting on All New Criminal Laws

The next reform, a mandatory reporting requirement on all new federal criminal laws, would work hand-in-hand with the reform ensuring Judiciary Committee jurisdiction over all new and modified criminal offenses and penalties. This reform, similar to a bill Illinois Congressman Don Manzullo introduced in 2001, would require the federal government to provide a public report that includes much of the information necessary to assess the purported justification and benefits of all new criminalization.

The 4,450 statutory criminal offenses and tens of thousands of regulatory criminal offenses that are scattered throughout tens of thousands of pages of the United States Code and the Code of Federal Regulations cover an unimaginably broad range of conduct. Given its scope, all or almost all inherently wrongful conduct is already criminalized at the federal level and can be adequately charged using one (or several) of the existing criminal offenses. Because the length of federal prison sentences has skyrocketed over the past two decades, it is safe to assume that federal fines and prison sentences are generally severe enough to satisfy the needs of justice. Yet Congress continues to create an average of one new crime a week—over 400 new federal crimes just from 2000 to 2007—and continues to propose new and stiffer penalties at a similar rate.

> Congress continues to create an average of one new crime a week—over 400 new federal crimes just from 2000 to 2007—and continues to propose new and stiffer penalties at a similar rate.

The federal government should be required to account for and justify any new or modified criminal offenses or penalties. Over the past half-century, the political pressures to criminalize and the benefits therefrom have proved to be increasingly difficult to resist for most Members of Congress of both major parties. Federal regulators who criminalize conduct do not even have the restraint of accountability to the voters who elected them to check their reflexive impulses to add criminal offenses and penalties to the Code of Federal Regulations. Federal officials have lost sight of what should be criminalized and how to ensure that punishment fits the crime. More public accountability is needed.

> The federal government should be required to account for and justify any new or modified criminal offenses or penalties.

This reform would impose a requirement on the federal government to engage in basic but thorough reporting on the grounds and justification for all new and modified criminal offenses and penalties. The requirement would probably take the form of changes in rules governing both chambers of Congress and statutory reporting requirements governing the federal agencies that create and modify criminal offenses and penalties.

For every new or modified criminal offense or penalty that Congress passes, this procedural reform proposal could require, for example, that the report include:

- A description of the problem that the new or modified criminal offense or penalty will purportedly redress, including a description of the perceived gaps in existing law, the wrongful conduct that is currently going unpunished or underpunished, and the specific crimes motivating the legislation;

- The express constitutional authority under which the federal government purports to act;

- An analysis of whether the criminal offenses or penalties are consistent with constitutional and prudential considerations of federalism;

- An assessment of any overlap between the conduct to be criminalized and conduct already criminalized by federal and state law;

- A comparison of the new law's penalties and the penalties under existing federal and state laws for similar conduct that is similarly egregious and harmful;

- An analysis of the impact on the federal budget and federal resources, including the judiciary, to enforce the new offense and penalties to the degree required to solve the problem the new criminalization purports to address; and

- An explanation of how the *mens rea* requirement of the criminal offense should to be interpreted and applied to each of the material elements of the offense.

A second set of provisions of this reform proposal should require Congress to collect information reported by the executive branch on criminalization. This information should be compiled and reported annually and, at a minimum, should include:

- All new criminal offenses and penalties the federal government added to federal regulations, as well as an enumeration of the specific statutory authority under which the agency engaged in the criminalization, and

- For each criminal referral that administrative agencies make to the Justice Department, the provisions of the United States Code and of federal regulations on which the agency based the referral, the number of counts alleged or charged under each statutory and regulatory provision, and the ultimate disposition of each count.

The reporting requirements in this procedural reform proposal would increase Congress's responsibility to deliberate over and provide factual and constitutional justification for every expansion of the federal criminal law. Frequently, congressional proposals seek to create new federal crimes that merely duplicate existing federal criminal statutes and unnecessarily provide redundant penalties for crimes already punished under state law. As it stands, there is no comprehensive means for Congress to determine whether these laws are necessary and, further, whether they dilute the impact of the unique role that has historically been allocated to federal criminal jurisdiction.

These reforms are procedural and thus would not, in and of themselves, change the substance of any criminal offense or penalty. Nonetheless, their benefits would be substantial.

First, they would give Americans the information they need to form their own judgments about the efficacy of criminal law. To achieve that end, the laws should require the federal government to provide information in its possession that is otherwise difficult if not impossible to compile. Researchers and advocates could then use this information to conduct more thorough studies of criminalization in America.

Second, these reforms would require and provide an opportunity for legislators and affected Americans to consider issues of both overcriminalization and overfederalization of crime. They place squarely before Congress and the public concrete information about the impact of new federal crimes and provide an opportunity to stop and think about very basic principles that are relevant to efforts as wide-ranging and diverse as criminal intent reform and federal sentencing policy.

Third, because these reforms are substantively neutral, they do not negatively affect any constituency. A broad range of individuals and organizations, including The Heritage Foundation, the National Association of

Criminal Defense Lawyers, the Federalist Society, the ACLU, the Washington Legal Foundation, the American Bar Association, and the Cato Institute are working together on projects to combat overcriminalization and the overfederalization of crime. These reforms are good-government measures that are attractive to such a diverse set of groups because they facilitate openness, deliberation, and full participation by average Americans in the political process that controls the greatest power government routinely uses against its own citizens.

Finally, and most important, these reforms would begin the process of reclaiming criminal law from overcriminalization. They would start us on the

> The time to roll back the tide of criminal law that is choking American freedom is now.

path toward a fairer and more just criminal law—one that punishes wrongdoers but defends the innocent. We look forward to a day when Americans will no longer have to fear for their liberty at the hands of their government for trivial offenses like eating a French fry in the subway.

The road ahead is a long one. Reform will not come overnight. But the time to take the first steps and roll back the tide of criminal law that is choking American freedom is now.

Baker, "Revisiting"]; see also John Baker, "Measuring the Explosive Growth of Federal Crime Legislation" (The Federalist Society for Law and Public Policy Studies (May 2004)) [hereinafter Baker, "Measuring"].

[4] Paul Rosenzweig, "Civil Sanctions and the Labor–Management Reporting and Disclosure Act," United States House of Representatives, Committee on Education and the Workforce, Subcommittee on Employer–Employee Relations, June 27, 2002 (at http://edworkforce.house.gov/hearings/107th/eer/lmrdatwo62702/rosenzweig.htm).

[5] American Bar Association, "The Federalization of Criminal Law" (Washington, D.C.; ABA, 1998), Appendix C; see also Ronald L. Gainer, "Federal Criminal Code Reform: Past and Future," 2 Buff. Crim. L. Rev. 46, 53 (1998).

[6] Federalization of Criminal Law at 9 & 11 (Chart 2).

[7] Gainer, Federal Criminal Code, at 53.

[8] See Act of April 30, 1789, 1 Stat. 112. This statute—the first criminal statute in the United States—contained 28 separate sections. See generally Currie, The Constitution in Congress: The Federalist Period 1789–1801, at 93–97 (U. Chicago Press 1997). The number 30 is used because a couple of miscellaneous criminal provisions in other statutes are known to have been adopted.

[9] The data in this chart are derived from estimates made in "The Federalization of Criminal Law," in 1998, and the two later studies, Baker "Revisiting" and Baker "Measuring," by Professor John S. Baker, Jr.

[10] Federalization of Criminal Law at 10.

[11] James D. Calder, The Origin and Development of Federal Crime Control Policy (1983), pp. 20–24, 198–203 (describing events leading to enactment of criminal laws in the 1920s and early 1930s); Kathleen F. Brickey, "The Commerce Clause and Federalized Crime: A Tale of Two Thieves," 543 Annals Am. Acad. Pol. & Soc. Sci. 27, 30 (1996) (recounting events leading to passage of federal carjacking legislation).

[12] Franklin E. Zimiring & Gordon Hawkins, "Toward a Principled Basis for Federal Criminal Legislation," 543 Annals Am. Acad. Pol. & Soc. Sci. 15, 20–21 (1996).

[13] Administrative Office of United States Courts, "Federal Judicial Caseload Statistics," Table D-2. Defendants, at http://www.uscourts.gov/caseload2008/contents.html (accessed October 5, 2009).

[14] Id.

[15] Id. All categories pale, however, in comparison to the principal area of federal effort—the prosecution of drug offenses, which resulted in nearly 29,000 individuals being charged in the one-year period ending in March 2008. Id.

[16] See Paul Rosenzweig, "Sentencing of Corporate Fraud and White Collar Crimes," United States Sentencing Commission (March 25, 2003) (available at http://www.ussc.gov/hearings/3_25_03/rosensweig_test.pdf) (accessed April 15, 2003).

[17] United States v. Dotterweich, 320 U.S. 277, 286 (1943) (Murphy, J., dissenting).

[18] 4 Blackstone, Commentaries on the Laws of England, 78–79 (1769) (emphasis in original deleted); see also e.g. State v. Rider, 90 Mo. 54, 1 S.W. 825 (1886) ("The mere intent to commit a crime is not a crime. An attempt to perpetrate it is necessary to constitute guilt in law.").

[19] E.g. Rex. v. Scofield, Cald 397 (1784); Rex v. Higgins, 2 East 5 (1801). For a more contemporary statement of this truism, see Gray v. State, 43 Md. App. 238, 403 A.2d 853 (1979).

[20] E.g. Gebardi v. United States, 287 U.S. 112 (1932) (acquiescence of woman traveling interstate insufficient to sustain Mann Act conviction); State v. Kimbrell, 294 S.C. 51, 362 S.E.2d 630 (1987) (mere presence at criminal act insufficient to sustain conviction).

[21] See American Law Institute, Model Penal Code § 2.01 (1985). Thus, involuntary acts (e.g. reflex, convulsion, movement while asleep or under hypnosis) are not considered an adequate basis for criminal liability. Id. § 2.01(2).

[22] E.g. 18 U.S.C. § 2(a).

[23] E.g. 18 U.S.C. § 2(b); Parnell v. State, 323 Ark. 34, 912 S.W.2d 422 (1996).

[24] E.g. State v. Hanks, 39 Conn. App. 333, 665 A.2d 102 (1995). The necessity of at least one act in furtherance of the conspiracy serves to differentiate the criminal conspiracy from mere thought. E.g. People v. Swain, 12 Cal.4th 593, 909 P.2d 994 (1996). Once an individual joins a conspiracy, he is criminally liable for all the reasonably foreseeable consequences of acts done in furtherance of the conspiracy. E.g. Pinkerton v. United States, 328 U.S. 640 (1946).

[25] 2 Ld. Raym. 1574, 92 Eng. Rep. 518 (1730).

[26] Id.

[27] Joseph Beale, "The Proximate Consequences of an Act," 33 Harv. L. Rev. 633, 637 (1920).

[28] E.g., Commonwealth v. Hall, 322 Mass. 523, 78 N.E.2d 644 (1948) (mother left child in attic); State v. Fabritz, 276 Md. 416, 348 A.2d 275 (1975) (failure to summon medical treatment). In most instances, this common-law duty has now been codified in statute.

[29] United States v. Schaick, 134 F. 592 (2d Cir. 1904).

[30] Compare Commonwealth v. Teixera, 396 Mass. 746, 488 N.E.2d 775 (1986) (no liability for failure to support absent financial ability to pay) with Rex v. Russell, [1933] Vict.L.R. 59 (Victoria 1932) (parent liable for failing to prevent drowning of children by wife).

[31] See Jones v. United States, 308 F.2d 308 (1962) (no criminal liability without finding of a legal duty of care); cf. Barber v. Superior Court, 147 Cal.App.3d 1006, 195 Cal.Rptr. 484 (1983) (no criminal liability for doctor to remove life support at request of wife and children).

[32] People v. Robbins, 83 A.D.2d 271, 443 N.Y.S.2d 1016 (1981); see also Commonwealth v. Konz, 450 A.2d 638 (Pa. 1982) (husband forgoes insulin, wife has no duty).

[33] See Model Penal Code § 2.01(3) (1962) ("Liability for the commission of an offense may not be based on an omission unaccompanied by action unless: (a) the omission is expressly made sufficient by the law defining the offense; or (b) a duty to perform the omitted act is otherwise imposed by law.").

[34] See e.g. Commonwealth v. Putch, 18 Pa. D&C 680 (Cty. Ct. 1932) (owner liable for acts of "his driver"); Moreland v. State, 164 Ga. 467, 139 S.E. 77 (1927) (owner liable for act of chauffer).

[35] 320 U.S. 277 (1943).

[36] Id. at 285–86 (Murphy, J. dissenting).

[37] Id. at 284.

[38] Id. at 280. This phrase, among the most famous in the Supreme Court's corporate criminal law oeuvre, lies at the heart of the conception of a "public welfare offense"—a subject addressed below.

[39] Id. at 284–85. The inference that Congress thought this necessary rests on a false assumption—that in the absence of congressional criminalization, no regime exists for deterring the introduction of adulterated products into the stream of commerce. This ignores the availability of tort liability and other civil liability regimes. Indeed, the availability of alternate methods of calibrated deterrence calls into question the entire justification for managerial liability. Later in this chapter, we discuss the general decline of legal distinctions between torts and crimes.

[40] Id. at 286 (Murphy, J., dissenting).

[41] United States v. Park, 421 U.S. 658 (1975).

[42] Id. at 666, n. 10. The "responsible relation" doctrine is, remarkably, without limit. Even at its inception, the Court said it could not define or "even indicate by way of illustration" the class of employees who stood in responsible relation to a crime. Rather, it left such definition to "the good sense of prosecutors, the wise guidance of trial judges, and the ultimate judgment of juries." Dotterweich, 320 U.S. at 285.

[43] Id. at 670.

[44] Id. at 672. This demonstrates the absence of coherent limits to the pure deterrence rationale for altering social conduct. The arguments advanced are equally supportive of a severe sentence (e.g. life imprisonment), which no society, in good conscience, would impose for these offenses.

[45] Responsible corporate officer cases are numerous. For a sampling see e.g., United States v. Hong, 242 F.3d 528 (4th Cir. 2001); United States v. Iverson, 162 F.3d 1015 (9th Cir. 1998); United States v. Hansen, 262 F.3d 1217 (11th Cir. 2001); United States v. MacDonald & Watson Waste Oil Co., 933 F.2d 35 (1st Cir. 1991); United States v. White, 766 F.Supp. 873 (E.D. Wash. 1991). In addition to the environmental and FDA cases noted in the text, the responsible corporate officer doctrine has also been applied in tax cases. See Purcell v. United States, 1 F.3d 932 (9th Cir. 1993). No barrier to its application in other regulatory contexts (e.g., OSHA, SEC, or Foreign Corrupt Practices Act) is apparent. For one of the earlier, and most troubling, applications of concepts of vicarious liability, one that Justice Murphy called "unworthy of the traditions of our people" and an "abandonment of our devotion to justice," see In re Yamashita, 327 U.S. 1, 28, 29 (1946) (Murphy, J. dissenting) (convicting Japanese General of war crimes for acts of units under his command even though he lacked the capacity to command his troops because all communications had been destroyed during the U.S. invasion of the Philippines). The prevalence of such charges today contrasts with the rarity of criminal charges against corporate officers at the turn of the century. E.g. United States v. Wise, 370 U.S. 405, 407 n.1 (1962) (from 1890 to 1914, fewer than two corporate officers were indicted each year for violations of the Sherman Antitrust Act). The modern use

of such charges has, in some instances, been statutorily sanctioned. See e.g. 33 U.S.C. § 1319(c)(6) (defining a "person" to include "any responsible corporate officer").

[46] See United States v. Weitzenhoff, 35 F.3d 1275, 1293 (9th Cir. 1993) (Kleinfeld, J., dissenting from denial of rehearing en banc) ("If we are fortunate, sewer plant workers…will continue to perform their vitally important work despite our decision. If they knew they risk three years in prison, some might decide that their pay…is not enough to risk prison for doing their jobs.").

[47] Hanousek, 176 F.3d 1124. Like the "responsible relation" doctrine, the requirement of "but for" causation is one that has almost no limit. Virtually any act that bears any relationship, however small, to an event is capable of being characterized as a "but for" cause of that event.

[48] 13 Cox Crim. Cas. 550 (1877).

[49] Roscoe Pound, Introduction to Sayre, Cases on Criminal Law (1927).

[50] Dotterweich, 320 U.S. at 286 (Murphy, J. dissenting).

[51] Morissette v. United States, 342 U.S. 246, 252 (1952). Despite the difficulties courts have in defining what intent is, there is a substantial commonsense component to the inquiry. Recall the Holmesian aphorism: "even a dog distinguishes between being stumbled over and being kicked." See Oliver Wendell Holmes, The Common Law (1881).

[52] Morissette, 342 U.S. at 250–51.

[53] See Dobbs Case, 2 East P.C. 513 (1770); see also Thacker v. Commonwealth, 134 Va. 767, 114 S.E. 504 (1922) (defendant shot at a light and struck and killed a victim; not guilty of murder); State v. Peery, 224 Minn. 346, 28 N.W.2d. 851 (1947) (requiring proof of "intent to be lewd" in indecent exposure prosecution of defendant who was accidentally viewed through ground floor window by passers-by).

[54] The Model Penal Code (as its name suggests) is an attempt to form a uniform set of criminal rules for all 50 states. It has generally been successful. The Code defined four different types of "intent" from which a legislature might choose in defining a crime's scienter requirement: purpose, knowledge, recklessness, and negligence. To these four, one may add a fifth possibility: strict liability (or the proof of a crime without proof of any intent). Under the Code, "purpose" means the intent to do an act for the purpose of achieving a particular unlawful result. "Knowledge" indicates the intent to do an act, deliberately and not by mistake or accident, aware of the likeliness of the unlawful result. "Recklessness" means a callous and gross disregard for a risk created by an actor's conduct (what one might colloquially call "criminal negligence"). By contrast, "negligence" denotes simply a failure to take the care expected of a reasonable person in a similar situation. Each of these intent requirements thus connotes a progressively less directed and intentional form of conduct. The trend in criminal law has been to follow that progression; history tells the tale of diminished intent requirements for criminal laws.

[55] E.g. State v. Wickstrom, 405 N.W.2d 1 (Ct. App. Minn. 1987) (defendant hit victim, causing abortion of pregnancy; guilty of criminal abortion despite lacking intent to injure fetus).

[56] People v. Garland, 254 Ill.App.3d 827, 627 N.E#.2d 377, 380–81 (1993) ("Specific intent exists where from the circumstances the offender must have subjectively desired the prohibited result. General intent exists when the prohibited result may reasonably be expected to follow from the offender's voluntary act even without any specific intent by the offender.").

[57] E.g. United States v. United States Gypsum Co., 438 U.S. 422, 445–46 (1978). Notably, in this example, a corporate executive will at least know that his company's market share is increasing, alerting him to circumstances that might warrant inquiry. In complex health, safety, and environmental regulatory regimes, there is often nothing extrinsic that will alert the average business person to the proscribed nature of this conduct.

[58] Walker v. Superior Court, 47 Cal.3d 112, 115, 253 Cal.Rptr 1, 15–16, 763 P.2d 852, 866 (1988); see also State v. Gorman, 648 A.2d 967 (Me. 1994) (criminal negligence is gross deviation from standard of reasonable prudent person).

[59] See Gian-Cursio v. State, 180 So.2d 396 (Fla. Ct. App. 1965).

[60] See American Law Institute, Model Penal Code § 2.02(2)(d) (1985).

[61] Hanousek, 176 F.3d at 1120–21.

[62] The seminal case most frequently cited for the proposition is Shevlin-Carpenter Co. v. State of Minnesota, 218 U.S. 57 (1910) (State may "eliminate the question of intent" without violating the Due Process clause of the Fourteenth Amendment).

[63] Hopkins, "Mens Rea and the Right to Trial by Jury," 76 Calif. L. Rev. 391, 397 (1988).

[64] 1 Q.B. 702 (1866).

[65] Lafave & Scott, Criminal Law § 3.8, at 242 n.1 (2d ed. 1986).

[66] United States v. FMC Corporation, 572 F.2d 902, 904 (2d Cir. 1978).

[67] E.g. United States v. Freed, 401 U.S. 601 (possession of unregistered hand grenades); Dotterweich, 320 U.S. at 278 (sales under Food and Drug laws); United States v. Balint, 258 U.S. 250 (1922) (sale of narcotics).

[68] E.g. United States v. International Minerals & Chemical Corp., 402 U.S. 558, 565 (1971) ("[W]here…dangerous or deleterious materials are involved, the probability of regulation is so great that anyone who is aware that he is in possession of them or dealing with them must be presumed to be aware of the regulation.").

[69] See 33 U.S.C. § 1319(c)(4) (making it a crime to knowingly make a false statement in any certification required by the regulations promulgated by Environmental Protection Agency). Those regulations, in turn, require the compliance with permit requirements, which typically require the filing of a "discharge monitoring report." See 40 C.F.R. § 122.41(l)(4). As this brief exegesis demonstrates, even discerning that the law criminalizes the filing of a false report is itself a problematic endeavor.

[70] United States v. International Minerals & Chemical Corp., 402 U.S. 558, 569 (1971) (Stewart, J., dissenting).

[71] See Staples v. United States, 511 U.S. 600, 616 (1994) (citing e.g. Commonwealth v. Raymond, 97 Mass. 567 (1867) (fine up to $200 or 6 months in jail); Commonwealth v. Farren, 91 Mass. 489 (1864) (fine only); People v. Snowburger, 113 Mich 86, 71 N.W. 497 (1897) (fine up to $500 or incarceration in county jail).

[72] See Francis B. Sayre, "Public Welfare Offenses," 33 Colum. L. Rev. 55, 70 (1933); see also Morissette v. United States, 342 U.S. 256, 256 (1952) ("penalties commonly are relatively small, and conviction does no grave damage to an offender's reputation").

[73] E.g. People ex rel. Price v. Sheffield Farms-Slawson-Decker, Co., 225 N.Y. 25, 32–33, 121 NE 474, 477 (1918) (Cardozo, J.); id. at 35, 121 N.E. at 478 (Crane, J., concurring) (imprisonment for crime that requires no mens rea stretches law of regulatory offenses beyond its limitations).

[74] E.g. United States v. Weitzenhoff, 35 F.3d 1275 (9th Cir. 1994) (felony violation of Clean Water Act—no knowledge of regulations necessary).

[75] E.g. United States v. Ming Hong, 242 F.3d 528 (4th Cir. 2001) (misdemeanor convictions stacked for 3-year sentence).

[76] United States v. Weitzenhoff, 35 F.3d 1275, 1293 (9th Cir. 1993) (Kleinfeld, J., dissenting from denial of rehearing en banc).

[77] American Law Institute, Model Penal Code § 2.05 and Comments at 282–83 (1985).

[78] United States v. Hudson, 7 Cranch 32, 3 L.Ed. 259 (1812). It is perhaps a matter of more than historical interest that the Constitution specifically identified only three federal criminal offenses: treason, piracy, and forgery. The contemporary extent of federal criminal law would look quite odd to the Founders.

[79] Liparota v. United States, 471 U.S. 419 (1985).

[80] E.g. United States v. International Minerals & Chemical Corp., 402 U.S. 558, 563–64 (1971) ("A person thinking in good faith that he was shipping distilled water when in fact he was shipping some dangerous acid would not be covered"); United States v. Ahmad, 101 F.3d 386 (5th Cir. 1996) (defendant entitled to mistake of fact instruction).

[81] E.g. United States v. X-Citement Video, 513 U.S. 64, 72 (1994) (Due Process requires that scienter standard apply to "each of the statutory elements which criminalize otherwise innocent conduct"); cf. Ratzlaff v. United States, 510 U.S. 135 (1994) (to prove violation of anti-structuring law, government must prove knowledge of the law because deposit of funds in a bank is not inherently wrongful conduct putting one on notice of prohibitory criminal statutes); Staples v. United States, 511 U.S. 600 (1994) (mere possession of a gun insufficient to put defendant on notice as to existence of gun law prohibitions).

[82] See Francis B. Sayre, "Public Welfare Offenses," 33 Colum. L. Rev. 55 (1933).

[83] Herbert Packer, "Mens Rea and the Supreme Court," 1962 S.Ct. Rev. 104.

[84] See Liparota v. United States, 471 U.S. 419, 433 (1985).

[85] United States v. Dotterweich, 320 U.S. 277, 281 (1943).

[86] United States v. Weitzenhoff, 35 F.3d 1275 (9th Cir. 1993); but see United States v. Ahmad, 101 F.3d 386 (5th Cir. 1996).

[87] United States v. Hanousek, 528 U.S. 1102 (2000) (Thomas, J., dissenting from denial of certiorari) (quoting Staples v. United States, 511 U.S. 600, 613 n.6 (1994)).

[88] Id.

[89] John C. Coffee, Jr., "Does 'Unlawful' Mean 'Criminal'?: Reflections on the Disappearing Tort/Crime Distinction in American Law," 71 B.U.L. Rev. 193 (1991).

[90] See, e.g., United States v. Ward, 448 U.S. 242, 249–51 (1980) (permitting imposition of civil penalty even though language of statute was virtually identical to long-standing criminal statute). Ward has been interpreted to mean that the legislature is free to choose to characterize misconduct as civil or criminal, thereby giving enforcement officials the option of choosing which sanction to impose. Examples of regulatory structures that allow the discretionary imposition of administrative, civil, and criminal sanctions for virtually identical conduct abound. Compare e.g., 33 U.S.C. § 1319(g) (authorizing administrative penalties for violations of Clean Water Act); id. §§ 1319(b), (d) (civil penalties); id. § 1319(c) (criminal penalties).

[91] Coffee, "Tort/Crime Distinction," at 220.

[92] William J. Stuntz, "The Pathological Politics of Criminal Law," 100 Mich. L. Rev. 505, 507 (2001).

[93] Id. at 510.

[94] Id. at 600.

[95] Nash v. United States, 229 U.S. 373, 378 (1913).

[96] Dotterweich, 320 U.S. at 285.

Chapter 13

[1] For a detailed discussion of these issues, see Task Force on Federalization of Criminal Law, The Federalization of Criminal Law (Chicago: American Bar Association, 1998); John S. Baker, Jr., "Measuring the Explosive Growth of Federal Crime Legislation" (The Federalist Society for Law and Public Policy Studies (May 2004)); John Baker, "Nationalizing Criminal Law: Does Organized Crime Make It Necessary or Proper?" Rutgers Law Journal 16 (1985): 495; Brian Walsh, "Doing Violence to the Law: The Over-Federalization of Crime," Federal Sentencing Reporter 20 (June 2008): 295; Erik Luna, "The Overcriminalization Phenomenon," 54 American University Law Review 703 (2005).

[2] Henry M. Hart, Jr., "The Aims of the Criminal Law," reprinted in In the Name of Justice (Washington, D.C.: Cato Institute, 2009), at 6.

[3] United States v. International Minerals & Chemical Corp., 402 U.S. 558 (1971) (Stewart, J., dissenting).

[4] See Timothy Lynch, "Ignorance of the Law: Sometimes a Valid Defense," Legal Times, April 4, 1994.

[5] Hart, "The Aims of the Criminal Law," at 19.

[6] United States v. Wilson, 159 F.3d 280 (1998).

[7] Id., at 296 (Posner, J., dissenting).

[8] Id. The Wilson prosecution was not a case of one prosecutor using poor judgment and abusing his power. See, for example, United States v. Emerson, 46 F.Supp. 2d 598 (1999).

[9] See generally Ronald A. Cass, "Ignorance of the Law: A Maxim Reexamined," 17 William and Mary Law Review 671 (1976).

[10] Connally v. General Construction Company, 269 U.S. 385, 393 (1926) (internal quotation marks omitted).

[11] Papachristou v. City of Jacksonville, 405 U.S. 156, 162–63 (1972).

[12] James Madison, "Federalist Paper 62," in The Federalist Papers, ed. Clinton Rossiter (New York: New American Library, 1961),at 381.

[13] See Robert A. Anthony, "Unlegislated Compulsion: How Federal Agency Guidelines Threaten Your Liberty," Cato Institute Policy Analysis no. 312, August 11, 1998.

[14] William L. Gardner and Adam H. Steinman, "'Knowing' Remains the Key Word," National Law Journal, September 2, 1991, at 28.

[15] Quoted in William P. Kucewicz, "Grime and Punishment," 54 ECO (June 1993).

[16] Pennsylvania has protected its citizens from overzealous prosecutors with such a law for many years. See 1 Pa.C.S.A. 1208.

[17] Wayne R. LaFave and Austin W. Scott Jr., Criminal Law, 2nd. ed. (St. Paul, MN: West Publishing Co., 1986), at 193–94.

[18] Quoted in Morissette v. United States, 342 U.S. 246, 250 n. 4 (1952).

[19] Utah v. Blue, 53 Pac. 978, 980 (1898).

[20] Morissette v. United States, 342 U.S. 246, 251 (1952).

[21] Richard G. Singer, "The Resurgence of Mens Rea: III—The Rise and Fall of Strict Criminal Liability," 30 Boston College Law Review 337 (1989). See also Special Report: Federal Erosion of Business Civil Liberties (Washington: Washington Legal Foundation, 2008).

[22] Lambert v. California, 355 U.S. 225, 228 (1957).

[23] Herbert Packer, "Mens Rea and the Supreme Court," 1962 Supreme Court Review 109. See also Jeffrey S. Parker, "The Economics of Mens Rea," 79 Virginia Law Review 741 (1993); Craig S. Lerner and Moin A. Yahya, "'Left Behind' After Sarbanes–Oxley," 44 American Criminal Law Review 1383 (2007).

[24] Thorpe v. Florida, 377 So.2d 221 (1979).

[25] Id., at 223.

[26] See United States v. Yirkovsky, 259 F.3d 704 (2001).

[27] Id., at 705–06.

[28] In my view, Congress should not stand by secure in the knowledge that such precedents exist. Justice Anthony Kennedy has made this point quite well: "The legislative branch has the obligation to determine whether a policy is wise. It is a grave mistake to retain a policy just because a court finds it constitutional…. Few misconceptions about government are more mischievous than the idea that a policy is sound simply because a court finds it permissible. A court decision does not excuse the political branches or the public from the responsibility for unjust laws." Anthony M. Kennedy, "An Address to the American Bar Association Annual Meeting," reprinted in In the Name of Justice (Washington, D.C.: Cato Institute, 2009), at 193.

[29] See LaFave and Scott, Criminal Law, at 212.

[30] Francis Bowes Sayre, "Criminal Responsibility for the Acts of Another," 43 Harvard Law Review 689-90 (1930).

[31] Id., at 702.

[32] United States v. Park, 421 U.S. 658 (1975). Although many state courts have followed the reasoning of the Park decision with respect to their own state constitutions, some courts have recoiled from the far-reaching implications of vicarious criminal liability. For example, the Pennsylvania Supreme Court has held that "a man's liberty cannot rest on so frail a reed as whether his employee will commit a mistake in judgment." Commonwealth v. Koczwara, 155 A.2d 825, 830 (1959). That Pennsylvania ruling, it must be emphasized, is an aberration. It is a remnant of the common-law tradition that virtually every other jurisdiction views as passé.

[33] United States v. Park, 421 U.S. 658, 666 (1975).

[34] Id., at 672.

[35] "[T]he willfulness or negligence of the actor [will] be imputed to him by virtue of his position of responsibility." United States v. Brittain, 931 F.2d 1413, 1419 (1991); United States v. Johnson & Towers, Inc., 741 F.2d 662, 665 n. 3 (1984). See generally Joseph G. Block and Nancy A. Voisin, "The Responsible Corporate Officer Doctrine—Can You Go to Jail for What You Don't Know?" Environmental Law (Fall 1992).

[36] Hanousek v. United States, 528 U.S. 1102 (2000) (Thomas, J., dissenting from the denial of certiorari).

[37] See Susan S. Kuo, "A Little Privacy, Please: Should We Punish Parents for Teenage Sex?" 89 Kentucky Law Journal 135 (2000).

[38] Bennis v. Michigan, 516 U.S. 442 (1996).

[39] Department of Housing and Urban Development v. Rucker, 535 U.S. 125 (2002).

[40] See e.g. Maryland v. Smith, 823 A.2d 644, 678 (2003) ("[T]he knowledge of the contents of the vehicle can be imputed to the driver of the vehicle.").

Chapter 14

[1] This chapter is excerpted, with permission, mostly from Professor Baker's article, "Reforming Corporations Through Threats of Federal Prosecution," 89 Cornell Law Rev. 310 (2004).

[2] Edwin H. Sutherland, White Collar Crime: The Uncut Version (1983).

[3] See id. at 52–53. As detailed in the chapter before this one, mens rea is Latin for "guilty mind" and generally is used to identify the concept of criminal intent. Traditionally, criminal intent—that is, the requirement for a purposeful wrongful act—was a part of the very definition of a crime.

[4] Sutherland, at 52–53.

[5] Id. at 7.

[6] See id. at 265 n. 7 ("The term 'white collar' is used here to refer principally to business managers and executives, in the sense in which it was used by a president of General Motors who wrote 'An Autobiography of a White Collar Worker.'").

[7] Gilbert Geis & Colin Goff, Introduction to Sutherland, at xviii.

[8] Id.

[9] See id. at 53.

[10] See id. at 6.

[11] Id. at 7.

[12] Id. at 53.

[13] See id. at 49–50.

[14] See id. at 56–57.

[15] The same act committed by people with different states of mind traditionally (and morally) has had different legal consequences. Accidentally wandering onto someone else's property on a hike may be a civil tort, requiring compensation to be paid to the property owner if any damage was done, but it is not a criminal trespass. Likewise, an accidental bump in a crowd might constitute a slight civil battery (another tort) but not a criminal battery.

[16] See Sutherland, at 60.

[17] See 1 Wayne R. LaFave & Austin W. Scott, Jr., Substantive Criminal Law § 3.4(a), at 297 (1986).

[18] Jackson v. Virginia, 443 U.S. 307, 315–316 (1979).

[19] See Sutherland, at 6.

[20] Id. at 55.

[21] See id. at 54–55, 60.

[22] Id. at 53 (emphasis added).

[23] Id.

[24] See LaFave & Scott, § 3.4(a), at 297.

[25] See Sutherland, at 55.

[26] Morissette v. United States, 342 U.S. 246, 250–51 (1952).

[27] Jerome Hall, General Principles of Criminal Law, at 278–83 (2d ed. 1960).

[28] See Paul W. Tappan, "Who Is the Criminal?" 12 Am. Soc. Rev. 96, 98–99 (1947) ("Apparently the criminal may be law obedient but greedy; the specific quality of his crimes is far from clear.").

[29] Id. at 98. In his foreword to the 1961 edition of Professor Sutherland's book White Collar Crime, Professor Donald R. Cressey commented that the book "clearly was not an attempt to extend the concept, 'crime,' despite the beliefs of some reviewers." Edwin H. Sutherland, White Collar Crime iv (2d ed. 1961). He characterized the criticism of Tappan and another critic as "extraneous." Id. Professor Jerome Hall, however, has written that "Tappan's attack was devastating." Hall, at 276.

[30] Tappan, at 100.

[31] See Julie R. O'Sullivan, Federal White Collar Crime 54 (2001).

[32] Ilene H. Nagel & Winthrop M. Swenson, "The Federal Sentencing Guidelines for Corporations: Their Development, Theoretical Underpinnings, and Some Thoughts About Their Future," 71 Wash. U. L.Q. 205, 216 & n. 51 (1993). Co-author Winthrop M. Swenson "was responsible for the staff group that developed the basis for the organizational guidelines." Win Swenson, The Organizational Guidelines' "Carrot and Stick" Philosophy, and Their Focus on "Effective" Compliance (Sept. 7, 1995), in U.S. Sentencing Comm'n, Corporate Crime in America: Strengthening the "Good Citizen"

Corporation: Proceedings of the Second Symposium on Crime and Punishment in the United States (1995), at 29.

[33] See Hall, at 275.

[34] Id. at xvi.

[35] Marshall B. Clinard & Peter C. Yeager, Corporate Crime at 18 (1980).

[36] See id. at 17.

[37] Letter from Eric H. Jaso, Counselor to the Assistant Attorney General, Criminal Division, DOJ, to the Honorable Diana E. Murphy, Chair, United States Sentencing Commission (Oct. 1, 2002), at http://www.usdoj.gov/dag/cftf/ sentencing_guidelines.htm (emphasis added).

[38] See Geis & Goff, Introduction to Sutherland, at xxv.

[39] Id. at xvi.

[40] Sutherland, at 264 (emphasis added).

[41] Edwin H. Sutherland & Donald R. Cressey, Criminology 51 (10th ed. 1978); Edwin H. Sutherland et al., Criminology 66 (11th ed. 1992) (emphasis added).

[42] 18 U.S.C. §§ 1961–1968 (2000).

[43] See Nicholas R. Mancini, "Mobsters in the Monastery? Applicability of Civil RICO to the Clergy Sexual Misconduct Scandal and the Catholic Church," 8 Roger Williams U. L. Rev. 193, 195–96 (2002) (discussing application of RICO to Catholic Church and other corporations).

[44] See id. at 232–33.

Chapter 15

[1] New York State Criminal Justice, 2008 Crimestat Report 1 (May 2009).

[2] See Heather Mac Donald, "Don't Cut Cops: Safety Remains City's Job No. 1," NY Post, Jul. 7, 2009.

[3] See Paul H. Robinson and Markus Dirk Dubber, An Introduction to the Modern Penal Code 3 (1999), available at http://www.law.upenn.edu/fac/phrobins/intromodpencode.pdf.

[4] N.Y. Penal L. § 15.10.

[5] See N.Y. Penal L. § 15.15.

[6] The following New York Consolidated Laws contain criminal offenses: Agriculture and Markets; Alcoholic Beverage Control; Arts and Cultural Affairs; Banking; Business Corporation; Civil Rights; Civil Service; Cooperative Corporation; Correction; County; Defense Emergency Act; Domestic Relations; Education; Election; Energy; Environmental Conservation; Estates, Powers, and Trusts; Executive; Family Court; General Business; General City; General Municipal; General Obligations; Highway; Indian; Insurance; Judiciary; Labor; Legislative; Local Finance; Lost and Strayed Animals; Mental Hygiene; Military; Multiple Dwelling; Multiple Residence; Municipal Home Rule; Navigation; New York Civil Court; New York Criminal Court; Not-for-Profit Corporation; Parks, Recreation, and Historic Preservation; Public Authorities; Public Health; Public Land; Public Officers; Public Service; Racing, Pari-

Mutuel Wagering, and Breeding; Railroad; Real Property; Real Property Actions and Proceedings; Real Property Tax; Retirement and Social Security; Second Class Cities; Social Services; Senate Finance; Tax; Town; Transportation; Transportation Corporations; Uniform Justice Court; Vehicle and Traffic; Village; Volunteer Ambulance Workers' Benefit; Volunteer Firefighters' Benefit; and Workers Compensation.

[7] The following New York unconsolidated laws contain criminal offenses: Boxing, Sparring and Wrestling; General City Model; Local Emergency Housing Rent Control Act; New York City Health and Hospitals Corporation Act; NYS Financial Emergency Act for the City of New York; Police Certain Municipalities; Regulation of Lobbying Act; and Yonkers Financial Emergency Act.

[8] See N.Y. Envt'l Conservation L. § 71-4001.

[9] See N.Y. Agr. & Mkts. L. art. 3 § 41; N.Y. Ins. L. § 109; N.Y. Labor L. art. 7 § 213.

[10] N.Y. Gen. Bus. L. § 352-c (b).

[11] See N.Y. Penal L. § 460.

[12] See N.Y. Penal L. § 470.

[13] See 2008 Annual Report, New York General Assembly, Committee on Codes, available at http://assembly.state.ny.us/comm/Codes/2008Annual/report.pdf.

[14] A.9673/S.7994; ch. 510.

[15] N.Y. Penal L. § 240.30 (1).

[16] Press Release, Assemblyman Mike Spano, March 6, 2008.

[17] See, e.g., People v. Morgenstern, 140 Misc. 2d 861 (1988).

[18] See New York City Bar Association, Statement on New York State Legislation Regulating the Sale or Distribution of Video Games Based on Violent Content or Rating, June 4, 2007, available at http://www.nycbar.org/pdf/report/video_games_legislation_memo.pdf.

[19] See N.Y. Penal L. § 235.22.

[20] See District of Columbia v. Heller, 554 U.S. ___; 128 S. Ct. 2783 (2008). The Court recently agreed to decide the extension question.

[21] See Madison Gray, A Brief History of New York's Rockefeller Drug Laws, Time (Apr. 2, 2009), available at http://www.time.com/time/nation/article/0,8599,1888864,00.html.

[22] Id.

[23] See, e.g., Sally Satel, "Do Drug Courts Really Work?" City Journal (Summer 1998), available at http://www.city-journal.org/html/8_3_a3.html.

[24] See Press Release, Governor Paterson Signs Rockefeller Drug Reforms into Law, Apr. 24, 2009, available at http://www.ny.gov/governor/press/press_0424091.html.

[25] See generally 2009 N.Y. Laws ch. 56.

[26] See Satel, "Drug Courts."

[27] Nicolas Thompson, "The Sword of Spitzer," Legal Affairs (May–June 2004), available at http://www.legalaffairs.org/issues/May-June-2004/feature_thompson_mayjun04.msp.

[28] 244 N.Y. 33 (1926).

[29] Thompson, "Spitzer."

[30] The following firms each settled with Spitzer: Bear Stearns, Credit Suisse First Boston, Deutsche Bank, Goldman Sachs, J.P. Morgan Chase, Lehman Brothers, Merrill Lynch, Morgan Stanley, Salomon Smith Barney, and UBS Warburg.

[31] See Theo Francis, "Spitzer Charges Bid-Rigging in Insurance," Wall St. J. (Oct. 15, 2004).

[32] Id.

[33] See E.J. McMahon, New York State's Fiscal Reckoning (Autumn 2008).

[34] Henry G. Manne, "Regulation 'In Terrorem,'" Wall St. J. (Nov. 24, 2004), available at http://online.wsj.com/article/0,,SB110108317665080424-email,00.html.

[35] Cf. "Payola in Radio and Television Broadcasting," 22 J.L. & Econ. 269 (1979).

[36] Andrew G. Simpson, Greenberg, "AIG's Risky Subprime Activity 'Exploded' After He Left," Insurance Journal (Oct. 10, 2008), available at http://www.insurance-journal.com/news/national/2008/10/10/94544.htm.

[37] Lynnley Browing, "AIG's House of Cards," Portfolio.com (Sept. 28, 2008), at http://www.portfolio.com/news-markets/top-5/2008/09/28/AIGs-Derivatives-Run-Amok?page=2#page=2.

[38] See Nicole Gelinas, "Andrew Cuomo's Civil Approach," City Journal (Aug. 12, 2008), available at http://www.city-journal.org/2008/eon0812ng.html.

[39] See Marie Gryphon, "Banking on a Scapegoat," Nat'l Rev. Online (Oct. 7, 2009), at http://www.manhattan-institute.org/html/miarticle.htm?id=5423.

[40] See 2008 Crimestat Report.

[41] See id. at 1.

[42] Id. at 2.

[43] See Heather Mac Donald, "New York Cops: Still the Finest," City Journal (Summer 2006), available at http://www.city-journal.org/html/16_3_ny_cops.html.

[44] See George L. Kelling and Catherine M. Coles, Fixing Broken Windows: Restoring Order and Reducing Crime in Our Communities (1996).

[45] Mac Donald, "Finest."

[46] See Heather Mac Donald, "The NYPD Diaspora," City Journal (Summer 2008), available at http://www.city-journal.org/2008/18_3_nypd.html.

Chapter 16

[1] John C. Coffee, Jr., "Does 'Unlawful' Mean 'Criminal'?: Reflections on the Disappearing Tort/Crime Distinction in American Law," 71 B.U. L. Rev. 193 (1991).

[2] Aguirre v. State, 22 S.W.3d 463, 472 (Tex. Crim. App 1999).

[3] Remarks by State Rep. Mary Denny, Republican Club of Austin, March 5, 2005.

[4] United States v. Cordoba-Hincapie, 825 F. Supp 485 515–16 (E.D.N.Y. 1993).

[5] Henry M. Hart, Jr., "The Aims of the Criminal Law," 23 Law & Contemp. Problems 401, 423 (1958).

[6] See Erin M. Davis, "The Doctrine of Respondeat Superior: An Application to Employers' Liability for the Computer or Internet Crimes Committed by Their Employees," 12 Alb. L.J. Sci. & Tech. 683, 707 (2002).

[7] Many legislators are rightfully reluctant to create new causes of action because of the abuses in the civil justice system, such as class actions where trial lawyers, not plaintiffs, receive the vast majority of the awards. However, there are many ways to avoid such excesses: The right to sue can be limited to individual causes of action and exclude class actions; caps on damages and attorney fees' can be imposed; and binding arbitration can be required with any appeal limited to the question of whether the arbitrator's decision was clearly an abuse of discretion.

[8] See joint interim study report at http://www.house.state.tx.us/committees/reports/79interim/joint/joint_CriminalJuri_GeneralInvest.pdf.

[9] Speech by State Rep. Harold Dutton at Texas Public Policy Foundation policy primer, audio available at http://www.texaspolicy.com/audio/2005-12-07-pp.html.

[10] Criminal negligence is equivalent to gross negligence, which is a higher standard than ordinary civil negligence. Texas Penal Code 6.03(d) provides: "A person acts with criminal negligence, or is criminally negligent, with respect to circumstances surrounding his conduct or the result of his conduct when he ought to be aware of a substantial and unjustifiable risk that the circumstances exist or the result will occur. The risk must be of such a nature and degree that the failure to perceive it constitutes a gross deviation from the standard of care that an ordinary person would exercise under all the circumstances as viewed from the actor's standpoint."

Chapter 17

[1] Mr. Thornburgh would like to thank Brian W. Stolarz, Associate, K&L Gates, for his assistance in this project.

[2] See Erik Luna, "The Overcriminalization Phenomenon," 54 American University Law Review, 703, 713. Professor Luna stated that "[g]iven the moral gravity of decision-making in criminal justice and the unparalleled consequences that flow from such determinations, criminal liability and punishment must always be justifiable in inception and application." Id. at 714; see also Julie O'Sullivan, "Symposium 2006: The Changing Face of White-Collar Crime: The Federal Criminal 'Code' is a Disgrace: Obstruction Statutes as a Case Study," 96 J. Crim. L. & Criminology 643, 657 (2006) (stating that "[c]riminal liability imports a condemnation, the gravest we permit ourselves to make. To condemn when fault is absent is barbaric.").

[3] See Morissette v. United States, 342 U.S. 246, 251 (1952).

[4] See John S. Baker, Jr., "Measuring the Explosive Growth of Federal Crime Legislation," at 10 (Federalist Society for Law and Public Policy Studies, May 2004).

[5] See John S. Baker, Jr., "Revisiting the Explosive Growth of Federal Crimes," at 7 (The Heritage Foundation Legal Memorandum, No. 26, June 16, 2008).

[6] See Brian W. Walsh, "Enacting Principled, Nonpartisan Criminal-law Reform," at 2-3 (The Heritage Foundation, January 9, 2009) (stating that possible reforms to remedying offenses with unclear or non-existent criminal intent requirements are to apply a default criminal intent to criminal statutes that do not have any such requirement, to mandate that any introductory or blanket criminal intent requirement be applied to

all material elements of the criminal offense, and to codify the rule of lenity, which resolves ambiguity in criminal statutes in favor of the defendant.)

[7] See Brian Walsh, "Exploring the National Criminal Justice Commission Act of 2009," Congressional Testimony before the Subcommittee on Crime and Drugs of the Committee on the Judiciary, United States Senate, June 11, 2009 at 14 (stating that "[i]f criminal-law experts and the Justice Department itself cannot ever count them, the average American has no chance of knowing what she must do to avoid violating federal criminal law.").

[8] See Paul Rosenzweig, "Overcriminalization: An Agenda for Change," 54 American University Law Review, 809, 819. Professor Rosenzweig also stated that although many scholars have sought to provide an estimate on the number of federal crimes, the Congressional Research Service, the arm of Congress charged with conducting research, "has proffered that it is impossible to know the exact number." Id.

[9] See Luna, at 722 ("[l]ike all other professionals, police and prosecutors seek the personal esteem and promotion that accompany success, typically measured by the number of arrests for the former and convictions for the latter. To put it bluntly, beat cops do not become homicide detectives by helping little old ladies across the street, and district attorneys are not reelected for dismissing cases or shrugging off acquittals.").

[10] See Sorich v. United States, 129 S.Ct. 1308, 1310 (2009) (Scalia, J., dissenting). Justice Scalia also quoted a recent dissent in the Second Circuit Court of Appeals that asked "[h]ow can the public be expected to know what the statute means when the judges and prosecutors themselves do not know, or must make it up as they go along?") (citing United States v. Rybicki, 354 F.3d 124, 160 (Jacobs, J., dissenting)); see also Judge Alex Kozinski and Misha Tseytlin, "You're (Probably) a Federal Criminal," In the Name of Justice (Timothy Lynch, Ed.) (2009) (stating that "[c]ourts have had little success limiting the 'intangible right to honest services' doctrine," and "it is unsurprising that courts have been unable to successfully confine this doctrine, since any number of actions could reasonably be seen as depriving an employer or agent of 'the intangible right to honest services.'").

[11] Id. (emphasis added).

[12] O'Sullivan, at 670 (stating that "[t]he same principles that demand that Congress take the laboring oar in identifying the conduct that will be subject to penal sanction—beforehand and with reasonable specificity and clarity—also, of course, bars prosecution law-making.").

[13] See New York Central & Hudson River Railroad v. United States, 212 U.S. 481 (1909).

[14] See Dick Thornburgh, "The Dangers of Over-Criminalization and the Need for Real Reform: The Dilemma of Artificial Entities and Artificial Crimes," 44 American Criminal Law Review, (Fall 2007).

[15] See Politicalcartoons.com, http://www.politialcartoons.com/cartoon/5b7d87f6-41b7-9c8fcfa126a1776d.html (last visited July 15, 2009).

[16] See Thornburgh, at 1285; see also O'Sullivan, at 643 (stating that "[t]here actually is no federal criminal 'code' worthy of the name. A criminal code is defined as 'a

systematic collection, compendium, or revision of laws.' What the federal government has is a haphazard grab-bag of statutes accumulated over 200 years, rather than a comprehensive, thoughtful, and internally consistent system of criminal law."). Professor O'Sullivan also stated that "our failure to have in place even a the modestly coherent code makes a mockery of United States much-vaunted commitments to justice, the rule of law, and human rights." Id. at 644.

[17] See Walsh, "Principled, Non-partisan" (stating that "[t]he American Law Institute's Model Penal Code includes key provisions standardizing how courts interpret criminal statutes that have unclear or nonexistent criminal-intent requirements. Federal law should include similar provisions.").

[18] See generally Ronald L. Gainer, "Federal Criminal Code Reform: Past and Future," 2 Buffalo Criminal Law Review 45 (1998).

[19] See Washington Legal Foundation, "Federal Erosion of Business Civil Liberties," 2008 Special Report at 1–5 (stating that "regulatory agencies promulgate rules that not only depart from the intent of Congress, but also impose criminal penalties that dispense with the showing of criminal intent," and referencing a speech made by the former General Counsel of the Treasury about the agency's "invention" of a bank regulation designed to prevent a particular form of money laundering by eliminating mens rea and making bank employees strictly liable, contrary to the intent of Congress.).

[20] See Congressional Responsibility Act of 2005 (H.R. 931), introduced by Rep. J.D. Hayworth (R–AZ).

[21] Id. at p. 2.

[22] See generally Ronald L. Gainer, Creeping Criminalization and Its Social Costs, Legal Backgrounder, Washington Legal Foundation, Vol. 34 No. 13, Oct. 2, 1998.

[23] The Filip Memo revised the Principles of Federal Prosecution of Business Organizations, and the Principles are set forth in the United States Attorney's Manual. Section 9-28.500 (A) of the Manual, entitled "Pervasiveness of Wrongdoing Within the Corporation," states that "[a] corporation can only act through natural persons, and it is therefore held responsible for the acts of such persons fairly attributable to it. Charging a corporation for even minor misconduct may be appropriate where the wrongdoing was pervasive and was undertaken by a large number of employees, or by all the employees in a particular role within the corporation, or was condoned by upper management. On the other hand, it may not be appropriate to impose liability upon a corporation, particularly one with a robust compliance program in place, under a strict respondeat superior theory for the single isolated act of a rogue employee." Id. (emphasis added); see also August 28, 2008 Memorandum by Mark Filip, Deputy Attorney General, available at www.usdoj.gov/dag/readingroom/dag-memo-08282008.pdf (last viewed July 20, 2009).

[24] See Walsh, "Principled, Non-partisan," at 4 (stating that "[w]hat is needed [regarding the attorney–client privilege] is a permanent solution with the force of law that applies to all federal agencies—i.e., comprehensive legislation with provisions like those in the bipartisan Attorney–Client Privilege Protection Act that passed the House last year by a unanimous voice vote.").

Chapter 18

[1] Alan M. Dershowitz, Foreword to Harvey Silverglate, Three Felonies a Day: How the Feds Target the Innocent, at xix, xx (2009).

[2] See Herbert Wechsler, "The Challenge of a Model Penal Code," 65 Harv. L. Rev. 1097, 1098 (1952) ("Whatever view one holds about the penal law, no one will question its importance in society. This is the law on which men place their ultimate reliance for protection against all the deepest injuries that human conduct can inflict on individuals and institutions. By the same token, penal law governs the strongest force that we permit official agencies to bring to bear on individuals.").

[3] Testimony of Michael Lieberman, Anti-Defamation League, before the Senate Committee on the Judiciary (June 25, 2009).

[4] As Professor John Baker notes in his most recent study, 17 of 91 entirely new crimes enacted from 2000 through 2007 lacked any mens rea requirement at all.

[5] United States v. Bass, 404 U.S. 336, 348 (1971) (quoting Judge Henry Friendly).

[6] New York Central & Hudson River R.R. Co. v. United States, 212 U.S. 481 (1909).

[7] See United States v. Stein, 541 F.3d 130, 136 (2d Cir. 2008) (KPMG's policy, adopted at DOJ insistence, capping and then stopping payment of defendant's legal fees constitutes unjustifiable interference with defendant's right to counsel and violated Sixth Amendment).

[8] United States v. Calandra, 414 U.S. 338, 343 (1974).

[9] Selwyn Raab, "Donovan Cleared of Fraud Charges by Jury in Bronx," N.Y. Times, May 26, 1987, at A1.

[10] William J. Campbell, "Eliminate the Grand Jury," 64 J. Crim. L. & Criminology 174, 180 (1973).